Exam Ref DA-100
Analyzing Data with
Microsoft Power BI

Daniil Maslyuk

Exam Ref DA-100 Analyzing Data with Microsoft Power BI

Published with the authorization of Microsoft Corporation by:
Pearson Education, Inc.
Hoboken, New Jersey

ISBN-13: 978-0-13-681968-4
ISBN-10: 0-13-681968-0

Library of Congress Control Number: 2021935778

2 2021

TRADEMARKS

Microsoft and the trademarks listed at http://www.microsoft.com on the "Trademarks" webpage are trademarks of the Microsoft group of companies. All other marks are property of their respective owners.

WARNING AND DISCLAIMER

Every effort has been made to make this book as complete and as accurate as possible, but no warranty or fitness is implied. The information provided is on an "as is" basis. The author, the publisher, and Microsoft Corporation shall have neither liability nor responsibility to any person or entity with respect to any loss or damages arising from the information contained in this book or from the use of the programs accompanying it.

SPECIAL SALES

For information about buying this title in bulk quantities, or for special sales opportunities (which may include electronic versions; custom cover designs; and content particular to your business, training goals, marketing focus, or branding interests), please contact our corporate sales department at corpsales@pearsoned.com or (800) 382-3419.

For government sales inquiries, please contact governmentsales@pearsoned.com.

For questions about sales outside the U.S., please contact intlcs@pearson.com.

CREDITS

EDITOR-IN-CHIEF
Brett Bartow

EXECUTIVE EDITOR
Loretta Yates

DEVELOPMENT EDITOR
Songlin Qiu

SPONSORING EDITOR
Charvi Arora

MANAGING EDITORS
Sandra Schroeder

SENIOR PROJECT EDITOR
Tracey Croom

COPY EDITOR
Liz Welch

INDEXER
Timothy Wright

PROOFREADER
Betty Pessagno

TECHNICAL EDITOR
Claire Mitchell, Owen Auger

EDITORIAL ASSISTANT
Cindy Teeters

COVER DESIGNER
Twist Creative, Seattle

COMPOSITOR
codeMantra

To Dasha, Leonard, and William, who served as a great source of motivation and support.

—DANIIL MASLYUK

Contents at a glance

Contents

Chapter 3   Visualize the data   141

Acknowledgments

I would like to thank Loretta Yates for trusting me to write the second Power BI exam reference book, Charvi Arora for managing the project, Tracey Croom for managing the production, and everyone else at Pearson who worked on this book to make it happen. Also, I'd like to thank both technical editors, Claire Mitchell and Owen Auger, who checked the book for accuracy and helped reduce the number of errors.

A few people have contributed to my becoming a fan of Power BI. Gabriel Polo Reyes was instrumental in my being introduced to the world of Microsoft BI. Thomas van Vliet, my first client, hired me despite my having no prior commercial experience with Power BI and fed me many problems that led to my mastering Power BI.

About the author

 DANIIL MASLYUK is an independent business intelligence consultant, trainer, and speaker who specializes in Microsoft Power BI. Daniil blogs at xxlbi.com and tweets as @DMaslyuk.

Introduction

Exam DA-100: Analyzing Data with Microsoft Power BI, focuses on using Microsoft Power BI for data analysis. About one-fourth of the exam covers data preparation, which includes getting data from different data sources, and profiling, cleaning, transforming, and loading the data. Approximately 30 percent of the questions are related to data modeling: designing, developing, and optimizing a data model. Almost one-third of the book covers the skills necessary to visualize and analyze data, such as creating reports and dashboards, as well as performing advanced analysis. The remainder of the book discusses how to manage datasets and workspaces in the Power BI service.

The DA-100 exam is intended for business intelligence professionals, data analysts, and report creators who are seeking to validate their skills and knowledge in analyzing data with Power BI. Candidates should be familiar with how to get, model, and visualize data in Power BI Desktop, as well as share reports with other people.

This book covers every major topic area found on the exam, but it does not cover every exam question. Only the Microsoft exam team has access to the exam questions, and Microsoft regularly adds new questions to the exam, making it impossible to cover specific questions. You should consider this book a supplement to your relevant real-world experience and other study materials. If you encounter a topic in this book that you do not feel completely comfortable with, use the "Need more review?" links you'll find in the text to find more information and take the time to research and study the topic. Great information is available on MSDN, on TechNet, and in blogs and forums.

Organization of this book

This book is organized by the "Skills measured" list published for the exam. The "Skills measured" list is available for each exam on the Microsoft Learn website: *http://aka.ms/examlist*. Each chapter in this book corresponds to a major topic area in the list, and the technical tasks in each topic area determine a chapter's organization. If an exam covers six major topic areas, for example, the book will contain six chapters.

Preparing for the exam

Microsoft certification exams are a great way to build your résumé and let the world know about your level of expertise. Certification exams validate your on-the-job experience and product knowledge. Although there is no substitute for on-the-job experience, preparation through study and hands-on practice can help you prepare for the exam. This book is *not* designed to teach you new skills.

We recommend that you augment your exam preparation plan by using a combination of available study materials and courses. For example, you might use the Exam Ref and another study guide for your "at home" preparation and take a Microsoft Official Curriculum course for the classroom experience. Choose the combination that you think works best for you. Learn more about available classroom training and find free online courses and live events at *http://microsoft.com/learn*. Microsoft Official Practice Tests are available for many exams at *http://aka.ms/practicetests*.

Note that this Exam Ref is based on publicly available information about the exam and the author's experience. To safeguard the integrity of the exam, authors do not have access to the live exam.

Microsoft certifications

Microsoft certifications distinguish you by proving your command of a broad set of skills and experience with current Microsoft products and technologies. The exams and corresponding certifications are developed to validate your mastery of critical competencies as you design and develop, or implement and support, solutions with Microsoft products and technologies both on-premises and in the cloud. Certification brings a variety of benefits to the individual and to employers and organizations.

> **MORE INFO   ALL MICROSOFT CERTIFICATIONS**
>
> For information about Microsoft certifications, including a full list of available certifications, go to *www.microsoft.com/learn*.

Check back often to see what is new!

Companion files

Most of the chapters in this book include exercises that let you interactively try out new material learned in the main text. All files can be downloaded from the following page:

MicrosoftPressStore.com/ExamRefDA100PowerBI/downloads

There are two kinds of files:

1. Source files, required to work in Power Query Editor:
    - The Targets folder

- Inventory.xlsx
- WideWorldImporters.xlsx

2. The Power BI files folder, containing completed PBIX files.

All exercises assume you extracted the companion files to the C:\DA-100 folder.

Quick access to online references

Throughout this book are addresses to webpages that the author has recommended you visit for more information. Some of these links can be very long and painstaking to type, so we've shortened them for you to make them easier to visit. We've also compiled them into a single list that readers of the print edition can refer to while they read.

Download the list at *MicrosoftPressStore.com/ExamRefDA100PowerBI/downloads*.

The URLs are organized by chapter and heading. Every time you come across a URL in the book, find the hyperlink in the list to go directly to the webpage.

Errata, updates, & book support

We've made every effort to ensure the accuracy of this book and its companion content. You can access updates to this book—in the form of a list of submitted errata and their related corrections—at:

MicrosoftPressStore.com/ExamRefDA100PowerBI/errata

If you discover an error that is not already listed, please submit it to us at the same page.

For additional book support and information, please visit
www.MicrosoftPressStore.com/Support.

Please note that product support for Microsoft software and hardware is not offered through the previous addresses. For help with Microsoft software or hardware, go to
http://support.microsoft.com.

Stay in touch

Let's keep the conversation going! We're on Twitter: *http://twitter.com/MicrosoftPress*.

CHAPTER 1

Prepare the data

Over the past five years, Microsoft Power BI has evolved from a new entrant in the data space to one of the most popular business intelligence tools used to visualize and analyze data. Before you can analyze data in Power BI, you need to prepare, model, and visualize the data. Data preparation is the subject of this chapter; we review the skills necessary to consume data in Power BI Desktop.

We start with the steps required to connect to various data sources. We then review the data profiling techniques, which help you "feel" the data. Later, we look at how you can clean and transform data by using Power Query—this activity often takes a disproportionate amount of time in many data analysis projects. Finally, we show how you can resolve data import errors after loading data.

Skills covered in this chapter:

- 1.1: Get data from different data sources
- 1.2: Profile the data
- 1.3: Clean, transform, and load the data

Skill 1.1: Get data from different data sources

No matter what your data source is, you need to get data in Power BI before you can work with it. Power BI can connect to a wide variety of data sources, and the number of supported data sources grows every month. Furthermore, Power BI allows you to create your own connectors, making it possible to connect to virtually any data source.

The data consumption process begins with an understanding of business requirements and data sources available to you. For instance, if you need to work with near-real-time data, your data consumption process is going to be different compared to working with data that is going to be periodically refreshed. As you'll see later in the chapter, different data sources support different connectivity modes.

This skill covers how to:

- Identify and connect to a data source
- Change data source settings
- Select a shared dataset or create a local dataset
- Select a storage mode
- Choose an appropriate query type
- Identify query performance issues
- Use Microsoft Dataverse
- Use parameters
- Use or create a PBIDS file
- Use or create a dataflow
- Connect to a dataset by using the XMLA endpoint

Identify and connect to a data source

There are over 100 native connectors in Power BI Desktop, and the Power BI team is regularly making new connectors available. When connecting to data in Power BI, the most common data sources are files, databases, and web services.

> **NEED MORE REVIEW?** **DATA SOURCES IN POWER BI**
>
> The full list of data sources available in Power BI can be found at *https://docs.microsoft.com/en-us/power-bi/power-bi-data-sources*.

To choose the right connector, you must know what your data sources are. For example, you cannot use the Oracle database connector to connect to a SQL Server database, even though both are database connectors.

> **NOTE** **COMPANION FILES**
>
> In our examples, we are going to use this book's companion files, which are based on a fictitious company called Wide World Importers. Subsequent instructions assume that you placed all companion files in the C:\DA-100 folder.

To review the skills needed to get data from different data sources, let's start by connecting to the WideWorldImporters.xlsx file from this book's companion files:

1. On the **Home** tab, select **Excel**.
2. In the **Open** window, navigate to the **WideWorldImporters.xlsx** file and select **Open**.

3. In the **Navigator** window, select all eight check boxes on the left; the window should look similar to Figure 1-1.

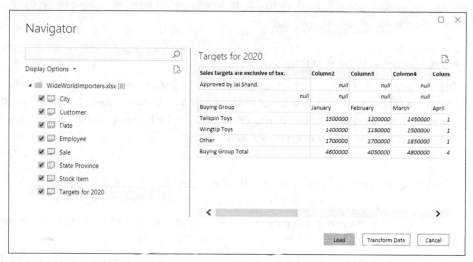

FIGURE 1-1 The Navigator window

4. Select **Transform Data**.

After you complete these steps, the Power Query Editor window opens automatically; you can see it in Figure 1-2.

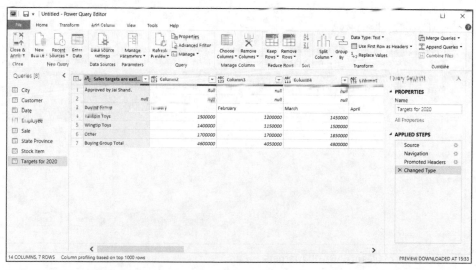

FIGURE 1-2 Power Query Editor

If in the Navigator window you chose **Load**, the Power Query Editor window would not open, and all Excel sheets you selected would be loaded as is.

Note that the Navigator window shows you a preview of the objects you selected. For example, in Figure 1-1 we see the preview of the Targets for 2020 sheet; its shape suggests we need to apply some transformations to our data before loading it, because it has some extraneous information in its first few rows.

> **NOTE   DATA PREVIEW RECENTNESS**
>
> To make query editing experience more fluid, Power Query caches data previews. Therefore, if your data changes often, you may not see the latest data in Power Query Editor. To refresh a preview, you can select **Home > Refresh Preview**. To refresh previews of all queries, you should select **Home > Refresh Preview > Refresh All**.

The Navigator window is not unique to the Excel connector; indeed, you will see the same window when connecting to a complex data source like a database, for instance.

We are going to transform our data later in this chapter. Before we do that, let's connect to another data source: a folder. While you are in Power Query Editor:

1. On the **Home** tab, select **New source**. If you select the button label instead of the button, select **More**.

2. In the **Get data** window, select **Folder** and then **Connect**.

3. Select **Browse**, navigate to C:\DA-100\Targets, and select **OK** twice. At this stage, you should see the list of files in the folder like in Figure 1-3.

FIGURE 1-3 List of files in C:\DA-100\Targets

4. Select **Combine & Transform Data**.

5. In the **Combine files** window, select **OK** without changing any settings.

At this stage, you have connected to two data sources: an Excel file and a folder, which contained several CSV files.

Although we did not specify the file type when connecting to a folder, Power Query automatically determined the type of files and applied the transformations it deemed appropriate. In addition to Excel and CSV files, Power BI can connect to several other file types, including JSON, XML, PDF, and Access database.

> **IMPORTANT FORMAT CONSISTENCY**
>
> It is important that the format of the files in a folder is consistent—otherwise, you may run into issues. Power Query applies the same transformations to each file in a folder, and it decides which transformations are necessary based on the sample file you choose in the Combine files window.

Power Query Editor

If you followed our instructions, your Power Query Editor window should look like Figure 1-4.

FIGURE 1-4 Power Query Editor after connecting to Excel and a folder

As you can see, after you instructed Power Query to automatically combine files from the folder, it created the Targets query and several helper queries, whose names are italicized—this means they won't be loaded. We will review the data loading options later in this chapter, and we will continue using the same queries we created in this example.

> **NOTE COMPANION FILES**
>
> You can review the steps we took by opening the file 1.1.1 Connect to data sources.pbix from the companion files folder.

Query dependencies

You can check the dependencies queries have by selecting **Query dependencies** on the **View** ribbon. The **Query dependencies** view provides a diagram like the one in Figure 1-5 that shows both data sources and queries.

FIGURE 1-5 Query dependencies view

To view the dependencies of a specific query, select a query, and Power BI will highlight both the queries that depend on the selected query as well as queries and sources that the query depends on.

The default layout is top to bottom; you can change the layout by using the **Layout** drop-down list.

Change data source settings

After you connect to a data source, sometimes you may need to change some settings associated with it. For example, if you moved the WideWorldImporters.xlsx file to a different folder, you would need to update the file path in Power BI to continue working with it.

One way to change the data source settings is to select the cog wheel next to the Source step under **Applied steps** in **Query Settings** in Power Query Editor. After you select the cog wheel, you can change the file path as well as the file type. The shortcoming of this approach is that you will need to change settings in each query that references the file, which can be tedious and error-prone if you have a lot of queries.

Another way to change the data source settings is by selecting **Data source settings** on the **Home** tab. This opens the **Data source settings** window, shown in Figure 1-6.

The **Data source settings** window allows you to change the source settings for all affected queries at the same time by selecting **Change Source**. You can change and clear the permissions for each data source by selecting **Edit Permissions** and **Clear Permissions**, respectively. Permissions include the credentials used for connecting to a data source and the privacy level. Privacy levels are relevant when combining data from different sources in a single query, and we will look at them later in this chapter.

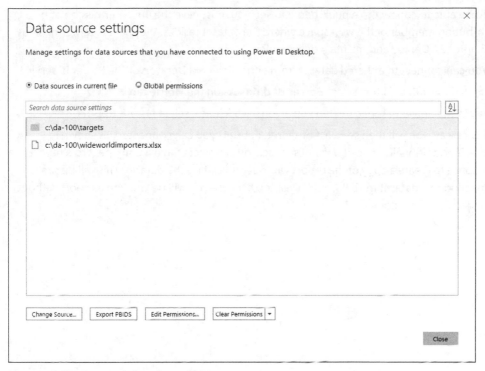

FIGURE 1-6 The Data source settings window

Select a shared dataset or create a local dataset

So far in this chapter, we have been creating our own dataset, which is also known as a *local* dataset. If a dataset already exists that you or someone else prepared and published to the Power BI service, you can connect to that dataset, also known as a shared dataset. Using a shared dataset has several benefits:

- You ensure consistent data across different reports.
- When connecting to a shared dataset, you are not copying any data needlessly.
- You can create a copy of an existing report and modify it, which takes less effort than starting from scratch.

REAL WORLD USING SHARED DATASETS

Sometimes different teams want to see the same data by using different visuals. In that case, it makes sense to create a single dataset and different reports that all connect to the same dataset.

To be able to connect to a published dataset, you must have the Build permission or be a contributing member of the workspace where the dataset resides. We will review permissions in Chapter 5, "Deploy and maintain deliverables."

You can connect to a shared dataset from either Power BI Desktop or the Power BI service:

- In Power BI Desktop, select **Power BI datasets** on the **Home** tab.
- In the Power BI service, when you are in a workspace, select **New** > **Report**.

Either way, you will then see a list of shared datasets you can connect to, as shown in Figure 1-7. Additionally, in the Power BI service, you can select **Save a copy** next to a report in a workspace to create a copy of the report without duplicating the dataset. This will be similar to connecting to a dataset from Power BI Desktop because you will be creating a report without an underlying data model.

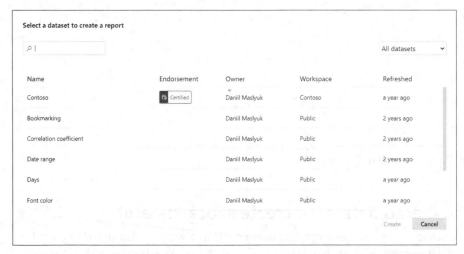

FIGURE 1-7 List of available datasets

After you are connected to a shared dataset in Power BI Desktop, some user interface buttons will be grayed out or missing because this connectivity mode comes with limitations. For example, when you connect to a shared dataset, Power Query Editor is not available, and the Data view is missing. In the lower-right corner, you'll see the name and workspace you're connected to, as shown in Figure 1-8.

Connected live to the Power BI dataset: Contoso in Contoso

FIGURE 1-8 Power BI Desktop connected to a Power BI dataset

While the **Transform Data** button is inactive, you can select its label and select **Data source settings** to change the dataset you are connected to.

Note that you can still create measures, and they will be saved in your PBIX file but not in the shared dataset itself. That means other users who connect to the same shared dataset will not see the measures you created. These measures are known as *local* or *report-level* measures. Creating measures in general is going to be reviewed in Chapter 2, "Model the data."

Select a storage mode

The most common way to consume data in Power BI is to import it into the data model. When you import data in Power BI, you create a copy of it that is kept static until you refresh your dataset. Data from files and folders, which we connected to earlier in the chapter, can be imported only in Power BI. When it comes to databases, you can create data connections in one of two ways.

First, you can import your data, which makes the Power BI data model cache it. This method offers you the greatest flexibility when you model your data because you can use all the available modeling features in Power BI.

Second, you can connect to your data directly in its original source. This method is known as *DirectQuery*. With DirectQuery, data is not cached in Power BI. Instead, the original data source is queried every time you interact with Power BI visuals. Not all data sources support DirectQuery.

A special case of DirectQuery called Live Connection exists for Analysis Services (both Tabular and Multidimensional) and the Power BI service. This connectivity mode ensures that all calculations take place in the corresponding data model.

Importing data

When you import data, you load a copy of it into Power BI. Because Power BI is based on an in-memory columnar database engine, the imported data consumes both the RAM and disk space, because data is stored in files. During the development phase, the imported data consumes the disk space and RAM of your development machine. After you publish your report to a server, the imported data consumes the disk space and RAM of the server to which you publish your report. The implication of this is that you can't load more data into Power BI than your hardware allows. This becomes an issue when you work with very large volumes of data.

You have an option to transform data when you import it in Power BI, limited only by the functionality of Power BI. If you only load a subset of tables from your database, and you apply filters to some of the tables, only the filtered data gets loaded into Power BI.

After data is loaded into the Power BI cache, it is kept in a compressed state, thanks to the in-memory database engine. The compression depends on many factors, including data type, values, and cardinality of the columns. In most cases, however, data will take much less space once it is loaded into Power BI compared to its original size.

One of the advantages of this data connection method is that you can use all the functionality of Power BI without restrictions, including all transformations available in Power Query Editor, as well as all DAX functions when you model your data.

Additionally, you can combine imported data from more than one source in the same data model. For example, you can combine some data from a database and some data from an Excel file in a single table.

Another advantage of this method is the speed of calculations. Because the Power BI engine stores data in-memory in compressed state, there is little to no latency when accessing the data. Additionally, the engine is optimized for calculations, resulting in the best computing speed.

Data from imported tables can be seen in the **Data** view in Power BI Desktop, and you can see the relationships between tables in the **Model** view. The Report, Data, and Model buttons are shown in Figure 1-9 on the left.

FIGURE 1-9 Power BI Desktop when importing data

DirectQuery

When you use the DirectQuery connectivity mode, you are not caching any data in Power BI. All data remains in the data source, except for metadata, which Power BI caches. Metadata includes column and table names, data types, and relationships.

For most data sources supporting DirectQuery, when connecting to a data source, you select the entities you want to connect to, such as tables or views. Each entity becomes a table in your data model. The experience is similar to the Navigator window we saw earlier in the chapter when connecting to an Excel file, shown in Figure 1-1.

If you only use DirectQuery in your data model, the Power BI file size will be negligible compared to a file with imported data.

The main advantage of this method is that you are not limited by the hardware of your development machine or the capacity of the server to which you will publish your report. All data is kept in the data source, and all the calculations are done in the source as well.

Data from DirectQuery tables cannot be seen in the **Data** view of Power BI Desktop; if all tables in a data model are in DirectQuery mode, the **Data** view button will not be visible, though you can still use the **Model** view. A fragment of the interface when using DirectQuery is shown in Figure 1-10.

FIGURE 1-10 Power BI Desktop interface when using DirectQuery

Live Connection

A special case of DirectQuery, called Live Connection, is available for Power BI service datasets and Analysis Services data models. It differs from DirectQuery in a few ways:

- You cannot apply any transformations to data.
- It is not possible to define physical relationships in Live Connection.
- Data modeling is limited to only creating measures.

You may consider using Live Connection rather than importing data because of the enhanced data modeling capabilities and improved security features in the data source. More specifically, unlike DirectQuery with some databases, Live Connection always considers the username of the user who is viewing a report, which means security can be set up dynamically. Additionally, SQL Server Analysis Services can be configured to refresh as frequently as needed, unlike the scheduled refresh in the Power BI service, which is limited to eight times a day without Power BI Premium.

Composite models

A *composite model* is a data model that combines imported data and DirectQuery or that uses DirectQuery to connect to multiple data sources. For example, you could be getting the latest sales data from a database by using DirectQuery, and you could be importing an Excel spreadsheet with sales targets. You can combine both data sources in a single data model by creating a composite model.

> **IMPORTANT POTENTIAL SECURITY RISKS IN COMPOSITE MODELS**
>
> Building a composite model may pose security risks; for example, data from an Excel file may be sent to a database in a query, and a database administrator might see some data from the Excel file.

For each table in a composite model, the *storage mode* property defines how the table is stored in the data model. To view the property, you can hover over a table in the **Fields** pane in the **Report** or **Data** view; alternatively, you can view or change it in the **Model** view in the

Advanced section of the **Properties** pane once you select a table. Storage mode can be set to one of the following options:

- Import
- DirectQuery
- Dual

The *Dual* mode means a table is both cached and retrieved in DirectQuery mode when needed, depending on the storage mode of other tables used in the same query. This mode is useful whenever you have a table that is related to some imported tables and other tables whose storage mode is DirectQuery. For example, consider the data model from Table 1-1.

TABLE 1-1 Sample data model

Table Name	Data Source	Storage Mode
Sales	Database	DirectQuery
Date	Database	Dual
Targets	Excel file	Import

In this model, the Date table is related to both the Sales and the Targets table. When you use data from the Date and Sales tables, it is retrieved directly from the database in Direct-Query mode; when you use Date and Targets together, no query is sent to the database, which improves the performance of your reports.

IMPORTANT **CHANGING STORAGE MODE**

If you change the storage mode from DirectQuery or Dual to Import, there is no going back. If you need to set the storage mode of a table to Dual, you must create a table by using DirectQuery first.

Choose an appropriate query type

To get the best user experience, you should import data if you can. However, there are several scenarios in which you may consider DirectQuery over importing data:

- If the size of the data model is too large to fit into memory, DirectQuery may be a viable option. Keep in mind that performance will depend on the data source's hardware.

- If the underlying data changes frequently and reports must always show the most recent data, then DirectQuery could be the solution. Again, the data source must be able to return the results in reasonable time. Otherwise, there might not be a point in querying for the latest data.

- In case a company's policy mandates that data reside only in its original source, Direct-Query would be preferable over importing data.

Implications of using DirectQuery

Using DirectQuery entails some implications to the available functionality, described next.

REPORT PERFORMANCE VARIES

When using DirectQuery, the report performance depends on the underlying source hardware. If it can return queries in less than five seconds, then the experience is bearable yet still might feel slow to users who are accustomed to the speed of the native Power BI engine. If the data source is not fast enough, the queries might even time out, making the report unusable. Whether the data source can handle the additional load from frequent querying should also be considered. With DirectQuery, each visual a user interacts with can send a query to the data source, and this happens to every user who is working with a report at the same time.

NOT EVERY QUERY TYPE IS USABLE

Not every kind of query can be used in DirectQuery mode. When a user interacts with a visual in a report that uses DirectQuery, all the necessary queries to retrieve the data are combined and sent to the data source. For this reason, it is not possible to use native queries with common table expressions or stored procedures.

LIMITED DATA TRANSFORMATION FUNCTIONALITY

Compared to data transformations available with imported data, the data transformation functionality is limited when using DirectQuery due to performance considerations. The transformations need to be applied every time there is an interaction with a visual, not once per data refresh, as in the case of importing data. Only those transformations that can be efficiently translated to the data source query language are allowed. If you try to apply transformations that are not allowed, you will get the error shown in Figure 1-11 and be prompted to either cancel the operation or import data.

FIGURE 1-11 Error message saying the step is not supported in DirectQuery mode

DATA MODELING LIMITATIONS

The data modeling experience is limited in DirectQuery as well. Data modeling includes creating measures, calculated columns, hierarchies, and relationships; renaming and hiding columns; formatting measures and columns; and defining default summarization and sort order of columns. The following are limitations associated with data modeling in DirectQuery:

1. With DirectQuery, there are no built-in date tables that are created for every date/datetime column like in Import mode by default. Date tables are required for Time Intelligence calculations, and if the data source has a date table, it can instead be used for Time Intelligence purposes.

2. Calculated columns are limited in two ways. First, they can only use the current row of the table or a related row in a many-to-one relationship, which rules out all aggregation functions. Second, calculated columns can use only some of the functions that return

scalar values. More specifically, only functions that can be easily translated into the data source's native language are supported. For example, you can create a "Month Name" column in a Sales table with the RELATED function, but you cannot count the number of rows in the Sales table for each row in the Date table in a calculated column because that would require an aggregation function like COUNTROWS. Usually, IntelliSense, Microsoft's autocomplete feature, will list only the supported functions.

3. Calculated tables are not supported in DirectQuery mode.

4. Parent-child functions, such as PATH, are not supported in DirectQuery. If you need to create a hierarchy of employees or a chart of accounts, consider building it in the data source.

5. Building clusters, which relies on DAX functions, is not supported in DirectQuery.

Table 1-2 summarizes the similarities and differences between three data connectivity modes available in Power BI.

TABLE 1-2 Data connectivity modes compared

	Imported Data	**DirectQuery**	**Live Connection**
Maximum data model size	Tied to license Power BI Pro: 1 GB limit per dataset Power BI Premium: capacity based	Limited only by the underlying data source hardware	Power BI service: same dataset size limits as Import Data Other sources: Limited only by underlying data source hardware
Number of data sources	Unlimited	Unlimited	Only one
Data refresh	Tied to license; Power BI Pro: up to 8 times a day at 30- minute intervals Power BI Premium: unlimited	Report shows the latest data available in the source	Report shows the latest data available in the source
Performance	Best	Varies depending on data source; almost always slower compared to imported data and Live Connection	Best
Data transformation	Fully featured	Limited to what can be translated to data source language	None
Data modeling	Fully featured	Highly restricted	Analysis Services and Power BI service: measures can be created without restrictions
Security	Row-level security can be applied based on current user login	Row-level security defined at data source is only available for some data sources; row-level security can still be done in Power BI Desktop	Can leverage data source security rules based on current user's login

EXAM TIP

Be prepared to know when DirectQuery or Live Connection data connectivity modes are appropriate based on a client's business requirements.

Identify query performance issues

Several reasons could be responsible for poor performance when connecting to data in Power BI. Power BI Desktop has a few features that can help identify those issues.

View native query

When you get data in Power BI from some data sources, like databases, Power Query will do its best to translate the transformations you perform into the native language of the data source—for example, SQL. This feature of Power Query is known as *query folding*. Most of the time, this will make getting data more efficient. For instance, if you connect to a database and get a subset of columns from a table, Power Query may only retrieve those columns from the data source instead of loading all columns and then locally removing the ones you don't want.

In some cases, it may be possible to view the query that Power Query sent to the data source to retrieve the data you wanted. For this, you need to right-click a query step in Power Query Editor and select **View Native Query**. The window that opens looks like Figure 1-12.

```
Native Query

select [_].[SupplierID] as [SupplierID],
    case
        when [_].[PurchaseOrderID] is null
        then -1
        else [_].[PurchaseOrderID]
    end as [PurchaseOrderID],
    [_].[PaymentMethodID] as [PaymentMethodID],
    [_].[TransactionDate] as [TransactionDate],
    [_].[AmountExcludingTax] as [AmountExcludingTax],
    [_].[TaxAmount] as [TaxAmount],
    [_].[OutstandingBalance] as [OutstandingBalance],
    [_].[FinalizationDate] as [FinalizationDate]
from
(
    select [_].[SupplierID],
        [_].[PurchaseOrderID],
        [_].[PaymentMethodID],
        [_].[TransactionDate],
        [_].[AmountExcludingTax],
        [_].[TaxAmount],
        [_].[OutstandingBalance],
        [_].[FinalizationDate]
    from [Purchasing].[SupplierTransactions] as [_]
    where [_].[TransactionDate] >= convert(datetime2, '2016-01-01 00:00:00')
) as [_]

                                            OK
```

FIGURE 1-12 Native Query window

In the query shown in Figure 1-12, we connected to a SQL Server database, applied a filter, selected a few columns, and replaced a value. Because these operations can be translated to SQL, Power Query decided to do the transformations in the source instead of performing them after loading the whole table, which led to better performance.

You cannot edit the native query; it is provided for your information only. If you want Power BI to issue a specific query, you must provide a SQL statement when connecting to a database.

If the **View Native Query** option is grayed out, it means that the data source does not support query folding or that some query step could not be translated into the data source's native language. For example, if we applied the *Clean* transformation to a text column, the query would not fold, because there is no direct equivalent in SQL yet.

> **IMPORTANT** **POWER QUERY STEPS ORDER**
>
> The order of steps in Power Query matters. If you must have a transformation that cannot be folded, it's best to reorder your steps to fold as many steps as possible.

Query diagnostics

Power BI contains the query diagnostics toolset, which can help you identify performance bottlenecks. Query diagnostics allow you to see the queries that you emit while authoring or refreshing a dataset. They are especially useful for working with data sources that support query folding. By using query diagnostics, you can look at all queries that happen during data refreshes or while you author queries, or you can analyze a single step in detail.

To review how to use query diagnostics, let's connect to an OData feed first. It's a feed from Microsoft based on their fictitious AdventureWorks company.

1. Create a new Power BI Desktop file.

2. Select **Get data** > **OData feed**.

3. Enter **https://services.odata.org/AdventureWorksV3/AdventureWorks.svc/** in the **URL** box and select **OK**.

4. If prompted, in the credentials window, ensure **Anonymous** is selected and select select **Connect**.

5. Select the **CompanySales** check box in the **Navigator** window and select **Transform Data**.

Now that you are connected to an OData feed, you can apply some transformations and see the effect on our query. To start recording traces in Power Query, select **Start diagnostics** on the **Tools** ribbon; when finished, select **Stop diagnostics**. Alternatively, you can analyze a single step—for this, you must select the **Diagnose step** button on the **Tools** ribbon, or you can right-click a step and select **Diagnose**. We are going to analyze a single step in the following way:

1. Filter the **ProductCategory** column to **Bikes** by using the filter button on the column header.

2. Right-click the **ProductCategory** column header and select **Remove**.

3. In the **Query Settings** pane, right-click the last step and select **Diagnose**.

After Power Query finishes recording the traces, it creates a new query group called Diagnostics (like in Figure 1-13) that contains several queries whose names start with *CompanySales_Removed Columns*, all ending with the current date and time. The queries are sources from JSON files stored locally on your computer. The *Detailed* query contains more rows and columns than the Aggregated query, which is a summary query.

Among other information available in the recorded traces, you will see the time it took for a query to run and whether a native query was sent to a data source, which can help you understand if query folding took place. In Aggregated and Detailed queries, you can find the **Data Source Query** column, which contains the query sent to the data source, if available.

Occasionally, you won't be able to see the native query by using the **View Native Query** feature discussed earlier in this chapter, but you will see a native query sent to a data source when using query diagnostics. We can check whether query folding took place by following the next steps:

1. In the *Aggregated* diagnostics query, filter the **Operation** column to only include **CreateResult**.

2. Go to the **Data Source Query** column and select the only column cell.

You should see the result shown in Figure 1-13.

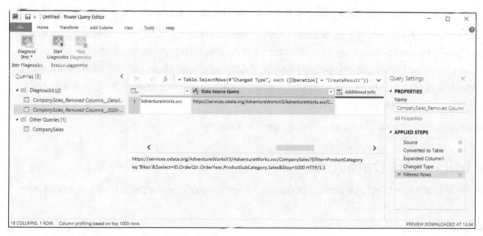

FIGURE 1-13 Native query sent to OData feed

The full query is as follows:

```
https://services.odata.org/AdventureWorksV3/AdventureWorks.svc/
CompanySales?$filter=ProductCategory eq 'Bikes'&$select=ID,OrderQtr,OrderYear,
ProductSubCategory,Sales&$top=1000 HTTP/1.1
```

Note that query folding occurs; the filter we placed on the **ProductCategory** column is included in the query and the **ProductCategory** column is not included in the query result. If you only relied on the **View Native Query** feature, you would not see the query because the option would be grayed out.

Some query diagnostics may require that you be running Power BI Desktop as administrator. If you are unable to record some traces, like full data refreshes, due to IT policies, you can still record traces when previewing and authoring queries in Power Query Editor. For this, go to **File** > **Options and settings** > **Options** > **Global** > **Diagnostics** > **Query diagnostics** and select **Enable in Query Editor**.

> **NEED MORE REVIEW?** **USING QUERY DIAGNOSTICS**
>
> For advanced information on how you can use the feature, including details on how to understand and visualize the recorded traces, see "Query Diagnostics" on Microsoft Docs at *https://docs.microsoft.com/en-us/power-query/QueryDiagnostics*.

Incremental refresh

If you work with large volumes of imported data in Power BI, sometimes it might be a good idea to implement *incremental refresh*, which keeps the bulk of your data static and only refreshes the most recent data, reducing the load on the data source during data refresh.

When you configure incremental refresh, you need to be sure that the underlying source supports it—otherwise, incremental refresh may not provide any benefits, and the whole table will be reloaded during each data refresh. If dataset or dataflow refresh history shows abnormally long refresh time even though incremental refresh was configured, chances are the underlying source does not support it.

We review incremental refresh in more detail in Chapter 5.

Use Microsoft Dataverse

Power Platform has a family of products that offer similar experiences when you get data in Power BI:

- Power BI dataflows
- Microsoft Dataverse (formerly known as Common Data Service)
- Power Platform dataflows

The Power Platform dataflows connector allows you to get Power BI dataflows, too. All three products store data in tables, also known as entities. Microsoft Dataverse also offers a set of standardized tables that you can map your data to, or you can create your own tables.

Connecting to Power BI or Power Platform dataflows only requires you to sign in, and then you'll see the entities you have access to.

To connect to Microsoft Dataverse, you'll need to know the server address, which usually has the following format: **https://environment.crm.dynamics.com/**.

NEED MORE REVIEW?   **FINDING SERVER ADDRESSES**

If you want to learn how to find the server name, see the step-by-step tutorial here: *https://docs.microsoft.com/en-us/powerapps/maker/common-data-service/ data-platform-powerbi-connector.*

Additionally, you'll need maker permissions to access the Power Apps portal and read permissions to access data within entities. Afterward, the connection experience is similar to connecting to a database.

Use parameters

Query parameters can simplify certain tasks, like changing a data source address or placing a filter in a query. Here are some examples of when you'd use parameters:

- Switching between the development and production environments when getting data from a database
- Configuring Incremental refresh, which is reviewed in Chapter 5
- Creating custom functions by using the user interface
- Using report templates

NEED MORE REVIEW?   **TEMPLATES IN POWER BI DESKTOP**

Power BI report templates can be used as a starting point when you analyze data in Power BI. Power BI report templates are out of the scope of this book. More information on how you can create and use report templates is available at *https://docs.microsoft.com/en-us/power-bi/ desktop-templates.*

Creating parameters

To create a new parameter in Power Query Editor, on the **Home** ribbon select **Manage parameters** > **New parameter**. You will then see the **Parameters** window shown in Figure 1-14.

FIGURE 1-14 The Parameters window

For each parameter, you can configure the following options:

- **Name**   This will become the parameter name by which you can reference it.
- **Description**   This will show up when you hover over the parameter in the **Queries** pane or when you open a report template that contains the parameter.
- **Required**   This determines whether the parameter value can be empty.
- **Type**   This is the data type of the parameter. Not all Power Query data types are available. For example, *whole number* cannot be selected; instead, you can choose *decimal number* for numerical parameters.
- **Suggested values**   You can choose one of these three options:
  - **Any value**   This is the default setting, and it allows any value within the limits of the parameter type.
  - **List of values**   This allows you to type a list of values from which you can choose a parameter. When you use this option, you may also specify the default value, which will be selected if you open a template with this parameter.
  - **Query**   When this option is selected, you will need to use a query of type list that will feed the list of values.
- **Current value**   This is the value the parameter returns when you reference it.

Using parameters

Let's follow an example on how to use parameters in practice:

1. Create a new Power BI Desktop file.
2. Open **Power Query Editor** by selecting **Transform data** on the **Home** ribbon.
3. Create a new parameter as follows:
   - Name: **Year**
   - Type: **Decimal number**
   - Current value: **2006**

You can leave all other parameter options as is.

Now that you have created the new parameter, let's connect to the **CompanySales** table from the AdventureWorks OData feed:

1. Still in **Power Query Editor**, select **New source** > **OData feed**.
2. Enter **https://services.odata.org/AdventureWorksV3/AdventureWorks.svc/** in the **URL** box and select **OK**.
3. Select the **CompanySales** check box and select **OK**.

In the lower-left corner of Power Query Editor, note that the **CompanySales** query, which you've just created, returns 235 rows. We are now going to use our parameter to filter the query.

1. Select the filter button on the **OrderYear** column header and select **Number filters** > **Equals**. You will be presented with the filter options in Figure 1-15.

FIGURE 1-15 Filter rows options

2. Select the top **1.2** drop-down list next to **equals** and select **Parameter**. Note that the **Year** parameter we created earlier is automatically selected because it is the only parameter.

3. Select **OK**.

The query now returns 50 rows, because it is filtered to only show rows where **OrderYear** is **2006**—the current value of the **Year** parameter.

Editing parameters

You can *edit* parameters in Power BI Desktop or the Power BI service. Editing a parameter refers to changing its current value, as opposed to managing a parameter, which refers to changing any parameter attribute.

To continue with our example, you can edit the **Year** parameter by selecting it in the **Queries** pane and changing its current value to **2007**. Note how the **CompanySales** query now returns 96 rows instead of 50.

NOTE **COMPANION FILES**

You can review this example by opening 1.1.8 Parameters.pbix from the companion files folder.

NOTE **EDITING MULTIPLE PARAMETERS**

If you had several parameters, it would be more convenient to select **Manage parameters >
Edit parameters** to edit all the parameters at once.

Also note that if you used query diagnostics, you would see that query folding occurred since Power BI issued the following query to the data source:

```
https://services.odata.org/AdventureWorksV3/AdventureWorks.svc/
CompanySales?$filter=OrderYear eq 2007&$top=1000 HTTP/1.1
```

You can also edit parameters after publishing your report to the Power BI service. This is done in the dataset settings, as shown in Figure 1-16.

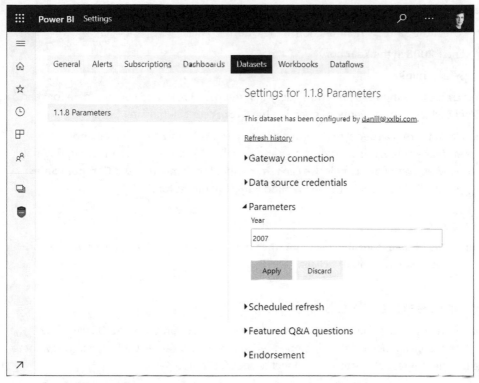

FIGURE 1-16 Editing parameters in the Power BI service

After you change the parameter value, select **Apply**.

NEED MORE REVIEW? **POWER BI SERVICE**

We review the Power BI service in more detail in Chapter 5.

Creating functions

Power Query allows you to create your own functions, which can be useful when you want to apply the same logic multiple times. One way to create a custom function is by converting a query to a function. If your query already uses parameters, then those will become the parameters of the new function.

Let's continue our AdventureWorks example and create a function that will output sales for a particular year based on the year you enter:

1. Right-click the **CompanySales** query and select **Create function**.
2. In the **Function name** box, enter **SalesByYear**.
3. Select **OK**.

This creates the **SalesByYear** group of queries, which contains the **Year** parameter, the **CompanySales** query, and the **SalesByYear** function.

Now test the new function:

1. Select the **SalesByYear** function in the **Queries** pane.
2. Enter **2008** in the **Year** box.
3. Select **Invoke**.

This creates the **Invoked Function** query that returns 73 rows and contains data for year 2008 only, which you can verify by selecting the **OrderYear** column filter button.

Note that there is a special relationship between the **SalesByYear** function and **CompanySales** query: updating the latter also updates the former, which in turn updates all function invocations. For example, we can remove the **ID** column from the **CompanySales** query, and it will disappear from the **Invoked Function** query, too.

EXAM TIP

You should be able to identify scenarios when query parameters can be beneficial based on the business requirements of a client.

Use or create a PBIDS file

If you've already connected to data in Power BI Desktop, you can export PBIDS files, which have data source connection details embedded in them. They can be useful when you want to make it easier for report creators to connect to specific data sources.

You can export a PBIDS file from **Data source settings** by selecting **Export PBIDS**. Refer to "Change data source settings," earlier in the chapter, for steps on how to open data source settings.

In the Wide World Importers example, if you export the *Targets* folder data source, you'll get a PBIDS file with the following code:

```
{
  "version": "0.1",
  "connections": [
    {
      "details": {
        "protocol": "folder",
        "address": {
          "path": "c:\\da-100\\targets"
        },
        "authentication": null,
        "query": null
      },
      "options": {},
      "mode": null
    }
  ]
}
```

When you open a PBIDS file, the experience is the same as when you connect to the data source in a new Power BI Desktop file.

> **NOTE CREDENTIALS**
>
> PBIDS files do not contain credentials, so users still need to be able to access the data sources.

Use or create a dataflow

In addition to Power BI Desktop, Power Query can be found in the Power BI service: you can prep, clean, and transform data in dataflows. Dataflows can be useful when you want your Power Query queries to be reused across your organization without the queries necessarily being in the same dataset. For this reason, you cannot create a dataflow in your own work-space, because only you have access to it.

To create a dataflow in a workspace, select **New > Dataflow**. From there, you have several choices:

- **Add new entities**   Define new tables from scratch by using Power Query.
- **Add linked entities**   Linked entities are tables in other dataflows that you can reuse to reduce duplication of data and improve consistency across your organization.
- **Import model**   If you have a previously exported dataflow model file, you can import it.
- **Create and attach**   Attach a Common Data Model folder from your Azure Data Lake Storage Gen2 account and use it in Power BI.

The Power Query Online interface (Figure 1-17) looks similar to Power Query Editor in Power BI Desktop.

FIGURE 1-17 Power Query interface when editing a dataflow

Once you finish authoring your queries, you can select **Save & close** and enter the name of the new dataflow. After saving, you'll need to refresh the dataflow by selecting **Refresh now** from the dataflow options in the workspace—otherwise, it won't contain any data. When a dataflow finishes refreshing, you can connect to it from Power BI Desktop and get data from it.

Connect to a dataset by using the XMLA endpoint

When you use Power BI Premium, you can use the XML for Analysis (XMLA) endpoint to connect to your datasets. By using XMLA endpoints, you can get data from a Power BI dataset and use a client tool other than Power BI to interact with the data. For example, you can visualize the data in Microsoft Excel, or you can use a third-party tool to edit your dataset.

To use the XMLA endpoints, **Allow XMLA endpoints and Analyze in Excel with on-premises datasets** must be enabled in the Power BI admin portal. The **XMLA Endpoint** setting in Power BI Premium capacity settings must also be set to **Read Only** or **Read Write**; the latter is required for editing datasets.

When making a connection by using the XMLA endpoint, you connect to a Power BI workspace as if it were a server, with datasets acting as databases. To get the workspace connection address, go to the workspace settings and select **Premium,** then **Copy** under **Workspace Connection**, as shown in Figure 1-18.

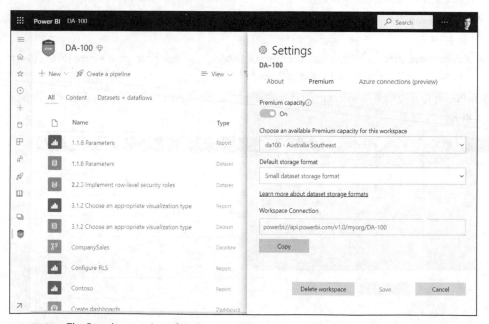

FIGURE 1-18 The Premium section of workspace settings

The address will have the following format:

```
powerbi://api.powerbi.com/v1.0/myorg/Your Workspace Name
```

You can then use the address as a server address when making a connection in your client tool. Most client tools will allow you to select a dataset after you connect to your workspace. Some client tools require setting an initial catalog—in this case, use the name of a dataset you want to connect to.

> **NOTE**   **USING AZURE B2B AND XMLA ENDPOINT**
>
> If you're an external user in someone's tenant and want to connect to their dataset by using the XMLA endpoint, you'll need to replace *myorg* with their domain name; the workspace connection string will look like *powerbi://api.powerbi.com/v1.0/contoso.com/Your Workspace Name*.

Skill 1.2: Profile the data

When performing data analysis, you will find it useful to see the overall structure or shape of data, which you can achieve by profiling data. Data profiling allows you to describe its content and consistency. It's advisable to do data profiling before working with data, because you can discover limitations in the source data and then decide if a better data source would be required. If you analyze the data without profiling it, you may miss outliers, and your results may not be representative of what's really happening.

Power Query has column profiling capabilities that can be used to profile your data before you even load it. These include column quality, column value distribution, and column profile.

> **This skill covers how to:**
> - Identify data anomalies
> - Examine data structures and interrogate column properties
> - Interrogate data statistics

Identify data anomalies

Power Query provides different functionality for identifying data anomalies depending on what you are looking for: you might be looking for unexpected values, such as prices over $10,000 when you analyze sales of a retail store, or you may be looking for missing or error values. In this section, we cover missing or error values, and later in the chapter we look at how you can identify unexpected values.

When you look at a table in Power Query Editor, you can check the quality of each column. By default, each column will have a colored bar under its header, which shows how many valid, error, and empty values there are in each column. To show the exact percentages, select **View** > **Data preview** > **Column quality**.

Figure 1-19 shows the **Employee** query from our earlier Wide World Importers example with the **Column quality** feature enabled.

1²₃ Employee Key ▼	1²₃ Parent Employee Key ▼	A⁸C Employee ▼	A⁸C Title ▼	A⁸C Email ▼
● Valid 100%	● Valid 85%	● Valid 100%	● Valid 100%	● Valid 100%
● Error 0%	● Error 0%	● Error 0%	● Error 0%	● Error 0%
● Empty 0%	● Empty 15%	● Empty 0%	● Empty 0%	● Empty 0%
1	0	null Unknown	N/A	N/A
2	3	4 Hudson Onslow	Salesperson	hudson.onslow@wideworldimporters.com
3	4	19 Isabella Rupp	Manager	isabella.rupp@wideworldimporters.com
4	6	4 Sophia Hinton	Salesperson	sophia.hinton@wideworldimporters.com
5	7	4 Amy Trefl	Salesperson	amy.trefl@wideworldimporters.com
6	8	12 Anthony Grosse	Salesperson	anthony.grosse@wideworldimporters.com
7	12	19 Henry Forlonge	Manager	henry.forlonge@wideworldimporters.com
8	13	12 Hudson Hollinworth	Salesperson	hudson.hollinworth@wideworldimporters.com
9	14	20 Lily Code	Salesperson	lily.code@wideworldimporters.com
10	15	20 Taj Shand	Salesperson	taj.shand@wideworldimporters.com
11	16	20 Archer Lamble	Salesperson	archer.lamble@wideworldimporters.com
12	19	null Jai Shand	Director	jai.shand@wideworldimporters.com
13	20	19 Jack Potter	Manager	jack.potter@wideworldimporters.com

FIGURE 1-19 Column quality

Note how the **Parent Employee Key** column has 85% valid values and 15% empty ones. If we didn't expect any empty values in the column, this would prompt us to investigate the issue. For the column quality purposes in Power Query, empty values are *null* values or empty strings. There are no errors in this query, so the Error percentage is always 0%.

If we now go to the **Customer** query and check the Postal Code column, we'll see that there are <1% error values. Note that Power Query won't tell you the percentage of valid or missing values when there are errors in a column. For now, we'll leave this error as is, and we're going to fix the error in this column later in this chapter.

To copy the column quality metrics, right-click the area under the column header and select **Copy quality metrics**.

Examine data structures and interrogate column properties

In addition to column quality, you can look at column value distribution. To enable this feature, select **View** > **Data preview** > **Column distribution**. In Figure 1-20, you can see the **Stock Item** query with this feature enabled.

FIGURE 1-20 Column distribution

Note that you can now see how many distinct and unique values each column has, as well as the distribution of column values in the form of a column chart under each column header. Column profiling is shown irrespective of the column type, which you can see to the left of a column's name.

The distinct number refers to how many different values there are in a column once duplicates are excluded. The unique number shows how many values occur exactly once. The number of distinct and unique values will be the same only if all values are unique.

The column charts show the shape of the data—you can see whether the distribution of values is uniform or if some values appear more frequently than others. For example, in Figure 1-20, you can see that the **Selling Package** column mostly consists of one value, with four other values appearing significantly less frequently.

To copy the data behind a column chart, right-click a column chart and select **Copy value distribution**. This will provide you with a list of distinct values and the number of times they appear in the column.

Knowing the column distribution can be particularly useful to identify columns that don't add value to your analysis. For example, in the **State Province** query, you can see that the following columns have only one distinct value each:

- Country
- Continent
- Region
- Subregion

Depending on your circumstances, you may choose to remove the columns to declutter your queries.

> **NOTE UNDERSTANDING VALUE DISTRIBUTION**
>
> The distribution of values is based on the current query only and none others. For example, the distribution of the **Stock Item Key** column values will be different in the **Stock Item** and **Sale** queries. It's also worth remembering that the distribution of values may be different if you choose to profile the entire dataset as opposed to the first 1,000 rows.

Interrogate data statistics

You can also profile columns to get some statistics and better understand your data. To enable this feature, select **View** > **Data preview** > **Column profile**. After you enable this feature, select a column header to see its profile. For example, Figure 1-21 shows the profile of the **Unit Price** column from the **Stock Item** query.

FIGURE 1-21 Column profile

You can now see two new areas in the lower part of Power Query Editor:

- **Column statistics**   This shows various statistics for the column. In addition to the total count of values and the number of error, empty, distinct, and unique values, you can see other statistics, such as minimum, maximum, average, and the number of zero, odd, and even values, among others. You will see different statistics depending on the column type. For instance, for text columns, you will see the number of empty strings in addition to the number of empty values. You can copy the statistics by selecting the ellipsis next to **Column statistics** and selecting **Copy**.

- **Value distribution** This is a more detailed version of the column chart you can see under the column name. You can now see which column refers to which value, and you can hover over a column to apply filters based on the corresponding value. You can copy the value distribution as text by selecting the ellipsis on the **Value distribution** header and selecting **Copy**. Also when you select the ellipsis, you can group the values depending on the data type. For example, you can group columns of type Date by year, month, day, week of year, and day of week. Text values can be grouped by text length. Whole numbers can be grouped by sign or parity (odd or even), whereas decimals can be grouped by sign only.

> **NEED MORE REVIEW?** **PROFILING TABLES**
>
> If you want to profile the whole table at once, you can use the **Table.Profile** function, which is not available when you are using the user interface alone, though you can write your own code to use it. We are reviewing the Advanced editor, where you can write custom code, later in this chapter.

Skill 1.3: Clean, transform, and load the data

Unless you are connecting to a dataset that someone has already prepared for you, in many cases you must clean and transform data before you can load and analyze it.

Power BI contains a powerful ETL (extract, transform, load) tool: Power Query. Power Query, also known as Get & Transform Data, first appeared as an add-in for Excel 2010; starting with Excel 2016, it has been an integral part of Excel. You can see Power Query in several other Microsoft products, including Power Apps and Power Automate.

When you connected to various data sources and worked inside Power Query Editor earlier in this chapter, you were using Power Query. Besides connecting to data, Power Query can perform sophisticated transformations to your data. In this book, Power Query refers to the engine behind Power Query Editor.

Power Query uses a programming language called M, which is short for "mashup." It is a functional, case-sensitive language. The latter point is worth noting because M is case-sensitive, unlike the other language of Power BI we are going to cover later, DAX. In addition, M is a completely new language that, unlike DAX, does not resemble Excel formula language in any way.

This skill covers how to:

- Resolve inconsistencies, unexpected or null values, and data quality issues and apply user-friendly value replacements
- Evaluate and transform column data types
- Identify and create appropriate keys for joins
- Apply data shape transformations to table structures
- Combine queries
- Apply user-friendly naming conventions to columns and queries
- Leverage the Advanced Editor to modify Power Query M code
- Configure data loading
- Resolve data import errors

Resolve inconsistencies, unexpected or null values, and data quality issues and apply user-friendly value replacements

If you followed the Wide World Importers example earlier in the chapter, you recall that the **Postal Code** column in the **Customer** query had an error in it. Power Query offers several ways to deal with errors or other unexpected values:

- Replace values
- Remove rows
- Identify the root cause of error

Replace values

You can replace undesirable values with different values by using the Power Query user interface. This approach can be appropriate when there are error values in the data source that you cannot fix. For example, when connecting to Excel, the #N/A values will show up as errors. Unless you can fix the errors in the source, it may be acceptable to replace them with some other values.

Since errors are not values as such, the procedure to replace them is different compared to replacing other unexpected values.

To replace errors:

1. Right-click a column header and select **Replace Errors**.
2. Enter the value you want to replace errors with in the **Value** box.
3. Select **OK**.

You can only replace errors in one column at a time when using the user interface.

To replace a value in a column:

1. Right-click a column header and select **Replace Values**.

2. Enter the value you want to replace in the **Value To Find** box.

3. Enter the replacement value in the **Replace With** box.

4. Select **OK**.

You can also right-click a value in the column and select **Replace Values**. This way, the **Value To Find** box will be prepopulated with the selected value.

For text columns, you can use the advanced options shown in Figure 1-22.

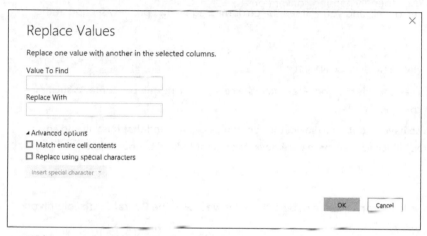

FIGURE 1-22 Replace Values options

- **Match entire cell contents**   With this option checked, Power Query won't replace values where the **Replace with** value is only part of the **Value To Find** value.

- **Replace using special characters**   Use this to insert special character codes, such as a carriage return or a nonbreaking space, in the **Replace With** or **Value To Find** box.

To replace values in multiple columns at once, you must select multiple columns before replacing values. To do so, hold the **Ctrl** key and select the columns whose values you want to replace. If you want to select a range of columns based on their order, you can select the first column, hold the **Shift** key, and select the last column.

The type of the replacement value must be compatible with the data type of the column—otherwise, you may get errors.

> **NOTE   NULL VALUES IN POWER QUERY**
>
> Null values are special values in Power Query. If you want to replace a value with a null, or vice versa, enter the word **null** in the relevant box, and Power Query will recognize it as a special value rather than text.

Remove rows

If there are errors in a column, you may wish to remove the rows entirely, depending on the business requirements. To do so, you can right-click a column header and select **Remove Errors**. Note that this will only remove rows where there are errors in the selected column. If you wish to remove all rows in a table that contain errors in any column, you can select the table icon to the left of the column headers and select **Remove Errors**.

Identify the root cause of error

When you see an error in a column, you can check the error message behind the error. To do so, select the error cell, and you will see the error message in the preview section at the bottom.

> **NOTE** **CHECKING THE CELL CONTENTS**
>
> In general, you can use this method—selecting the cell—to see nested cell contents such as errors, lists, records, and tables.
>
> Though you also have an option to select the hyperlink, keep in mind that this will add an extra query step, which you will have to remove if you want to load the query later.

Figure 1-23 shows the error message behind the error we saw in the **Postal Code** column of the **Customer** query.

FIGURE 1-23 Error message

After seeing this error message, you know that the error happened because Power Query tried to convert **N/A**, which is text, into a number. To confirm this, you can go one step back by selecting the **Promoted Headers** step in the list of **Applied steps**—the cell will show N/A, so you must transform the column type to **Text** to prevent the error from happening, as covered in the next section.

Although errors can happen for a variety of reasons, and not all errors occur because of type conversions, reading the error message will usually give you a good idea of what's going on.

Evaluate and transform column data types

If the data source does not communicate the type of each column, by default Power Query will do its best to detect the data types automatically if types are not available. So, for example, you'll get column types from a database, but not from a JSON file, so Power Query will try to detect types. It's important to note that the process is not perfect because Power Query does not always consider all values. As you saw earlier, Power Query may detect data types incorrectly.

> **NOTE** **DISABLING AUTOMATIC TYPE DETECTION**
>
> If you find the automatic type detection undesirable, you can turn it off at **File** > **Options and settings** > **Options** > **Current file** > **Data load** > **Type detection**.

Power Query supports the following data types:

- Decimal Number
- Fixed Decimal Number
- Whole Number
- Percentage
- Date/Time
- Date
- Time
- Date/Time/Timezone
- Duration
- Text
- True/False
- Binary

Continuing our Wide World Importers example, we now know that there is an error in the **Postal Code** column of the **Customer** query due to data type conversion. Power Query scanned the first few rows and, seeing whole numbers, decided that the type of the column is **Whole Number**, which you can see from the icon on the left side of the column header.

In our example, you should transform the **Postal Code** column type to Text to accommodate both numeric and text values.

To transform the column type, right-click a column header, then select **Change type** and select the desired data type. Alternatively, you can select the column type icon on the column header, and then select the data type you want to transform the column to.

After you try to change the type of the **Postal Code** column, you will see the message shown in Figure 1-24.

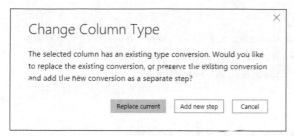

FIGURE 1-24 Change Column Type dialog box

Since Power Query has already automatically changed the type of the column before, you now have the option to either replace the conversion by selecting **Replace current** or add a new conversion on top of the existing one by selecting **Add new step**.

In this case, you should replace the current conversion because otherwise Power Query will try to convert the error value to Text, and it will still be an error. After you select **Replace current**, you will not see any errors, and you will be able to see the column distribution and other statistics.

> **NOTE CACHING IN POWER QUERY**
>
> If you still see errors after transforming type to Text, you should navigate to another query and come back to Customer. This is because Power Query sometimes caches the output and does not immediately update it.

Adding a new conversion step is appropriate in case you cannot convert the type in one step. For example, if you've got data in a CSV file, and there's a column that contains Date/Time values, you will not be able to set the column type to Date. Instead, you should set the data type to Date/Time first, and then add a new conversion step that changes the type to Date. This way, you will get no errors.

If you want Power Query to detect the type of one or more specific columns automatically, you can select the columns, then select **Transform** > **Any Column** > **Detect Data Type**.

Using locale

Occasionally, you will need to transform data by using a certain locale. For example, if your computer uses the DMY date format and you receive data in MDY format, you'll need to change type with the locale. To do so, right-click a column header and select **Change Type** > **Using Locale**. From there, you'll need to select the data type and locale from drop-down lists.

Identify and create appropriate keys for joins

Power BI allows you to combine data from different tables in several ways. Most commonly, you combine tables, or you create relationships between them.

Combining tables requires a join in the query, which in Power Query is also known as *merge*. Relationships, which you create in the model, not in Power Query, create implicit joins when visuals calculate values. The choice between the two depends on the business requirements and is up to the data modeler. In this section, we are discussing the keys you need for either operation.

When you join tables, you need to have some criteria to join them, such as keys in each table. For example, you join the *City* and *Sale* tables by using the *City Key* column in each table. Though it's handy to have keys named in the same way, it's not required. For instance, you can join the *Sale* table with the *Date* table by using the *Invoice Date Key* from the *Sale* table and the *Date* column from the *Date* table.

Each table can be on the *one* or the *many* side during a join. If a table is on the *one* side, it means the key in the table has a unique value for every row, and it's also known as the *primary key*. If a table is on the *many* side, it means that values in the key column are not necessarily unique for every row and may repeat, and such a key is often called a *foreign key*.

You can join tables that are both on the *one* side, but such situations are rare. Usually one table is on the *one* side and one table is on the *many* side. You can also perform joins when both tables are on the *many* side, though you should be aware that if you do it in Power Query, you will get duplicate rows.

Keys for joins in Power Query

Power Query allows you to perform joins based on one or more columns at once, so it's not necessary to create composite keys to merge tables in Power Query.

For joins in Power Query, column types are important. For example, if a column is of type Date, then you won't be able to merge it with a column of type Date/Time even if the Date/Time column has no Time component.

Keys for relationships

For relationships, Power BI is more forgiving of the data type. If columns that participate in a relationship are of different types, Power BI will do its best to convert them in one type behind the scenes. Although the relationship may still work, it's always best to have the same data type for columns that are in a relationship.

Power BI only allows you to create physical relationships between two tables on a single pair of columns. This means that in case you have a composite key in a table, you'll need to combine the key columns in a single column before you can create a physical relationship between two tables. You can do it in Power Query or by creating a calculated column in DAX.

> **NEED MORE REVIEW?** **CALCULATED COLUMNS AND DAX**
>
> If you use DirectQuery, some calculated columns can still be translated into the native language of the data source efficiently. For example, the COMBINEVALUES function in DAX translates well into SQL. We review DAX in Chapter 2.

There are two ways of combining columns in Power Query:

- Create a new column   This option keeps the original columns. To add a new merged column, select the columns you want to combine and select **Add column** > **From Text** > **Merge Columns**.

- Merge columns in-place   This option removes the original columns. To merge existing columns, select the columns you want to merge and select **Transform** > **Text Column** > **Merge Columns**.

> **IMPORTANT**   **COLUMN SELECTION ORDER**
>
> The order in which you select columns matters: the order of the text in the merged column follows the order of column selection. In other words, if you select column A first and then column B, the result will be different compared to your selecting column B first and then column A.

Either way, you'll be presented with the options shown in Figure 1-25.

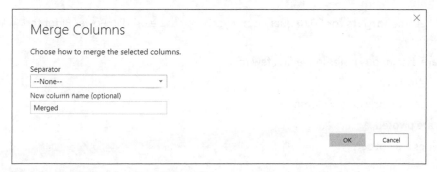

FIGURE 1-25 Merge columns options

You can use one of the predefined separators from the **Separator** drop-down list, or you can specify your own by selecting **Custom** from the drop-down list. You're also given an option to enter the new column name. After you specify the options, select **OK**.

Apply data shape transformations to table structures

Few data sources provide data in shapes that are ready to be used by Power BI. You'll often need to transform your data, especially if you work with files. In this section, we review common table transformations in Power Query by transforming the Wide World Importers queries that contain sales targets: **Targets for 2020** and **Targets**.

> **NOTE   COMPANION FILES**
>
> If you want to follow along with the example, use 1.1.1 Connect to data sources.pbix from the companion files folder.

In Figure 1-26, you can see the first four columns of the **Targets for 2020** query. There are 14 columns and seven rows in this query, which you can check by looking at the lower-left corner of Power Query when viewing the query.

> **NOTE   QUERY ROW COUNT**
>
> The row count is based on the query preview, and it may not account for all rows. You'll get a more accurate figure in the Data view after you load data.

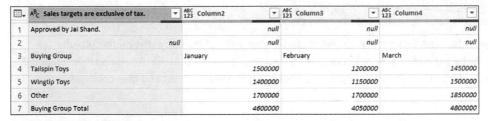

	A^B_C Sales targets are exclusive of tax.	ABC 123 Column2	ABC 123 Column3	ABC 123 Column4
1	Approved by Jai Shand.	null	null	null
2	null	null	null	null
3	Buying Group	January	February	March
4	Tailspin Toys	1500000	1200000	1450000
5	Wingtip Toys	1400000	1150000	1500000
6	Other	1700000	1700000	1850000
7	Buying Group Total	4600000	4050000	4800000

FIGURE 1-26 Targets for 2020

As you can see, the **Targets for 2020** query is not yet ready to be used in Power BI for the following reasons:

- There are extraneous notes in the first few rows.
- There are totals.
- There is no date or month column.
- Values are pivoted.
- Data types are not set.

In Figure 1-27, you can see the Targets query.

	ABC Source.Name	ABC Buying Group	1²₃ Target Excluding Tax (Millions)
1	2017.csv	Tailspin Toys	9
2	2017.csv	Wingtip Toys	9
3	2017 csv	Other	9
4	2018.csv	Tailspin Toys	15
5	2018.csv	Wingtip Toys	15
6	2018.csv	Other	18
7	2019.csv	Tailspin Toys	15
8	2019.csv	Wingtip Toys	15
9	2019.csv	Other	21

FIGURE 1-27 Targets query

There are several issues with this query, too:

- Targets are provided at year level, but we need them to be at month level.
- Years come from file names and have the .csv extension suffix.
- Targets are in millions instead of dollars.

After you transform each query, you must combine them. In our example, we're aiming for a single table with the following columns:

- **End of Month** You'll need to make a relationship with the *Date* table later, and you can use a column of type Date for that.
- **Buying Group** Only three values and no totals.
- **Target Excluding Tax** In dollars, for each month.

Working with query steps

To start getting the **Targets for 2020** query in the right shape, let's undo some of the automatic transformations done by Power Query. By looking at the **Applied steps** pane, you can see that after navigating to the right sheet in the Excel file, Power Query has promoted the first row to headers, even though the row did not contain column names. It also changed column types, considering column names as valid column values, which led to incorrect data type selection.

1. Right-click the **Promoted Headers** step in the **Applied steps** pane.
2. Select **Delete Until End**.
3. Select **Delete**.

This removes the **Promoted Headers** step and all subsequent steps. The **Delete Until End** option is especially useful when you have more than two steps you want to remove.

As Figure 1-28 shows, you can now see some notes left by a sales planner in the first two rows. Note that columns are now not typed.

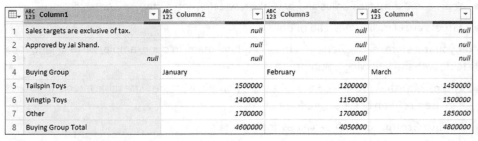

	ABC 123 Column1	ABC 123 Column2	ABC 123 Column3	ABC 123 Column4
1	Sales targets are exclusive of tax.	null	null	null
2	Approved by Jai Shand.	null	null	null
3	null	null	null	null
4	Buying Group	January	February	March
5	Tailspin Toys	1500000	1200000	1450000
6	Wingtip Toys	1400000	1150000	1500000
7	Other	1700000	1700000	1850000
8	Buying Group Total	4600000	4050000	4800000

FIGURE 1-28 Targets for 2020 with automatic transformations undone

Reducing rows and columns

Since the first three rows don't contain any meaningful data, we can remove them. In addition to filtering columns, the Power Query user interface offers the following options for row reduction:

- **Keep Rows**
  - **Keep Top Rows**   Keeps the specified number of top rows. Works on the whole table only.
  - **Keep Bottom Rows**   Keeps the specified number of bottom rows. Works on the whole table only.
  - **Keep Range of Rows**   Skips a specified number of top rows and then keeps the chosen number of rows. Works on the whole table only.
  - **Keep Duplicates**   Keeps rows that appear more than once. This option can work on the whole table, meaning all column values will have to match for rows to be considered duplicates, or it can work on selected columns only, so values will only need to match in specified columns for duplicates to be kept.
  - **Keep Errors**   Keeps rows that contain errors. This option can work on the whole table or selected columns only.

- **Remove Rows**
  - **Remove Top Rows**   Removes a specified number of top rows. Works on the whole table only.
  - **Remove Bottom Rows**   Removes a specified number of bottom rows. Works on the whole table only.
  - **Remove Alternate Rows**   Removes rows following a user-supplied pattern: it starts with a specified row, then alternates between removing the selected number of rows and keeping the chosen number of rows. Works on the whole table only.
  - **Remove Duplicates**   Removes rows that are duplicates of other rows. Can work on the whole table or selected columns only.
  - **Remove Blank Rows**   Removes rows that completely consist of empty strings or nulls. Works on the whole table only; if you need to remove blank values from a specific column, you can select the filter button to the right of a column's name and select **Remove Empty**.
  - **Remove Errors**   Removes rows that contain errors. Can work on the whole table or selected columns only.

Since notes can potentially change, it's best not to remove them by filtering out specific values. In our case, **Remove Top Rows** is appropriate.

1. Select **Remove Rows** on the **Home** ribbon.
2. Select **Remove Top Rows**.
3. Enter **3** in the **Number of rows** box.
4. Select **OK**.

Now that we have removed the top three rows, we can use the first row for the column names by selecting **Use First Row as Headers** on the Home ribbon. The result should look like Figure 1-29.

	ABC Buying Group	123 January	123 February	123 March
1	Tailspin Toys	1500000	1200000	1450000
2	Wingtip Toys	1400000	1150000	1500000
3	Other	1700000	1700000	1850000
4	Buying Group Total	4600000	4050000	4800000

FIGURE 1-29 Targets for 2020 with unnecessary rows removed and headers in place

NEED MORE REVIEW?   REMOVING TOP ROWS DYNAMICALLY

In practice, the number of rows with notes or other unneeded information may not be consistent. In such cases, you must specify the number of rows you want to remove dynamically. We're going to review one way to do that by modifying the M code later in this chapter.

Note how Power Query automatically detected column types, this time correctly since only the first column is a text column and all the other columns are numeric.

Next, you can see that the last row is a total row, and the last column, **Year Target**, is a total column. You need to remove both, because keeping them may result in incorrect aggregation later in Power BI.

There are several ways to remove the last row, and which way is best depends on several factors:

- If you're sure that the last row is always going to be a total row, you can remove it in the same way that you removed the top three rows earlier.

- If, on the other hand, you're not sure that the total row is always going to be there, it's safer to filter out a specific value from the **Buying Group** column—in our example, **Buying Group Total**.

- Depending on business logic, you can also apply a text filter that excludes values that end with the word "Total." This kind of filter relies on actual Buying Group column values not ending with "Total."

> **NEED MORE REVIEW?**   **CASE SENSITIVITY IN POWER QUERY**
>
> Since Power Query is case-sensitive by default, you must exclude the word "Total"; filtering out "total" won't work. We'll show you how to protect your code against this issue later in this chapter when we review the Advanced Editor.

Let's say you're sure that only the total row label ends with the word "Total," so we can apply a corresponding filter to the **Buying Group** column:

1. Select the filter button on the **Buying Group** column header.
2. Select **Text Filters** > **Does Not End With**.
3. Enter **Total** in the box next to the drop-down list that shows **does not end with**.
4. Select **OK**.

The last row is now filtered out, and you should remove the last column as well, since it contains totals for the year. To do so, select the **Year Target** column and press the **Delete** key.

With the totals gone, Power Query Editor should show "13 columns, 3 rows" in the lower-left corner. However, the current **Targets for 2020** query still does not meet our goals because we don't have a single date or month column. Instead, targets for each month appear in a separate column. We'll address this issue next.

Pivoting columns, unpivoting columns, and transposing

The current **Targets for 2020** query is sometimes called pivoted because attributes appear on both rows and columns and the same measure is scattered across multiple columns—just like in an Excel PivotTable.

Power Query provides several options when it comes to pivoting and unpivoting:

- **Pivot column**   This creates a new column for each value in the column you pivot. One scenario when this option can be useful is when you have different measures mixed in the same column. For example, if you have *Quantity* and *Price* as text labels in one column and numeric quantity and price values in another column, you could pivot the first column to create separate Quantity and Price columns with numeric quantity and price values, respectively.

- **Unpivot columns**   The selected columns will be transformed into two: Attribute, containing old column names, and Value, containing old column values. In general, unpivoting is useful when the source data has been prepared by using a PivotTable or similar method. This specific option is appropriate when the list of columns you want to unpivot is known in advance.

- **Unpivot other columns**   All columns except the selected ones will be unpivoted. This option is particularly useful when you only know the list of columns that don't need to be unpivoted. For example, if you have a file where monthly data is added as columns every month and you want to unpivot months, then you could use this option.

- **Unpivot only selected columns**   Despite the names of the previous two options, Power Query tries to recognize when you want to unpivot the selected columns or other columns, so this option allows you to be strict about which columns are unpivoted.

Furthermore, Power Query offers the **Transpose** feature, which allows you to transpose tables, treating rows as columns and columns as rows. This operation can be useful when you have multiple levels of headers; you can transpose your table, merge the columns that contain headers, and transpose again, so there will be only one row of headers.

IMPORTANT   **TABLE TRANSPOSITION AND COLUMN NAMES**

When transposing tables, remember that you lose column names during the operation, so if you want to keep them, you must demote headers to first row. You can do so by selecting the **Use First Row as Headers** drop-down and then selecting **Use Headers as First Row**.

For our Wide World Importers example, right-click the **Buying Group** column and select **Unpivot other columns**. This puts all column headers except for **Buying Group** in a single column called **Attribute**, and it puts all values in the **Value** column. The result should look like Figure 1-30.

	ABC Buying Group	ABC Attribute	123 Value
1	Tailspin Toys	January	1500000
2	Tailspin Toys	February	1200000
3	Tailspin Toys	March	1450000
4	Tailspin Toys	April	1100000
5	Tailspin Toys	May	1550000
6	Tailspin Toys	June	1300000
7	Tailspin Toys	July	1350000

FIGURE 1-30 Unpivoted months

As you can see, months now appear in a single column, which is what we want for Power BI. Now you need to transform month names into date values so you can create a relationship with the Date table later.

Adding columns

You can add a new column in Power Query by using one of the following options on the **Add column** ribbon:

- **Column From Examples**   This option allows you to type some examples in a new column, and Power Query will try its best to write a transformation formula to accommodate the examples.

- **Custom Column**   You can type your own M formula for the new column.

- **Invoke Custom Function**   This option invokes a custom function for every row of a table.

- **Conditional Column**   This option provides an interface where you can specify the if-then-else logic for your new column.

- **Index Column**   This option creates a sequential column that starts and increments with the values you specify. By default, it will start with 0 and increment by 1 for each row.

- **Duplicate Column**   This option creates a copy of a column you select.

In addition to these options, you can use data type–specific transformations to add columns, most of which are also available on the **Transform** ribbon. The difference between the **Add Column** and **Transform** ribbons is that the former will add a new column whereas the latter will transform a column in place.

TARGETS FOR 2020

In the **Targets for 2020** query, you must transform month names into dates, and you'll use the **Custom Column** option for this:

1. Select **Add Column** > **Custom Column**.

2. Enter **Start of Month** in the **New column name** box.

   Enter **Date.From([Attribute] & " 2020")** in the **Custom column formula** box. The Custom Column window should look like Figure 1-31.

3. Select **OK**.

4. Right-click the **Attribute** column and select **Remove**.

When entering a custom column formula, you can use the columns available in the table by double-clicking them in the Available columns list on the right; this will insert a column reference into your formula.

FIGURE 1-31 Custom Column window

Once you complete these steps, the result should look like Figure 1-32.

	A^B_C Buying Group	1²₃ Value	ABC 123 Start of Month
1	Tailspin Toys	1500000	01-Jan-20
2	Tailspin Toys	1200000	01-Feb-20
3	Tailspin Toys	1450000	01-Mar-20
4	Tailspin Toys	1100000	01-Apr-20
5	Tailspin Toys	1550000	01-May-20
6	Tailspin Toys	1300000	01-Jun-20
7	Tailspin Toys	1350000	01-Jul-20
8	Tailspin Toys	1350000	01-Aug-20

FIGURE 1-32 Targets for 2020 with Start of Month column

> **IMPORTANT CUSTOM COLUMN TYPES**
>
> The **Custom column** feature creates a column without a data type; you must set the data type manually before loading to ensure that the data is loaded correctly.

As you can see, the **Start of Month** column you've just created has no column type, and you may want to make it the first column instead of the last. Additionally, you have to rename the **Value** column.

1. Select the **ABC123** icon on the **Start of Month** column header and select **Date**.
2. Right-click the **Start of Month** column and select **Move** > **To Beginning**.
3. Double-click the **Value** column header.
4. Enter **Target Excluding Tax** and press the Enter key.

The **Targets for 2020** query is now finished, and we need to transform the **Targets** query next.

TARGETS

In the **Targets** query, you have yearly targets, and you need to have monthly targets. Let's say that, according to business rules, it's all right to divide the yearly target evenly across months for years prior to 2020, which this query contains.

There are a few ways to solve this problem, one of which is adding a new column that contains months and expanding it:

1. Select **Add New Column** > **Custom Column**.

2. Enter **Months** in the **New column name** box.

3. Enter **{1..12}** in the **Custom column formula** box.

4. Select **OK**.

The result should look like Figure 1-33.

	ABC Source.Name	ABC Buying Group	123 Target Excluding Tax (Millions)	ABC123 Months
1	2017.csv	Tailspin Toys	9	List
2	2017.csv	Wingtip Toys	9	List
3	2017.csv	Other	9	List
4	2018.csv	Tailspin Toys	15	List
5	2018.csv	Wingtip Toys	15	List
6	2018.csv	Other	18	List
7	2019.csv	Tailspin Toys	15	List
8	2019.csv	Wingtip Toys	15	List
9	2019.csv	Other	21	List

FIGURE 1-33 Months custom column added to the Targets query

In M, braces signify a list, and double period signifies a range. When you used **{1..12}** as a custom column formula, you put a list of numbers from 1 to 12, inclusive, in each cell of the new column. Therefore, you see the *List* hyperlinks in the **Months** column cells. Because custom columns by default don't have a data type set, you see ABC123 as the column type, even though in reality it is of type List.

If you select any **List** hyperlink, you'll navigate to a new step that contains one such list. You can also preview the contents of a cell without navigating to the list by selecting a cell without selecting a hyperlink.

You can expand the new column by selecting the double-arrow button on the column header. You'll then see two options:

- **Expand to New Rows**   This option duplicates each table row by the number of list items in the row's list.

- **Extract Values**   This option keeps the number of rows in the table the same, and it concatenates the list items by using a separator you specify, which can be one of the predefined ones or a custom value you provide.

In our example, you use the **Expand to New Rows** option. The result should look like Figure 1-34.

	ABC Source.Name	ABC Buying Group	123 Target Excluding Tax (Millions)	ABC 123 Months
1	2017.csv	Tailspin Toys	9	1
2	2017.csv	Tailspin Toys	9	2
3	2017.csv	Tailspin Toys	9	3
4	2017.csv	Tailspin Toys	9	4
5	2017.csv	Tailspin Toys	9	5
6	2017.csv	Tailspin Toys	9	6
7	2017.csv	Tailspin Toys	9	7
8	2017.csv	Tailspin Toys	9	8
9	2017.csv	Tailspin Toys	9	9
10	2017.csv	Tailspin Toys	9	10
11	2017.csv	Tailspin Toys	9	11
12	2017.csv	Tailspin Toys	9	12
13	2017.csv	Wingtip Toys	9	1
14	2017.csv	Wingtip Toys	9	2

FIGURE 1-34 Expanded Months column

Before you can create a column of type Date, you'll have to transform the first column, which contains file names. Each file is named after a year and has a .csv extension. There are multiple ways to extract the year number from the column. The most appropriate way depends on the business requirements. In our example, you can extract the first four characters:

1. Select the **Source.Name** column.
2. On the **Transform** ribbon, select **Text Column** > **Extract** > **First Characters**.
3. Enter **4** in the **Count** box.
4. Select **OK**.
5. Right-click the **Source.Name** column header and select **Change Type** > **Whole Number**.

Now that you have the year number, you can construct a date from it:

1. On the **Add Column** ribbon, select **Custom Column**.
2. Enter **Start of Month** in the **New column name** box.
3. Enter **#date([Source.Name], [Months], 1)** in the **Custom column formula** box.
4. Select **OK**.
5. Right-click the **Start of Month** column and select **Change Type** > **Date**.

In the new Start of Month column, we've got dates now, as desired. You can now clean up the query:

1. Hold the **Ctrl** key and select the following columns in order:
   A. **Start of Month**
   B. **Buying Group**
   C. **Target Excluding Tax (Millions)**
2. Right-click the header of any of the selected columns and select **Remove Other Columns**.

The **Target** query now has three columns. The only problem left in this query is to correct the **Target Excluding Tax (Millions)** column:

1. Select the **Target Excluding Tax (Millions)** column.
2. On the **Transform** ribbon, select **Number Column** > **Standard** > **Multiply**.
3. Enter **1000000** in the **Value** box and select **OK**.
4. Similarly, select **Number Column** > **Standard** > **Divide**, enter **12** in the **Value** box and select **OK**.
5. Double-click the **Target Excluding Tax (Millions)** column header, enter **Target Excluding Tax**, and press the **Enter** key.

The result should look like Figure 1-35.

	Start of Month	ABC Buying Group	1.2 Target Excluding Tax
1	01-Jan-17	Tailspin Toys	750000
2	01-Feb-17	Tailspin Toys	750000
3	01-Mar-17	Tailspin Toys	750000
4	01-Apr-17	Tailspin Toys	750000
5	01-May-17	Tailspin Toys	750000
6	01-Jun-17	Tailspin Toys	750000
7	01-Jul-17	Tailspin Toys	750000
8	01-Aug-17	Tailspin Toys	750000

FIGURE 1-35 Transformed Target query

Note how the column names are now the same as those in the **Targets for 2020** query—this is on purpose. You are now ready to combine the two queries into one.

Combine queries

There are two main ways to combine queries in Power Query:

- **Append** This stacks queries vertically. In SQL, it's like UNION ALL.
- **Merge** This combines queries horizontally based on the keys you supply. In SQL, it's like JOIN.

Append

When you append queries, you combine tables vertically. As a result, you get a taller table. Usually the tables will have the same columns, though this is not strictly necessary. The resulting table will have all columns from all queries, and if some columns were missing in one of the original queries, then they will be populated with *null* values if values are missing.

You can append queries in two ways:

- **Append Queries** This option appends one or more queries to the selected query and does not create any new queries. This is the default option if you select **Append Queries** without selecting the drop-down button.

- **Append Queries as New** This creates a new query that contains concatenated rows of the original queries. You can select this option after selecting the drop-down button.

In the Wide World Importers example, let's append the **Targets for 2020** and **Targets** queries:

1. Select the **Targets** query from the **Queries** pane.

2. Select **Append Queries**. You should see the options shown in Figure 1-36.

FIGURE 1-36 Options when appending

3. Select **Targets for 2020** from the **Table to append** drop-down list.

4. Select **OK**.

As a result, you will see a new step in the **Applied steps** pane called **Appended Query**. Unless you scroll down, you will not see any new rows because they are appended to the end of the query. In the lower-left corner, you can note the change in the number of rows, which increased to 144 from 108 in the previous step.

To meet our goal of having the **End of Month** column in the **Targets** query, let's transform the **Start of Month** column:

1. Right-click the **Start of Month** column and select **Transform** > **Month** > **End of Month**.

2. Rename the **Start of Month** column to **End of Month**.

Note how you need to apply the transformation only once, even though the current query consists of two queries—**Targets** and **Targets for 2020**.

For now, you can leave the **Targets for 2020** query as is, although it would be undesirable to load it since now there's duplicated data in the **Targets for 2020** and **Targets** queries. We will address this issue later in the "Configure data loading" section.

Merge

As discussed earlier, when you merge queries you combine them horizontally; as a result, you get a wider table. When merging, you need a set of keys—columns that have matching values in both tables—telling Power Query which rows of the first table should be combined with which rows of the second table.

Like the Append Queries feature, you can either merge two queries without creating a new one or you can merge queries as new.

There are six kinds of joins in Power Query:

- **Left Outer**   All from first, matching from second
- **Right Outer**   All from second, matching from first
- **Full Outer**   All rows from both
- **Inner**   Only matching rows
- **Left Anti**   Rows only in first
- **Right Anti**   Rows only in second

You can see the visual representation of joins in Figure 1-37.

FIGURE 1-37 Joins available in Power Query

In case your data isn't perfect, Power Query allows you to use fuzzy matching when performing merges. You can use the following options:

- **Similarity threshold**   Can be valued from 0 to 1, where 0 will make all values match each other and 1 will allow exact matches only. The default is 0.8.
- **Ignore case**   Lowercase and uppercase letters will be treated as the same.
- **Match by combining text parts**   Power Query will try to combine separate words into one to find matches between keys.
- **Maximum number of matches**   This option will limit the number of rows from the second table that are matched against the first table, and it can be useful if you expect multiple matches.
- **Transformation table**   You can use a column with two columns—**From** and **To**—to map values during the matching process. For example, you can map *NZ* to *New Zealand*, and the two values will be considered the same for merge purposes.

For Wide World Importers, let's merge the **City** and **State Province** queries:

1. Select the **City** query in the **Queries** pane.
2. Select **Merge Queries** on the **Home** ribbon.
3. Select **State Province** in the drop-down list below the **City** query preview.
4. Select **State Province Key** in both tables. The columns should be highlighted as in Figure 1-38.

FIGURE 1-38 Merge options

5. Ensure **Left Outer** is selected from the Join Kind drop-down list.
6. Select **OK**.

After you complete these steps, you'll see a new column named **State Province** added to the **City** query. Note that the new column

- Is of type Table
- Has *Table* hyperlinks in each cell
- Has a double-arrow button instead of a filter button on its header

If you select any cell in the new column without selecting the hyperlink, you'll see a preview of the cell contents, and you'll see a table row in our case.

You can expand the new column by selecting the double-arrow button on its header. There are two ways to expand a table column:

- **Expand** You can select the columns from the joined table that you want to add to the current table. If there is more than one matching row in the joined table, the current table's rows will be duplicated after expansion.

- **Aggregate** This option aggregates rows and won't duplicate any rows in the current table. You can apply arithmetic and statistical functions to the columns of the joined table. For example, if it made business sense, you could take the average of **State Province Key** from the **State Province** table.

When expanding the table column, you can use the original column name as a prefix. This option can be useful if there are column names that are the same in both tables but their content is different. For instance, if you are merging the **Product** and **Product Category** tables and both have a column called **Name**, then you can use the original column name as a prefix to avoid confusion.

In our example, let's expand the merged column:

1. In the **City** query, select the double-arrow button on the **State Province** column header.

2. Clear the **Select All Columns** check box.

3. Select the **State Province** and **Sales Territory** check boxes.

4. Clear the **Use original column name as prefix** check box.

5. Select **OK**.

6. Rename the **State Province.1** column to **State Province**.

7. Remove the **State Province Key** column.

The result should look like Figure 1-39.

	1²₃ City Key	ᴬᴮC City	ᴬᴮC Location	ᴬᴮC State Province	ᴬᴮC Sales Territory
1	98700	Greenfield	POINT (-90.7126119999999s 35.6322013)	Arkansas	Southeast
2	98706	Grider	POINT (-89.9806435 35.6386903)	Arkansas	Southeast
3	101245	Schaal	POINT (-93.961022 33.8262286)	Arkansas	Southeast
4	101362	Wesson	POINT (-92.7626597 33.1154128)	Arkansas	Southeast
5	94161	Astor Park	POINT (-81.5720175 29.1535911)	Florida	Southeast
6	94175	Bakers Mill	POINT (-82.939302 30.5796601)	Florida	Southeast
7	94237	Bratt	POINT (-87.4274794 30.9657386)	Florida	Southeast
8	94308	Compass Lake	POINT (-85.3927045 30.5926937)	Florida	Southeast

FIGURE 1-39 City query with columns from the State Province query

You've merged the **City** and **State Province** queries, and you've got five useful columns as a result. You don't need the **State Province Key** column anymore, and the columns you didn't include from the **State Province** query all had one distinct value each.

As is the case for the **Targets for 2020** query, the information from the **State Province** query now appears in two queries, so there's some data duplication in our queries. Again, we'll address this later in the chapter.

Apply user-friendly naming conventions to columns and queries

When you create your data model in Power BI, you don't have to follow any naming conventions to make your data model work. Nevertheless, following user-friendly naming conventions will make your model easier to use and reduce confusion among users.

In Power BI, you are encouraged to name your tables, columns, and measures in ways that are commonly understood by people without a technical background. Contrary to the popular naming conventions in the database world, it's completely fine to use spaces in names, so it's not necessary to use underscores or camelCase in Power BI.

REAL WORLD   **DATA MODEL CLARITY**

Having a user-friendly data model is extremely important. In large companies, data modelers and report builders may be different people, and data models must be as easy to understand as possible for report builders.

Furthermore, report viewers can personalize visuals in the Power BI service; while doing so, they can browse the list of fields and tables available in the model, which makes following user-friendly naming conventions even more important.

If you retrieve data from views in a database, they may carry the schema and a prefix, and it's desirable to remove them. For example, if you connect to a view called **vw_Sales** in the **pbi** schema, it will be imported as **pbi vw_Sales** in Power BI by default. It's best to rename it to **Sales** for clarity, since neither **pbi** nor **vw_** may make sense to report builders and viewers.

The Wide World Importers tables contain user-friendly query and column names.

Leverage the Advanced Editor to modify Power Query M code

Although you can do a lot of transformations in Power Query Editor just by using the user interface, you can do even more by writing M queries yourself. M is a case-sensitive language that is behind the Power Query engine.

You can view and edit full M queries in the Advanced Editor. To open it, select **Advanced editor** on the **Home** ribbon in Power Query Editor. Alternatively, you can right-click a query in the **Queries** pane and select **Advanced editor**. For example, here you can see the code behind the **Date** query.

```
let
    Source = Excel.Workbook(File.Contents("C:\DA-100\WideWorldImporters.xlsx"), null,
true),
    Date_Sheet = Source{[Item="Date",Kind="Sheet"]}[Data],
    #"Promoted Headers" = Table.PromoteHeaders(Date_Sheet, [PromoteAllScalars=true]),
    #"Changed Type" = Table.TransformColumnTypes(#"Promoted Headers",{{"Date", type
date}, {"Month", type text}, {"Month Number", Int64.Type}, {"Quarter", type text},
{"Year", Int64.Type}, {"ISO Week Number", Int64.Type}})in
    #"Changed Type"
```

Note that the query starts with let and ends with the in construct. Although these are not necessary with very short queries, you will see let and in in queries that have multiple steps. After let, you can see variable definitions that correspond to query steps, and after in, you can see the reference to the final variable, which is what the query ultimately returns.

Usually, as is the case in the **Date** query, every step, except the first one, builds on the previous step by referring to it.

If you look at the query steps in the **Query Settings** pane, you will see slightly different step names:

1. Source

2. Navigation

3. Promoted Headers

4. Changed Type

The only step name that is the same is **Source**. The second step—**Navigation**—is different because Power Query groups all navigational steps into one and shows it as **Navigation**, so sometimes you'll see more than one step shown as **Navigation**. The last two step names are different because they contain spaces; when you have special characters in names, you need to put them inside quotation marks and prefix them with a hash.

Formula bar

An alternative to the Advanced Editor is the Formula bar. Instead of viewing the code of the whole query, you can see the formula of the selected step. To enable the Formula bar, select **Formula Bar** on the **View** ribbon. Figure 1-40 shows the formula of the last step in the **Date** query.

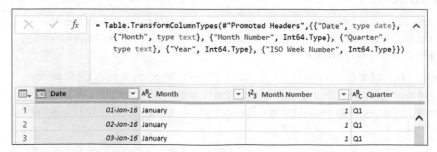

FIGURE 1-40 Last step formula in the Date query

Note that the formula corresponds to what you saw in the Advanced Editor for the **Changed Type** step.

> **NOTE** **FOLLOWING ALONG WITH THE EXAMPLES**
>
> If you want to follow along with the examples that follow, open 1.3.5 Combine queries.pbix from the companion files folder.

Earlier in the chapter, you removed the three top rows in the **Targets for 2020** query, which contained comments. At the time we noted that the number of extra top rows may change in the future and that you should protect your code against such changes. You can see what happens if one top row is removed in the following way:

1. Select the **Targets for 2020** query.
2. Select the **Navigation** query step.
3. On the Home ribbon, select **Remove Rows** > **Remove Top Rows**.
4. Select **Insert**.
5. Enter **1** in the Number of rows box.
6. Select **OK**.

You can see that the query now has a warning icon in the Queries pane, and if you go to the last step, you'll see the error message shown in Figure 1-41.

FIGURE 1-41 Error in the Targets for 2020 query

If you select **Go To Error**, you'll see that the error happened in the **Changed Type** step. The error happened because you promoted the wrong row to headers. To fix the issue, you must edit the formula of the **Removed Top Rows** step. The formula generated by the user interface, as seen in the Formula bar, is as follows:

```
= Table.Skip(#"Removed Top Rows1", 3)
```

The number of rows you remove is fixed, and since you removed an extra row before this query step, this step no longer produces the expected result. To protect your code against this, replace **3** in the step formula with the following:

```
each [Column1] <> "Buying Group"
```

This way, you instruct Power Query to remove all top rows that don't contain the value **Buying Group** in **Column1**. The full step formula is as follows:

```
= Table.Skip(#"Removed Top Rows1", each [Column1] <> "Buying Group")
```

Though the result has not changed, the query is now protected against someone inserting an extra line of comments at the top of the table.

Also in the **Targets for 2020** query, you removed the total row in the **Filtered Rows** step by excluding rows where the **Buying Group** column values end with **Total**. You can see the step formula here:

```
= Table.SelectRows(#"Changed Type", each not Text.EndsWith([Buying Group], "Total"))
```

Since Power Query is case-sensitive by default, your code may not work if someone writes *total* instead of *Total*. To protect your code against this, let's modify the formula step as follows:

```
= Table.SelectRows(#"Changed Type", each not Text.EndsWith([Buying Group], "Total",
Comparer.OrdinalIgnoreCase))
```

By using Comparer.OrdinalIgnoreCase, you instruct Power Query to ignore case differences and treat the words *total* and *Total* as the same.

> **NEED MORE REVIEW?**   **POWER QUERY M FORMULA LANGUAGE REFERENCE**
>
> The Advanced Editor and the Formula bar let you see which functions Power Query uses in formulas generated by the Power Query user interface. You can find the official Power Query M formula language reference here: *https://docs.microsoft.com/en-us/powerquery-m/*.

Configure data loading

When you develop your Power BI data model, you can use some helper queries in the process that you may not load to your model. For example, when you combine files from a folder, Power Query automatically creates some helper queries, which you can see in Figure 1-4 earlier in the chapter. The names of queries that aren't loaded are italicized.

If there's a query you don't want to load, right-click it in the **Queries** pane and clear the **Enable load** selection. If you have already loaded the query, you will see a warning that data loss may occur.

> **NOTE**   **COMPANION FILES**
>
> If you want to follow along with the example, open **1.3.6 Leverage Advanced Editor.pbix** from the companion files folder.

You may not want to load queries that were appended to or merged with another query. In the Wide World Importers example, you appended **Targets for 2020** to the **Targets** query, and you merged **State Province** with the **City** query. Because you had some data duplication as a result, it would be preferable to not load the **Targets for 2020** and **State Province** queries:

1. Right-click the **Targets for 2020** query and select **Enable load**.
2. Repeat the previous step for the **State Province** query.

The names of the queries should be italicized now, like in Figure 1-42.

FIGURE 1-42 Queries pane

Once you load the data, the two queries won't be loaded—they won't become tables. You can now load the data by selecting **Close & apply** on the **Home** ribbon.

Resolve data import errors

Occasionally, you may see errors after you load data in Power BI. If you followed previous examples, you would see the message shown in Figure 1-43 after you loaded data.

> **NOTE COMPANION FILES**
>
> If you want to follow along with the example, open 1.3.7 Configure data loading.pbix from the companion files folder.

FIGURE 1-43 Apply query changes information

Errors in this context refer to error values. Error values by themselves don't prevent queries from loading—you're merely notified about the number of error values for each query. Error values are loaded as blank values.

To view the rows that contain errors in Power Query, you can select the **View errors** hyperlink. This opens Power Query Editor, and it creates a new query called **Errors in Customers**, which contains one row. If you check the last column, **Postal Code**, you'll see the error you encountered earlier, shown in Figure 1-44.

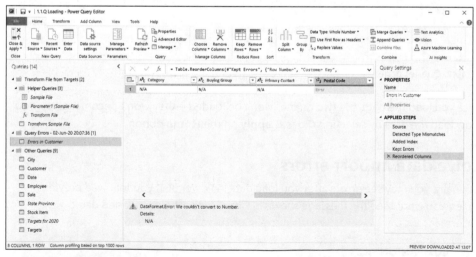

FIGURE 1-44 Postal Code error

The error happens because Power Query is trying to convert the "N/A" value, which is text, into a number. You can fix the issue by changing the data type of the **Postal Code** column:

1. Select the **Customer** query
2. Right-click the **Postal Code** column.
3. Select **Change Type** > **Text**.
4. Select **Replace current**.

If you return to the Errors in Customer query, you'll see that it's empty. To clean up the queries, you can delete the group that starts with **Query Errors**.

Once you select **Close & apply**, you'll see no error messages.

Chapter summary

In this chapter, you learned how to connect to data sources and select a storage mode and appropriate query type. You learned how to identify performance issues, use parameters, and profile the data. You also learned how to clean, transform, and load the data. Here are the key concepts from this chapter:

- Power BI has over 100 native connectors, with more being added all the time, and you can create your own connectors, too.
- You can change the data source settings, which include the location of the data source and the permissions associated with it. Changes apply to all queries that use the data source.
- Power BI Desktop performs best and allows you to use most of its features when you import data. In some cases, importing data is not feasible—for example, when there is too much data to import, or when data is updated very frequently and business requirements demand always showing the latest data. These issues can be addressed if the data source supports the DirectQuery connectivity mode. With DirectQuery, no data is imported into Power BI. Instead, all data remains in the source, and every time Power BI needs to calculate values, it sends queries in the data source's native query language. In some cases, you can apply certain types of transformations that can be translated to the native query language. There is a special case of DirectQuery called Live Connection, which is available with Analysis Services and Power BI service data models.
- You can create composite models by connecting to more than one data source in DirectQuery or by combining imported data and DirectQuery.
- Power Query allows you to perform query diagnostics, which can help identify performance issues in your queries. It can also show whether Power BI tries to translate its transformations into the data source's native language.
- You can connect to Microsoft Dataverse and dataflows, which use Power Query in the cloud. You can also create dataflows in the Power BI service.

- You can use parameters in your queries, which help you avoid making changes in several places manually. Parameters can also be useful to create your own functions.

- To make it easier for others to connect to the data sources you use, you can create PBIDS files that other users can reuse.

- When using Power BI Premium, you can connect to datasets in Power BI service by using the XMLA endpoint, which allows you to use tools other than Power BI to consume your data models. You can also use third-party tools to edit datasets in Power BI service by using the XMLA endpoint.

- Power Query offers several ways to profile your data, which includes column statistics and distribution, as well as the number of errors.

- Some of the most common operations you can perform in Power Query are
  - Replacing values
  - Reducing rows
  - Adding, removing, and splitting columns
  - Changing column type
  - Combining queries
  - Pivoting and unpivoting columns

- Power Query Editor uses a strongly typed, functional language called M, and it is rich in features with which you can perform basic and advanced transformations. Each transformation is recorded in a step, which can be reordered or deleted. The full query code can be edited in the Advanced Editor. Query dependencies can be seen in the Query dependencies view.

- Queries that don't need to be loaded can stay as queries if you disable their loading.

- If you see errors after loading your data, Power Query can show you the rows that contain errors, allowing you to correct them.

Thought experiment

In this thought experiment, demonstrate your skills and knowledge of the topics covered in this chapter. You can find the answers in the section that follows.

You are a data analyst at Contoso responsible for creating Power BI reports. Contoso has a development and a production environment, both of which use an Azure SQL Database. The production environment contains all historical data since 1990 and synchronizes with the OLTP system every five minutes; the development environment is only refreshed on demand. Additionally, some data is provided in CSV and Excel files.

Since Contoso is just starting with Power BI, they don't use Power BI Premium yet.

Based on background information and business requirements, answer the following questions:

1. To reduce the load on the production environment, you connect to the development database and develop your reports. Once you publish your report, you need to use the production data instead. Because you're developing your model iteratively, you need to switch between the environments back and forth. How can you minimize the time spent on changing data sources? The solution must allow for switching the source in the Power BI service.

   A. Create a parameter for database location and use it in queries.

   B. Change the data source in the Data Source settings.

   C. Change the data source in the Source step in each query.

2. You get data from a table in an Azure SQL Database that contains hundreds of millions of rows. Loading the full table takes half an hour. You would like to load a sample of 1,000 rows from the table. How can you achieve this? Your solution must minimize time spent on loading data.

   A. Use a report-level filter.

   B. Keep top rows.

   C. Provide your own SQL statement that has a TOP clause.

3. You get data from a CSV file with over 10,000 rows. You need to ensure one of the columns does not contain any missing values. Which Power Query features should you use?

   A. Column distribution

   B. Column quality

   C. Column profiling based on top 1,000 rows

   D. Column profiling based on the entire dataset

4. You are the only developer of Power BI reports in Contoso, and you're creating the first sales report. Your report must show data no later than 10 minutes from its arrival in the production environment. Which connectivity mode suits best? Your solution must minimize the resources spent.

   A. Import mode

   B. Live Connection

   C. DirectQuery

5. You need to combine the Customer and City tables, both of which have the CityKey column. Each row in the output table must contain a customer name and their city. Which Power Query feature should you use?

   A. Group by

   B. Merge

   C. Transpose

   D. Append

6. After you load data from an Excel file, you encounter the error shown in Figure 1-45.

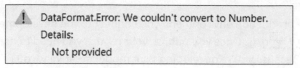

FIGURE 1-45 Error message

7. Which Power Query feature can you use to resolve the error? Your solution must retain all data from Excel.

   A. Replace errors

   B. Remove rows

   C. Change type (add new step)

   D. Change type (replace current)

Thought experiment answers

1. The answer is **A**. Using a parameter allows changing the source of all relevant queries at once, and it allows changing the source in the Power BI service. Although option B also allows changing the source of all affected queries, it does not allow changing the source in Power BI service. Option C requires you to change the source in each query separately, and you cannot change the source in the Power BI service this way.

2. The answer is **B** or **C**. Keeping top rows, if applied early in the query, will translate into SQL efficiently, resulting in fast data loading due to filtering taking place in the database. Using your own SQL statement with a TOP clause also filters data in the database, resulting in efficient data loading. Option A requires you to load all data first, which can take a long time.

3. The answer is **B** and **D**. Column distribution does not show the number of missing values, whereas column quality does. By default, column profiling is based on the first 1,000 rows; since there are over 10,000 rows in the CSV file, you need to perform column profiling on the entire dataset; otherwise, you risk missing some empty values at the end of the file.

4. The answer is **C**. The DirectQuery mode allows you to get the latest data as it arrives. Importing data requires refreshing the dataset, which would require Power BI Premium to refresh so frequently. Live Connection would require an Analysis Services model or a Power BI dataset, which are not available in Contoso.

5. The answer is **B**. Merge combines two tables by joining them based on a set of keys. Group by is for summarizing a single table. Transpose switches rows and columns of a single table. Append is best used to combine tables with mostly same columns.

6. The answer is **D**. The error is due to a text value being converted to a number, so changing the type to text instead of number would prevent the error from happening. Replacing an error will result in a number or null value, which would mean the original text value would be lost. Removing rows would also result in data loss. Changing type as a new step will not solve the problem as it will apply to the error value.

CHAPTER 2

Model the data

In the previous chapter, we reviewed the skills necessary to get and transform data by using Power Query Editor—the process also known as *data shaping*. In this chapter, we explore the skills needed to model data.

Power BI allows you to analyze your data to some degree right after you load it, but a strong understanding of data modeling helps you perform sophisticated analysis using rich data modeling capabilities, which includes creating relationships, hierarchies, and various calculations to bring out the true power of Power BI. In Chapter 1, "Prepare the data," in Power Query Editor we used the M language; once we loaded the data into the model, we used data analysis expressions, more commonly referred to as DAX, Power BI's native query language.

In this chapter, we discuss the skills necessary to design, develop, and optimize data models. Additionally, we look at DAX and how you can use it to enhance data models.

Skills covered in this chapter:

- 2.1: Design a data model
- 2.2: Develop a data model
- 2.3: Create measures by using DAX
- 2.4: Optimize model performance

Skill 2.1: Design a data model

A proper data model is the foundation of meaningful analysis. A Power BI data model is a collection of one or more tables and, optionally, relationships. A well-designed data model enables business users to understand and explore their data and derive insights from it. Before you create any visuals, you should complete this step by loading your data and defining the relationships between tables. Data modeling often occurs at the beginning phase of building a Power BI report to be able to create efficient measures that build upon your data model. In this section, we design a data model by focusing our attention on tables and their relationships.

This skill covers how to:

- Define the tables
- Configure table and column properties
- Define quick measures
- Flatten out a parent-child hierarchy
- Define role-playing dimensions
- Define a relationship's cardinality and cross-filter direction
- Design the data model to meet performance requirements
- Resolve many-to-many relationships
- Create a common date table
- Define the appropriate level of data granularity

Define the tables

Once a query is loaded, it becomes a table in a Power BI data model. Tables can then be organized into different data model types, also known as *schemas*. Here are the three most common schemas in Power BI:

- Flat (fully denormalized) schema
- Star schema
- Snowflake schema

There are other types of data models, though these three are the most common ones.

Flat schema

In the flat type of data model, all attributes are fully denormalized into a single table. Because there's only one table, there are no relationships, and in most cases there's no need for keys.

In our Wide World Importers example, you have a single table that contains all columns from all tables, meaning that the Sale and Targets columns will be in the same table. Because the tables have different data granularity, you run into problems when comparing actuals and targets.

> *NOTE* **DATA GRANULARITY**
>
> We review the concept of data granularity later in this skill section.

From the performance point of view, flat schemas are very efficient, though there are downsides:

- A single table can be cumbersome and confusing to navigate.
- Columns and data can often be duplicated, leading to a comparatively large file size.
- Mixing facts of different grains results in more complex DAX formulas.

Flat schemas are often used when connecting to a single, simple source. However, for more complex data models, flat schemas should be avoided in Power BI as much as possible.

Star schema

When you use a star schema, tables are conceptually classified into two kinds:

- **Fact tables**   These tables contain the metrics you want to aggregate. Fact tables have foreign keys, which are required to create relationships with dimensions, and columns that you can aggregate. In the Wide World Importers example, the Sale and Targets tables are fact tables. Fact tables are sometimes also known as data tables.

- **Dimension tables**   These tables contain the descriptive attributes that help you slice and dice your fact tables. A dimension table has a unique identifier—a key column— and descriptive columns. In the Wide World Importers example, City, Customer, Date, Employee, and Stock Item are dimension tables. Dimension tables are also sometimes known as lookup tables.

In a star schema, fact tables are surrounded by dimensions, as shown in Figure 2-1.

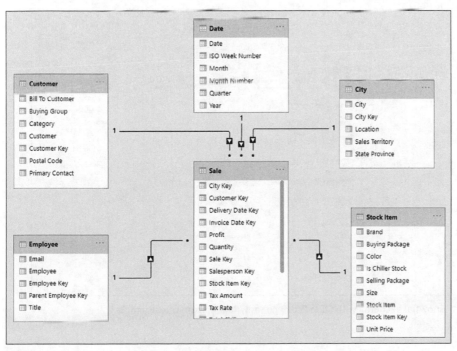

FIGURE 2-1 Star schema with Sale as the only fact table

The star schema has its name because it resembles a star, where the fact table is in the center and dimension tables are the star points. It's possible to have more than one fact table in a star schema, and it will still be a star schema.

In most cases, the star schema is the preferred data modeling approach in Power BI. It addresses the shortcomings of the flat schema:

- Fields are logically grouped, making the model easier to understand.
- There is less duplication of data, which results in more efficient storage.
- You don't need to write overly complex DAX formulas to work with fact tables that have a different grain.

Snowflake schema

The snowflake schema is similar to the star schema, except it can have some dimensions that "snowflake" from other dimensions. You can see an example in Figure 2-2.

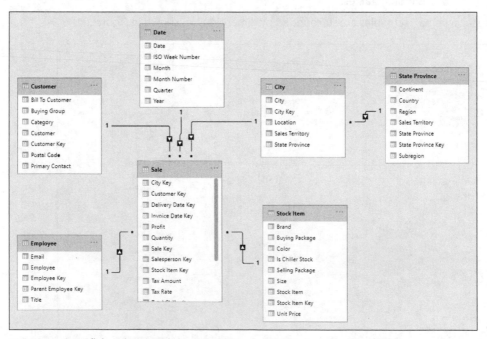

FIGURE 2-2 Snowflake schema with State Province snowflaking from the City table

In the Wide World Importers example, if you loaded the State Province query, the data model could be a snowflake schema. This is because the State Province table is related to the City dimension table, which in turn is related to the Sale fact table.

Snowflake schemas can be beneficial when there are fact tables that have different grains.

> **NOTE COMPANION FILE**
>
> You can see all three schemas in the 2.1.1 Define the tables.pbix file in the companion files folder.

> **NEED MORE REVIEW? DIMENSIONAL MODELING**
>
> In addition to fact and dimension tables, there are other types of tables such as factless facts, junk, and degenerate dimensions. For more information, see "Understand star schema and the importance for Power BI" at *https://docs.microsoft.com/en-us/power-bi/guidance/star-schema*.

Configure table and column properties

Both tables and columns have various properties you can configure, and you can do so in the **Model** view. To see the properties of a column or a table, select an object, and you see its properties in the **Properties** pane.

Table properties

For tables, depending on the storage mode, you can configure the following properties:

- **Name** Enter the table name.
- **Description** This property allows you to add a description of the table that will be stored in the model's metadata. It can be useful when you're building reports because you can see the description when you hover over the table in the Fields pane.
- **Synonyms** These are useful for the Q&A feature of Power BI, which we review in the next skill section. You can add synonyms so that the Q&A feature can understand that you're referring to a specific table even if you provide a different name for it.
- **Row label** This property is useful for both Q&A and featured tables, and it allows you to select a column whose values will serve as labels for each row. For example, if you ask Q&A to show "sales amount by product," and you select the Product Name column as the Row label of the Product table, then Q&A will show the sales amount for each product name.
- **Key column** If your table has a column that has unique values for every row, you can set the column as the key column.

- **Is hidden**   You can hide a table so that it disappears from the Fields pane.
- **Is featured table**   This property allows you to make a table *featured*, which will allow it to be used in Excel in certain scenarios.
- **Storage mode**   This property can be set to Import, DirectQuery, or Dual, as we covered in the previous chapter.

Column properties

For columns, depending on data type, you can configure the following properties:

- **Name**   Enter the column name.
- **Description**   This property is the same as for tables; you can add a column description.
- **Synonyms**   This property is the same as for tables; you can add synonyms to make the column work better with Q&A.
- **Display folder**   You can group columns from the same table into display folders.
- **Is hidden**   Hiding a column keeps it in the data model and hides it in the Fields pane.
- **Data type**   The available data types are different from those available in Power Query. For instance, Percentage, Date/Time/Timezone, and Duration are not available.
- **Format**   Different data types will show different formatting properties. For example, for numeric columns you'll see the following additional properties: Percentage format, Thousands separator, and Decimal places.
- **Sort by column**   You can sort one column by another. For example, you can sort month names by month numbers to make them appear in the correct order.
- **Data category**   This property can be useful for some visuals, and the default is Uncategorized. Depending on the data type, you can also select one of the following:
  - Address
  - City
  - Continent
  - Country/Region
  - County
  - Latitude
  - Longitude
  - Place
  - Postal Code
- **Summarize by**   This property determines how the column will be aggregated if you put it into a visual. The options you can choose depend on the data type. For most data types, in addition to Don't Summarize/None, you can choose Count and Count (Distinct)/Distinct Count, while for numeric columns, you can also choose Sum, Average,

Minimum/Min, and Maximum/Max. Power BI will try to automatically determine the appropriate summarization, but it's not always accurate.

■ **Is nullable** You can disallow null values for a column; if, during data refresh, a column is determined to get a null value, the refresh will fail.

NOTE MEASURE PROPERTIES

You can also configure measure properties, many of which are the same as column properties. Notable exceptions include Sort by column, Summarize by, and Is nullable—these properties aren't available for measures. We review measures in more detail later in this chapter.

Define quick measures

A *measure* in Power BI is a dynamic evaluation of a DAX query that will change in response to interactions with other visuals, enabling quick, meaningful exploration of your data. Creating efficient measures will be one of the most useful tools you can use to build insightful reports. If you are new to DAX and writing measures, or you are wanting to perform quick analysis, you have the option of creating a quick measure There are several ways to create a quick measure:

■ Select **Quick measure** from the **Home** ribbon.

■ Right-click or select the ellipsis next to a table or column in the **Fields** pane and select **New quick measure**. This method may prefill the quick measure form shown next.

■ If you already use a field in a visual, select the drop-down arrow next to the field in the Values section and select **New quick measure**. This method also may prefill the quick measure form shown next. If possible, this will add the new quick measure to the existing visualization. You'll be able to use this measure in other visuals too.

The following calculations are available as quick measures:

■ Aggregate per category
  ■ Average per category
  ■ Variance per category
  ■ Max per category
  ■ Min per category
  ■ Weighted average per category

- Filters
    - Filtered value
    - Difference from filtered value
    - Percentage difference from filtered value
    - Sales from new customers
- Time intelligence
    - Year-to-date total
    - Quarter-to-date total
    - Month-to-date total
    - Year-over-year change
    - Quarter-over-quarter change
    - Month-over-month change
    - Rolling average
- Totals
    - Running total
    - Total for category (filters applied)
    - Total for category (filters not applied)
- Mathematical operations
    - Addition
    - Subtraction
    - Multiplication
    - Division
    - Percentage difference
    - Correlation coefficient
- Text
    - Star rating
    - Concatenated list of values

Each calculation has its own description and a list of field wells. You can see an example in Figure 2-3.

FIGURE 2-3 Quick measures dialog box

> **NOTE HIDDEN FIELDS**
>
> If you have any hidden fields, you won't see them in the **Fields** section of the **Quick measures** dialog box.

For example, by using quick measures, you can calculate average profit per employee for Wide World Importers:

1.   Select **Quick measure** on the **Home** ribbon.
2.   From the **Calculation** drop-down list, select **Average per category**.
3.   Drag the **Profit** column from the **Sale** table to the **Base value** field well.
4.   Drag the **Employee** column from the **Employee** table to the **Category** field well.
5.   Select **OK**.

After you complete these steps, you can find the new measure called **Profit average per Employee** in the **Fields** pane.

If you select the new measure, you'll see its DAX formula:

```
Profit average per Employee =
AVERAGEX(
    KEEPFILTERS(VALUES('Employee'[Employee])),
    CALCULATE(SUM('Sale'[Profit]))
)
```

You can modify the formula, if needed. Reading the DAX can be a great way to learn how measures can be written.

Flatten out a parent-child hierarchy

Parent-child hierarchies are often used for employees, charts of accounts, and organizations. Instead of being composed of several columns, parent-child hierarchies are defined by two columns: node key and parent node key. In the Wide World Importers example, you can see a parent-child hierarchy in the Employee table, shown in Figure 2-4.

Employee Key	Parent Employee Key	Employee	Title
0		Unknown	N/A
3	4	Hudson Onslow	Salesperson
4	19	Isabella Rupp	Manager
6	4	Sophia Hinton	Salesperson
7	4	Amy Trefl	Salesperson
8	12	Anthony Grosse	Salesperson
12	19	Henry Forlonge	Manager
13	12	Hudson Hollinworth	Salesperson
14	20	Lily Code	Salesperson
15	20	Taj Shand	Salesperson
16	20	Archer Lamble	Salesperson
19		Jai Shand	Director
20	19	Jack Potter	Manager

FIGURE 2-4 Employee table

For our purposes, you can ignore the "Unknown" employee. By observing the Parent Employee Key values, note the following:

- Jai Shand is a director and has no "parent employee."
- Isabella Rupp, Henry Forlonge, and Jack Potter are all managers, and they all report to Jai Shand, their "parent employee."
- Isabella Rupp, Henry Forlonge, and Jack Potter all act as "parent employees" to various salespersons.
- There are three levels in the hierarchy: director level, manager level, and salesperson level.

If you were to create additional columns with each column containing a hierarchy level, you would need to merge the Employee table with itself in Power Query, which would widen the table and create a more complex query. In Power BI, you can also solve this problem by using DAX and calculated columns.

To create a calculated column in a table, right-click the table in the **Fields** pane and select **New column**. In the Wide World Importers example, you can use the following formula to create a calculated column in the Employee table:

```
Employee Path = PATH(Employee[Employee Key], Employee[Parent Employee Key])
```

This adds a new column that has all hierarchy levels listed, and you can see it in Figure 2-5.

Employee Key	Parent Employee Key	Employee	Title	Employee Path
0		Unknown	N/A	0
3	4	Hudson Onslow	Salesperson	19|4|3
4	19	Isabella Rupp	Manager	19|4
6	4	Sophia Hinton	Salesperson	19|4|6
7	4	Amy Trefl	Salesperson	19|4|7
8	12	Anthony Grosse	Salesperson	19|12|8
12	19	Henry Forlonge	Manager	19|12
13	12	Hudson Hollinworth	Salesperson	19|12|13
14	20	Lily Code	Salesperson	19|20|14
15	20	Taj Shand	Salesperson	19|20|15
16	20	Archer Lamble	Salesperson	19|20|16
19		Jai Shand	Director	19
20	19	Jack Potter	Manager	19|20

FIGURE 2-5 Employee Path column

The Employee Path column is only useful for technical purposes, so it can be hidden.

The next step is to add the following three calculated columns to the Employee table:

```
Director =
LOOKUPVALUE(
    Employee[Employee],
    Employee[Employee Key],
    PATHITEM(Employee[Employee Path], 1, INTEGER)
```

```
)
Manager =
LOOKUPVALUE(
    Employee[Employee],
    Employee[Employee Key],
    PATHITEM(Employee[Employee Path], 2, INTEGER)
)
Salesperson =
LOOKUPVALUE(
    Employee[Employee],
    Employee[Employee Key],
    PATHITEM(Employee[Employee Path], 3, INTEGER)
)
```

All three columns use the PATHITEM function to retrieve the employee key of the specified level and LOOKUPVALUE to look up the employee name based on their key.

After you add the columns, the table should look like the one in Figure 2-6.

Employee Key	Parent Employee Key	Employee	Title	Employee Path	Director	Manager	Salesperson
0		Unknown	N/A	0	Unknown		
3	4	Hudson Onslow	Salesperson	19|4|3	Jai Shand	Isabella Rupp	Hudson Onslow
4	19	Isabella Rupp	Manager	19|4	Jai Shand	Isabella Rupp	
6	4	Sophia Hinton	Salesperson	19|4|6	Jai Shand	Isabella Rupp	Sophia Hinton
7	4	Amy Trefl	Salesperson	19|4|7	Jai Shand	Isabella Rupp	Amy Trefl
8	12	Anthony Grosse	Salesperson	19|12|8	Jai Shand	Henry Forlonge	Anthony Grosse
12	19	Henry Forlonge	Manager	19|12	Jai Shand	Henry Forlonge	
13	12	Hudson Hollinworth	Salesperson	19|12|13	Jai Shand	Henry Forlonge	Hudson Hollinworth
14	20	Lily Code	Salesperson	19|20|14	Jai Shand	Jack Potter	Lily Code
15	20	Taj Shand	Salesperson	19|20|15	Jai Shand	Jack Potter	Taj Shand
16	20	Archer Lamble	Salesperson	19|20|16	Jai Shand	Jack Potter	Archer Lamble
19		Jai Shand	Director	19	Jai Shand		
20	19	Jack Potter	Manager	19|20	Jai Shand	Jack Potter	

FIGURE 2-6 The Director, Manager, and Salesperson columns in the Employee table

Note that some Manager and Salesperson column values are blank; Jai Shand, for example, is a director with nobody above him, so both Manager and Salesperson are blank. In the Wide World Importers example, this is not a big problem because only keys of salespersons are used in the Sale table. If this is undesirable, you can use the last parameter of LOOKUPVALUE, which provides the default value, as follows:

```
Manager =
LOOKUPVALUE(
    Employee[Employee],
    Employee[Employee Key],
    PATHITEM(Employee[Employee Path], 2, INTEGER),
    Employee[Director]
)
```

```
Salesperson =
LOOKUPVALUE(
    Employee[Employee],
    Employee[Employee Key],
    PATHITEM(Employee[Employee Path], 3, INTEGER),
    Employee[Manager]
)
```

Using the last parameter of LOOKUPVALUE in this case ensures that all columns have values.

> **NOTE   COMPANION FILE**
>
> You can see the final columns in the 2.1.4 Flatten PC hierarchy.pbix file in the companion files folder.

Define role-playing dimensions

In some cases, there may be more than one way to filter a fact table by a dimension. In the Wide World Importers example, the Sale table has two date columns: Invoice Date Key and Delivery Date Key, both of which can be related to the Date column from the Date table. Therefore, it is possible to analyze sales by invoice date or delivery date, depending on the business requirements. In this situation, the Date dimension is a role-playing dimension.

Although Power BI allows you to have multiple physical relationships between two tables, no more than one can be active at a time, and other relationships must be set as inactive. Active relationships, by default, propagate filters. The choice of which relationship should be set as active depends on the default way of looking at data by the business.

> **NEED MORE REVIEW?   ACTIVE AND INACTIVE RELATIONSHIPS**
>
> For a more thorough explanation of when you would use active or inactive relationships, see "Active vs inactive relationship guidance" at *https://docs.microsoft.com/en-us/power-bi/guidance/relationships-active-inactive*.

To create a relationship between two tables, you can drag a key from one table on top of the corresponding key from the other table in the **Model** view.

> **NOTE   AUTOMATIC DETECTION OF RELATIONSHIPS**
>
> By default, Power BI will try to detect relationships between tables automatically after you load data. In doing so, Power BI usually relies on identical column names, and the process is not always perfect. You can turn it off in **Options** > **Current file** > **Data load** if necessary.

In the Wide World Importers example, you can drag the **Date** column from the **Date** table on top of the **Invoice Date Key** column in the **Sale** table. Doing so creates an active relationship, signified by the solid line. Next, you can drag the **Date** column from the **Date** table on top of the **Delivery Date Key** column from the **Sale** table. This creates an inactive relationship, signified by the dashed line. The result should look like Figure 2-7.

FIGURE 2-7 Relationships between Sale and Date

If you hover over a relationship line in the Model view, it highlights the fields that participate in the relationship.

In the Wide World Importers model, you should also create the relationships listed in Table 2-1.

TABLE 2-1 Additional relationships in Wide World Importers

From: Table (Column)	To: Table (Column)
Sale (City Key)	City (City Key)
Sale (Customer Key)	Customer (Customer Key)
Sale (Salesperson Key)	Employee (Employee Key)
Sale (Stock Item Key)	Stock Item (Stock Item Key)

Inactive relationships can be activated by using the USERELATIONSHIP function in DAX, which also deactivates the default active relationship, if any. The following is an example of a measure that uses USERELATIONSHIP:

```
Revenue by Delivery Date =
CALCULATE(
    [Revenue],
    USERELATIONSHIP(
        'Date'[Date],
        Sale[Delivery Date Key]
    )
)
```

To use USERELATIONSHIP, you must define a relationship in the model first so that the function only works for existing relationships. This approach is useful for scenarios such as the Wide World Importers example, where you have multiple date columns within the same fact table.

NEED MORE REVIEW? **CALCULATE AND USERELATIONSHIP**

CALCULATE is the most important function in DAX, and we review it in more detail later in this chapter. It's important to be aware of certain limitations of USERELATIONSHIP. For more information, see "USERELATIONSHIP" at *https://docs.microsoft.com/en-us/dax/ userelationship-function-dax.*

If you have several measures that you want to analyze by using different relationships, this may result in your data model having many similar measures, cluttering your data model to a degree.

Another drawback of using USERELATIONSHIP is that you cannot analyze data by using two relationships at the same time. For instance, if you have a single Date table, it won't be possible to see which sales were invoiced last year and shipped this year.

An alternative to USERELATIONSHIP that addresses these drawbacks is to use separate dimensions for each role or relationship. In case of Wide World Importers, you would have Delivery Date and Invoice Date dimensions, which would make it possible to analyze sales by both delivery and invoice dates.

You have a few ways to create the new dimensions based on the existing Date table, one of which is to use calculated tables. For the Invoice Date table, the DAX formula would be as follows:

```
Invoice Date = 'Date'
```

The benefit of using calculated tables instead of referencing or duplicating queries in Power Query is that if you have calculated columns in your Date table, they will be copied in a calculated table, whereas you would have to re-create the same columns if you used Power Query to create the copies of the dimension.

When you're creating separate dimensions, it's best to rename the columns to make it clear where fields are coming from. For example, instead of leaving the column called Date, rename it to Invoice Date. You can do so by right-clicking a field in the **Fields** pane and selecting **Rename** or by double-clicking a field. Alternatively, you can rename fields by using a more complex calculated table expression. For example, you could use the SELECTCOLUMNS function in DAX to rename columns.

Define a relationship's cardinality and cross-filter direction

In the previous section, you saw how to create relationships between tables. In this section, we review the concepts of cardinality and cross-filter direction of relationships.

You can edit a relationship by double-clicking it in the Model view. For example, in Figure 2-8 you can see the options for one of the relationships between the Sale and the Date tables.

FIGURE 2-8 Relationship options

In the relationship options, you can select tables from drop-down lists. For each table, you get a preview of it, from which you can select a column that will be part of a relationship. Unlike for the Merge operation in Power Query, only one column from each table can be part of a relationship.

The **Make this relationship active** check box determines whether the relationship is active. Between two tables, there can be no more than one active relationship.

When using DirectQuery, the **Assume referential integrity** option is available, and it can improve query performance in certain cases.

NEED MORE REVIEW? **ASSUME REFERENTIAL INTEGRITY**

There are some requirements that data must meet for the Assume referential integrity option to work properly. For advanced details on this feature, including the requirements and implications of not meeting the requirements with this option set, see "Apply the Assume Referential Integrity setting in Power BI Desktop" at *https://docs.microsoft.com/en-us/power-bi/connect-data/desktop-assume-referential-integrity*.

Two options are worth reviewing in more detail: **Cardinality** and **Cross-filter direction**.

Cardinality

Depending on the selected tables and columns, you can select one of the following options:

- Many-to-one
- One-to-one
- One-to-many
- Many-to-many

Many-to-one and *one-to-many* are the same kind of relationship, and they only differ in the order in which the tables are listed. "Many" means that a key may appear more than once in the selected column, whereas "one" means a key value appears only once in the selected column. In our Wide World Importers example earlier, the Sale table was on the *many* side, whereas the Date table was on the *one* side; a single date appeared only once in the Date table, though there could be multiple sales on the same date in the Sale table.

One-to-one is a special kind of relationship in which a key value appears only once on both sides of the relationship. This type of relationship can be useful for splitting a single dimension with many columns into separate tables. You should use one-to-one only if you are confident that no duplicates will appear in this table, since duplicates would cause immediate errors in your data model.

NEED MORE REVIEW? **ONE-TO-ONE RELATIONSHIPS**

One-to-one relationships are rarely encountered in real life. For advanced information on this type of relationships in Power BI, see "One-to-one relationship guidance" at *https://docs.microsoft.com/en-us/power-bi/guidance/relationships-one-to-one*.

Many-to-many relationships in this context refer to direct relationship between two tables, neither of which is guaranteed to have unique keys. We review this type of relationship later in this chapter.

Cross-filter direction

This option determines the direction in which filters flow. For many-to-one and one-to-many relationships, you can select Single or Both.

- If you select **Single**, then the filters from the table on the "one" side will filter through to the table on the "many" side. This setting is signified by a single arrowhead on the relationship line in the Model view.

- If you select **Both**, then filters from both tables will flow in both directions, and such relationships are also known as *bidirectional*. This setting is signified by two arrowheads on the relationship line in the Model view, facing in opposite directions. When this option is selected, you can also select **Apply security filter in both directions** to make row-level security filters flow in both directions, too.

To illustrate the concept, consider the data model shown in Figure 2-9.

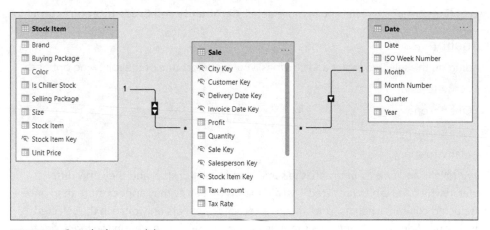

FIGURE 2-9 Sample data model

From this data model, you can create two table visuals as follows:

- Table 1: Distinct count of Stock Item by Year
- Table 2: Distinct count of Year by Stock Item

Both table visuals are shown in Figure 2-10. The first four rows are shown for Table 2 for illustrative purposes.

You can see that in Table 1, the numbers are different for different years and the total, whereas in Table 2, the Distinct Count of Year is showing 6 for all rows, including the total.

Table 1		Table 2	
Year	Distinct Count of Stock Item	Stock Item	Distinct Count of Year
2017	219	"The Gu" red shirt XML tag t-shirt (Black) 3XL	6
2018	219	"The Gu" red shirt XML tag t-shirt (Black) 3XS	6
2019	219	"The Gu" red shirt XML tag t-shirt (Black) 4XL	6
2020	227	"The Gu" red shirt XML tag t-shirt (Black) 5XL	6
Total	**228**	**Total**	**6**

FIGURE 2-10 Table visuals

The numbers are different in Table 1 because filters from the Date table can reach the Stock Item table through the Sale table; the Date table filters the Sale table because there is a one-to-many relationship; then the Sale table filters the Stock Item table because there is a bidirectional relationship. In 2017, 2018, and 2019, Wide World Importers coincidentally sold 219 stock items, whereas in 2020, they sold 227 stock items. At the total level you see 228, which is not the total sum of stock items sold across all years.

In Table 2, the numbers are the same because filters from the Stock Item table don't reach the Date table since there is no bidirectional filter. Even though you only had sales in four years, you see 6 across all rows, which is the number of years in the Date table.

It's also possible to set the cross-filter direction by using the CROSSFILTER function in DAX, as you can see in the following example:

```
Stock Items Sold =
CALCULATE(
    DISTINCTCOUNT('Stock Item'[Stock Item]),
    CROSSFILTER(
        Sale[Stock Item Key],
        'Stock Item'[Stock Item Key],
        BOTH
    )
)
```

The syntax of CROSSFILTER is similar to USERELATIONSHIP—the first two parameters are related columns. Additionally, there's the third parameter—direction—and it can be one of the following:

- **BOTH**   This option corresponds to **Both** in the relationship cross-filter direction options.
- **NONE**   This option deactivates the relationship, and it corresponds to the cleared **Make this relationship active** check box.
- **ONEWAY**   This option corresponds to **Single** in the relationship cross-filter direction options.

Bidirectional filters are sometimes used in many-to-many relationships with bridge tables when direct many-to-many relationships are not desirable.

Design the data model to meet performance requirements

The way you design a Power BI data model ultimately affects the performance of reports. A well-designed data model takes into consideration both business requirements and the constraints of data sources. Performance tuning is a broad topic; we cover some key concepts you should keep in mind while designing your data model:

- Storage mode
- Relationships
- Aggregations
- Cardinality

Storage mode

As you saw in the first chapter, Power BI supports several connectivity modes:

- Imported data
- DirectQuery
- Live Connection

Refer to the first chapter for more details.

Relationships

When you're using composite models, it's important to remember that relationships perform differently depending on the storage mode of the related tables.

You can use the concept of *islands* as an analogy of where data is queried to understand how data models work in practice. If you use two DirectQuery data sources, then each of them is a separate island. In contrast, all imported data resides in the same island regardless of where it originally came from, because all imported data is queried from memory. When you connect to data on the same island, you will have the fastest results since you don't need to "swim" to another island.

You can see different kinds of relationships ordered from fastest to slowest in the following list:

- One-to-many intra-island relationships
- Direct many-to-many relationships
- Many-to-many relationships with bridge tables
- Cross-island relationships

We review many-to-many relationships in detail in the next section.

Aggregations

When using DirectQuery, you can import some summarized data so that the most frequently queried data resides in memory and is retrieved quickly, whereas detailed data is queried from the data source. This feature is called *aggregations*, and we review it later in this chapter.

Cardinality

The term *cardinality*, in addition to defining relationships, also refers to the number of distinct values in a column. Power BI stores imported data in columns, not rows. For this reason, the cardinality of each column affects performance. In general, the fewer distinct values there are, the better performance. We review ways to reduce cardinality later in this chapter.

> **NEED MORE REVIEW?   MODEL DESIGN OPTIMIZATION**
>
> For further guidance on optimizing the model design, see "Optimize model design" at *https://docs.microsoft.com/en-us/power-bi/guidance/composite-model-guidance#optimize-model-design*.

Resolve many-to-many relationships

Many-to-many relationships occur very frequently in models. In general, many-to-many relationships happen in two cases:

- **Many-to-many relationships between dimensions**   For example, one client may have multiple accounts, and an account may belong to different clients.
- **Relationships between tables at different granularities**   For example, you may have a sales table at the date level and a targets table at the month level. Both tables could be related to a single date table. In this case, the relationship between the targets and date tables would be many-to-many since they are of different grain.

In the Wide World Importers example, a many-to-many relationship exists between the Date and Stock Item tables; on each date, multiple stock items could be sold, and each stock item could be sold on multiple dates. In this case, the relationship goes through the Sale table. Additionally, a many-to-many relationship exists between the Date dimension and the Targets fact table because the grain of the tables is different.

Power BI supports many-to-many relationships of two kinds:

- Direct many-to-many relationships
- Many-to-many relationships through a bridge table

Direct many-to-many relationships

As you saw earlier in this chapter, Power BI supports the many-to-many cardinality for relationships, allowing you to create a many-to-many relationship between two tables directly.

You will now create a relationship between the Targets table and the Customer table based on Buying Group, the same way you create other relationship types:

1. Go to the **Model** view.
2. Drag the **Buying Group** column from the **Customer** table on top of the **Buying Group** column from the **Targets** table.
3. Ensure the **Make this relationship active** check box is selected.
4. Set **Cross filter direction** to **Single (Customer filters Targets)**. Figure 2-11 shows how your options should look.
5. Select **OK**.

You can see asterisks on both sides of the relationship that indicate the many-to-many relationship.

This method performs well when the number of unique values on each side of a relationship is fewer than 1,000; otherwise, the method may be slow and creating a bridge table would be a more efficient solution. The technical details on why this happens are out of the scope of the exam.

Another limitation that this kind of relationships has is that you cannot use the RELATED function in DAX since neither table is on the "one" side.

FIGURE 2-11 Relationship options

This creates a relationship, as shown in Figure 2-12.

FIGURE 2-12 Relationship between Customer and Targets

Many-to-many relationships with bridge tables

A different way of creating a many-to-many relationship in Power BI is to use a bridge table. A *bridge table* is a table that allows you to create one-to-many relationships with each table that is in a many-to-many relationship. Bridge tables can be of two kinds:

- **A one-column table with unique values**   The bridge table is on the one side in each relationship. This is typical for relating facts or tables that have different grains.
- **A two-column table with unique combination of values**   The bridge table is on the many side in each relationship. This is common for many-to-many relationships between dimensions.

In the Wide World Importers example, the Date and Targets tables have different grains:

- Targets has one row per Buying Group and the end-of -month date.
- Date has one row per date.

Note that the Date table does not have a column that contains end-of-month dates. Dates are a special case, because you can create a one-to-many relationship between Date and Targets and avoid having a many-to-many relationship.

> **NOTE   DATE GRAIN MISMATCH**
>
> When you relate monthly Targets with the Date table, you need to pay attention to what values you'll be showing when you filter the Date table by dates. We address this issue later in this chapter in the section titled "Define the appropriate level of data granularity."

To illustrate this in practice, let's create a many-to-many relationship between Date and Targets based on End of Month date. First, add the End of Month column to the Date table:

1. Launch **Power Query Editor** by selecting **Transform Data** on the **Home** ribbon.
2. Select the **Date** column in the **Date** query.
3. On the **Add column** ribbon, select **From date & time** > **Date** > **Month** > **End of month**.

There are several ways to create a bridge table through Power Query, calculated tables in DAX, or importing a new table that all achieve the same outcome. For our requirement, let's create a bridge table between the Date and Targets table by using Power Query:

1. In Power Query Editor, right-click the **Date** query and select **Reference**.
2. Rename the newly created **Date (2)** query to **End of Month**.
3. Right-click the **End of Month** column header and select **Remove other columns**.
4. Right-click the **End of Month** column and select **Remove duplicates**.
5. On the **Home** ribbon, select **Close & apply**.

You can now relate the Date and Targets tables as shown in Table 2-2.

TABLE 2-2 Date, End of Month, and Targets relationships

From: Table (Column)	To: Table (Column)	Active	Cross Filter Direction
Date (End of Month)	End of Month (End of Month)	Yes	Both
Targets (End of Month)	End of Month (End of Month)	Yes	Single

You can see the relationships in Figure 2-13.

FIGURE 2-13 Date, End of Month, and Targets relationships

> **NOTE COMPANION FILE**
>
> You can see the final result in the 2.1.8 Resolve many-to-many relationships.pbix file in the companion files folder.

> **NEED MORE REVIEW? MANY-TO-MANY RELATIONSHIPS**
>
> For more examples of many-to-many relationships, see "Many-to-many relationship guidance" at *https://docs.microsoft.com/en-us/power-bi/guidance/relationships-many-to-many* and "Apply many-many relationships in Power BI Desktop" at *https://docs.microsoft.com/en-us/power-bi/transform-model/desktop-many-to-many-relationships*.

Create a common date table

By default, Power BI creates a calendar hierarchy for each date or date/time column from your data sources.

> **NEED MORE REVIEW? AUTO DATE/TIME HIERARCHIES**
>
> For detailed considerations and limitations of the auto date/time feature, see "Auto date/time guidance in Power BI Desktop" at *https://docs.microsoft.com/en-us/power-bi/guidance/auto-date-time*.

Although these can be useful in some cases, it's best practice to create your own date table, which has several benefits:

- You can use a calendar other than Gregorian.
- You can have weeks in the calendar.
- You can filter multiple fact tables by using a single date dimension table.

If you don't have a date table you can import from a data source, you can create one yourself. It's possible to create a date table by using Power Query or DAX, and there's no difference in performance between the two methods.

Creating a calendar table in Power Query

In Power Query, you can use the M language List.Dates function, which returns a list of dates, and then convert the list to a table and add columns to it. The following query provides a sample calendar table that begins on January 1, 2016:

```
let
    Source = #date(2016, 1, 1),
    Dates = List.Dates(Source, Duration.TotalDays(Date.AddYears(Source, 6) - Source),
#duration(1,0,0,0)),
    #"Converted to Table" = Table.FromList(Dates, Splitter.SplitByNothing(),
type table [Date = date]),
    #"Inserted Year" = Table.AddColumn(#"Converted to Table", "Year",
each Date.Year([Date]), Int64.Type),
    #"Inserted Month Name" = Table.AddColumn(#"Inserted Year", "Month Name",
each Date.MonthName([Date]), type text),
    #"Inserted Month" = Table.AddColumn(#"Inserted Month Name", "Month",
each Date.Month([Date]), Int64.Type),
    #"Inserted Week of Year" = Table.AddColumn(#"Inserted Month", "Week of Year",
each Date.WeekOfYear([Date]), Int64.Type)
in
    #"Inserted Week of Year"
```

If you want to add the calendar table to your model, start with a blank query:

1. In Power Query Editor, select **New Source** on the **Home** ribbon.
2. Select **Blank Query**.
3. With the new query selected, select **Query** > **Advanced Editor** on the **Home** ribbon.
4. Replace all existing code with the code above and select **Done**.
5. Give your query an appropriate name such as *Calendar* or *Date*.

The result should look like Figure 2-14, where the first few rows of the query are shown.

	Date	123 Year	ABC Month Name	123 Month	123 Week of Year
1	01-Jan-16	2016	January	1	1
2	02-Jan-16	2016	January	1	1
3	03-Jan-16	2016	January	1	2
4	04-Jan-16	2016	January	1	2
5	05-Jan-16	2016	January	1	2
6	06-Jan-16	2016	January	1	2
7	07-Jan-16	2016	January	1	2
8	08-Jan-16	2016	January	1	2
9	09-Jan-16	2016	January	1	2
10	10-Jan-16	2016	January	1	3

FIGURE 2-14 Sample calendar table built by using Power Query

You may prefer having a table in Power Query when you intend to use it in some other queries, since it's not possible to reference calculated tables in Power Query.

Creating a calendar table in DAX

If you choose to create a date table in DAX, you can use the CALENDAR or CALENDARAUTO function, both of which return a table with a single Date column. You can then add calculated columns to the table, or you can create a calculated table that has all the columns right away.

> **NOTE CALCULATED TABLES**
>
> We review the skills necessary to create calculated tables in Skill 2.2: Develop a data model.

The CALENDAR function requires you to provide the start and end dates, which you can hardcode for your business requirements or calculate dynamically:

```
Calendar Dynamic =
CALENDAR(
    MIN(Sale[Invoice Date Key]),
    MAX(Sale[Invoice Date Key])
)
```

The CALENDARAUTO function scans your data model for dates and returns an appropriate date range automatically.

To build a table similar to the Power Query table we built before, we can use the following calculated table formula in DAX:

```
Calendar =
ADDCOLUMNS(
    CALENDARAUTO(),
    "Year", YEAR([Date]),
    "Month Name", FORMAT([Date], "MMMM"),
    "Month", MONTH([Date]),
    "Week of Year", WEEKNUM([Date])
)
```

Define the appropriate level of data granularity

Data granularity refers to the *grain* of data, or the level of detail that a table can provide. For example, the Targets table in the Wide World Importers example provides a target figure for each month for each buying group, so the granularity is the month-buying group. If you filter the Targets table by a field that is at lower granularity—such as Customer or Date—you won't get any meaningful results. Figure 2-15 shows targets by date.

End of Month	Target Excluding Tax
⊟ **January 2017**	**2,250,000.00**
01-Jan-17	2,250,000.00
02-Jan-17	2,250,000.00
03-Jan-17	2,250,000.00
04-Jan-17	2,250,000.00
05-Jan-17	2,250,000.00
06-Jan-17	2,250,000.00
07-Jan-17	2,250,000.00

FIGURE 2-15 Targets by date

You can see that the same number is repeated at month level and date level, which can be confusing. To deal with this, you need to account for cases when targets are shown at unsupported levels of granularity.

There are a few ways of solving the problem. For example, you can make a measure return a result only when the unsupported grains are not filtered:

```
Total Target (filters) =
IF(
    NOT(
        ISFILTERED('Date'[Date])
        || ISFILTERED('Date'[ISO Week Number])
        || ISFILTERED(Customer[Customer Key])
        || ISFILTERED(Customer[Customer])
        || ISFILTERED(Customer[Primary Contact])
        || ISFILTERED(Customer[Postal Code])
```

```
        || ISFILTERED('Stock Item')
        || ISFILTERED(Employee)
        || ISFILTERED(City)
    ),
    SUM(Targets[Target Excluding Tax])
)
```

You can see the result in Figure 2-16.

End of Month	Target Excluding Tax	Total Target (filters)
⊟ **January 2017**	**2,250,000.00**	**2,250,000.00**
01-Jan-17	2,250,000.00	
02-Jan-17	2,250,000.00	
03-Jan-17	2,250,000.00	
04-Jan-17	2,250,000.00	
05-Jan-17	2,250,000.00	
06-Jan-17	2,250,000.00	
07-Jan-17	2,250,000.00	

FIGURE 2-16 Total Target measure used in a table

Although this approach can work in many cases, it has a downside. If new columns are introduced and they aren't at the supported level of granularity, then you'd need to modify your code. An alternative is to check the number of rows in the supported dimensions as follows:

```
Total Target (rows) =
VAR DateRows = COUNTROWS('Date')
VAR DateRowsAtMonthLevel =
    CALCULATE(
        COUNTROWS('Date'),
        REMOVEFILTERS('Date'),
        VALUES('Date'[End of Month])
    )
VAR CustomerRows = COUNTROWS(Customer)
VAR CustomerRowsAtBuyingGroupLevel =
    CALCULATE(
        COUNTROWS(Customer),
        REMOVEFILTERS(Customer),
        VALUES(Customer[Buying Group])
    )
VAR UnsupportedFilters =
    (DateRows <> DateRowsAtMonthLevel)
    || (CustomerRows <> CustomerRowsAtBuyingGroupLevel)
    || ISFILTERED('Stock Item')
    || ISFILTERED(Employee)
    || ISFILTERED(City)
```

```
VAR Result =
    IF(
        NOT(UnsupportedFilters),
        SUM(Targets[Target Excluding Tax])
    )
RETURN
    Result
```

You may still want to check whether unsupported tables are filtered, so you're still using ISFILTERED for some tables. The result, shown in Figure 2-17, is the same as for the previous measure.

End of Month	Target Excluding Tax	Total Target (filters)	Total Target (rows)
⊟ **January 2017**	**2,250,000.00**	**2,250,000.00**	**2,250,000.00**
01-Jan-17	2,250,000.00		
02-Jan-17	2,250,000.00		
03-Jan-17	2,250,000.00		
04-Jan-17	2,250,000.00		
05-Jan-17	2,250,000.00		
06-Jan-17	2,250,000.00		
07-Jan-17	2,250,000.00		

FIGURE 2-17 An alternative measure

> **NOTE COMPANION FILE**
>
> You can see the measures in the 2.1.10 Define the appropriate level of data granularity.pbix file in the companion files folder.

> **NOTE MEASURES**
>
> We review DAX measures in more detail in Skill 2.3: Create measures by using DAX.

Skill 2.2: Develop a data model

Data model development refers to enhancements you add to your model after you've loaded your data and created relationships between tables. In this section, we review the skills you need to create calculated tables, calculated columns, and hierarchies, and we show you how to configure row-level security for your report as well as set up the Q&A feature.

Apply cross-filter direction and security filtering

While editing table relationships, even if you set the relationship cross-filter direction to Both, by default the security filters are only applied in one direction. We mentioned earlier that there's an option to control security filtering called **Apply security filter in both directions**. This means that role filtering applied to a table will also be passed to the filtered table. When this option is disabled, only the table with the filter applied will be affected. This option exists because applying security filters affects the performance of your data model, so in some cases applying it may be undesirable.

> **NOTE   SECURITY FILTERS**
>
> Applying security filters refers to row-level security (RLS), a feature in Power BI that allows you to restrict access to data within a dataset based on a set of filters. We review RLS in detail later in this chapter.

Create calculated tables

Earlier in the chapter, you saw that one way to create a calendar table is to create a calculated table, which is an alternative to using Power Query. Calculated tables are defined by using DAX, and they're based on the data that is already loaded into the data model or on new data generated by using DAX. You won't see calculated tables in Power Query Editor.

Calculated tables are especially useful when you are doing the following:

- Cloning tables
- Creating tables that are based on data from different data sources
- Precalculating measures to improve report performance

This list is not exhaustive—there are other cases when you'll find calculated tables useful.

Cloning tables

As you saw earlier when we discussed creating a calculated table, to clone a table you also need to reference it by its name by using DAX. If you want to create a table called Invoice Date that's a clone of the Date table, follow these steps:

1. Go to the **Data** view.

2. Select **New table** on the **Home** ribbon.

3. Enter a calculated table expression. For example, this formula creates a table called Invoice Date by copying the Date table:

```
Invoice Date = 'Date'
```

4. Press **Enter**.

```
Invoice Date = 'Date'
```

Creating tables that are based on data from different data sources

In the previous section, you created a bridge table by using Power Query. In that case, you took distinct values from one column of one table and used the bridge table to relate two fact tables.

Sometimes you want to extract distinct values from more than one table because the distinct values may be different in different tables. In this case, you must take distinct values from both tables, and if they come from different data sources or from different "islands," or both, the performance may be slow. You can solve this issue by using a calculated table.

For example, you can retrieve the distinct Buying Group values from both the Customer and the Targets tables by using the following calculated table formula:

```
Buying Group =
DISTINCT(
    UNION(
        DISTINCT(Customer[Buying Group]),
        DISTINCT(Targets[Buying Group])
    )
)
```

The outer DISTINCT ensures there are no duplicates, and UNION combines values from two tables that come from different sources. UNION acts similarly to appending tables in Power Query, though they combine tables differently:

- UNION ignores column names and combines table columns based on their positions. The number of columns between tables must match.

- Appending tables in Power Query combines tables based on column names, and it's possible to combine tables that have a different number of columns.

In addition to UNION, other set functions available in DAX include EXCEPT and INTERSECT, which also require that tables have the same number of columns.

Since the data is already in memory, this process is usually much quicker compared to creating the same table using Power Query.

Precalculating measures to improve report performance

If you have complex measures that perform poorly, depending on the type of calculation you may want to precalculate them in a calculated table, and then create new measures that aggregate the precalculated values. This approach may not work for some types of calculations, though it usually helps with additive measures.

Aggregations, which we review later in the chapter, are an example of calculated tables that precalculate measures and improve performance.

NOTE   COMPANION FILE

You can see the calculated tables in the 2.2.2 Create calculated tables.pbix file in the companion files folder.

NEED MORE REVIEW?   USING CALCULATED TABLES

For more details on how to create calculated tables, see "Create calculated tables in Power BI Desktop" at *https://docs.microsoft.com/en-us/power-bi/transform-model/desktop-calculated-tables*.

Create hierarchies

Power BI allows you to group columns into hierarchies, which you can then use in visuals.

In the Wide World Importers example, you can create a hierarchy of employees:

1. Go to the **Model** view.
2. Right-click the **Director** column in the **Employee** table.
3. Select **Create hierarchy**.
4. Double-click the newly created hierarchy and rename it to **Employee Hierarchy**.
5. In the Fields pane, drag the **Manager** column on top of **Employee Hierarchy**.
6. Repeat the previous step for the **Salesperson** column.

Once the hierarchy is created, the result should look like Figure 2-18.

FIGURE 2-18 Employee Hierarchy

One column can be part of multiple hierarchies, and you can rename hierarchy items without affecting the original columns. At the same time, you do not need to sort a hierarchy element by another column, because it inherits this property from the original column. The original column can be hidden, if necessary.

A hierarchy can be created using existing columns only, and the columns must be in the same table. If you want to include columns from different tables in the same hierarchy, you'll have to bring the columns into one table. For this, you can use Power Query or the RELATED function in DAX, for example.

> **NEED MORE REVIEW? RELATED IN DAX**
>
> For more information on the RELATED function in DAX, including examples and require-ments for using the function, see "RELATED" at *https://docs.microsoft.com/en-us/dax/ related-function-dax.*

Apart from the convenience of dragging multiple fields to a visual at once in the right order, a hierarchy does not provide any special benefits in Power BI compared to using columns indi-vidually, since you can use both hierarchies and multiple individual columns together in fields to achieve the same result.

> **NOTE COMPANION FILE**
>
> You can see Employee Hierarchy in the 2.2.3 Create hierarchies.pbix file in the companion files folder.

Create calculated columns

Calculated columns are columns you create by using DAX. Similar to calculated tables, calcu-lated columns can use only the data already loaded into the model or new data generated by DAX, and they don't appear in Power Query Editor because they are generated after the data has been loaded into the model. By nature, creating calculated columns widens your table, and they are calculated after all your data is loaded, so multiple calculated columns can contribute to slow performance of your data model.

If you are experienced in Excel, creating calculated columns in DAX may remind you of creating columns in Excel, because DAX resembles the Excel formula language and there are many functions that appear in both DAX and Excel. There are some important differences, however:

- In DAX, there is no concept of a cell. If you need to get a value from a table, you must filter a specific column down to that value.
- DAX is strongly typed; it is not possible to mix values of different data types in the same column.

In our director, manager, and salesperson hierarchy example, you created calculated columns when you flattened out the parent-child hierarchy. In general, calculated columns are especially useful when you are:

- Creating columns that are going to be used as filters or categories in visuals
- Precalculating poorly performing measures

One way to create a calculated column is as follows:

1. Go to the **Data** view.
2. In the **Fields** pane, right-click a table where you want to create a calculated column.
3. Select **New column**.
4. Enter a calculated column expression by using DAX.
5. Press **Enter**.

Once you complete these steps, you'll be able to see the results immediately. The formula that you write is automatically applied to each row in the new column. You can reference another column from the same table in the following way:

```
'Table name'[Column name]
```

Though it's possible to reference a column within the same table by using only the column name, it's not considered a good practice and should be avoided.

For example, in Wide World Importers, you can calculate total cost in a calculated column in the Sale table by using the following expression:

```
Total Cost = Sale[Total Excluding Tax] - Sale[Profit]
```

If you want to reference a column from a related table that is on the one side of a relationship, you can use the RELATED function. For instance, in Wide World Importers, you can add a calculated column to the Sale table to calculate the price difference between the standard unit price and the price a product was sold for:

```
Unit Price Difference = RELATED('Stock Item'[Unit Price]) - Sale[Unit Price]
```

RELATED works on the many side of a relationship. If you want to add a column to the one side of a relationship and reference the related rows, you can use the RELATEDTABLE function. For instance, you can add a calculated column to the Customer table to count the number of related rows in the Sale table for each customer:

```
Sales Rows = COUNTROWS(RELATEDTABLE(Sale))
```

Implement row-level security roles

A common business requirement is to secure data so that different users who view the same report can see different subsets of data. In Power BI, this can be accomplished with the feature called row-level security (RLS).

Row-level security restricts data by filtering it at the row level depending on the rules defined for each user. To configure RLS, you first create and define each role in Power BI Desktop, and then assign individual users or Active Directory security groups to the roles in the Power BI service.

In this section, we discuss the skills necessary to implement row-level security roles in Power BI Desktop. We review assignment of roles in the Power BI service in Chapter 5, "Deploy and maintain deliverables."

Creating roles in Power BI Desktop

To see the list of roles configured in a dataset in Power BI Desktop, select **Manage roles** from the **Modeling** ribbon in the **Report** view. To create a new role, select **Create** in the **Roles** section. You'll then be prompted to specify table filters, as shown in Figure 2-19.

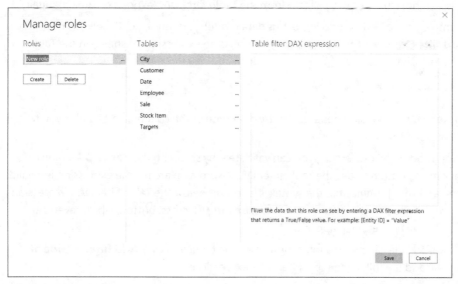

FIGURE 2-19 List of roles

When you create a role, you have the option to change the default name to a new one. It is important to give roles user-friendly names because you will see them in the Power BI service, and you should be able to assign users to the correct roles. All roles are listed in the Roles section of the Manage roles window.

If you right-click on a role or select the ellipsis next to a role, you'll be presented with the following options:

- **Create** This option creates a new role and is an alternative to the Create button below the list of roles.

- **Duplicate** Use this option to create a copy of the currently selected role.

- **Rename** Use this option to rename the currently selected role; you can also rename a role by double-clicking on its name.

- **Delete** Use this option to delete the currently selected role; you can also perform this action by selecting Delete below the list of roles.

For each role, you can define a DAX expression to filter each table. When row-level security is configured, these expressions will be evaluated against each row of the relevant table, and only those rows for which the expressions are evaluated as *true* will be visible.

You can either enter a table filter DAX expression yourself or use the ellipsis menu next to each table to add an expression that you can then customize. The menu can also be accessed by right-clicking on a table. The menu offers three options:

- **Add filter** This option lists all columns available in the table and allows you to hide all rows.

- **Copy table filter from** This option copies a table filter DAX expression from another role that has a filter expression defined for the table.

- **Clear table filter** This option removes any table filter DAX expression from the table. This is a shortcut to erasing all text from the Table filter DAX expression area manually.

For example, in the Wide World Importers data model, you can select the ellipsis next to **City** > **Add filter** > **[Sales Territory]**. Doing so inserts an expression, as shown in the Table filter DAX expression area:

```
[Sales Territory] = "Value"
```

The placeholder expression depends on the data type of the column, and it helps you to write the correct filter expression.

After you modify the expression, you can validate it by selecting the **Verify DAX expression** (check mark) button above the Table filter DAX expression area. If the expression is invalid, you will see a warning stating that the syntax is incorrect below the Table filter DAX expression area. Next to the check mark button is the **Revert changes** (cross) button, which reverts any changes that have not yet been applied.

If you want to hide all rows in a table, right-click the table and click **Add filter** > **Hide all rows**. This will add the following table filter DAX expression:

```
false
```

Because *false* is never going to be *true* for any row, no rows will be shown in this case.

You can configure row-level security in the Wide World Importers data model. First, create two roles as follows:

1. Create a new role and call it **Southeast**.

2. For the **Southeast** role, in the **City** table, enter the following table filter DAX expression:

   ```
   [Sales Territory] = "Southeast"
   ```

3. Select the **Verify DAX expression** button above the **Table filter DAX expression** area.

4. Right-click the **Southeast** role and select **Duplicate**.

5. Rename the new role to **Plains**.

6. For the Plains role, update the table filter DAX expression in the **City** table as follows:

```
[Sales Territory] = "Plains"
```

7. Select **Save**.

IMPORTANT   **DUPLICATING ROLES**

If you duplicate a role before you verify the last added table filter, the table filter will not be copied to the duplicate role.

Next, let's test the roles in Power BI Desktop.

Viewing as roles in Power BI Desktop

In Power BI Desktop, you can check what the users with specific roles will see even before you publish your report to the Power BI service and assign users to roles. To do so, once you have at least one role defined select **View as** on the **Modeling** ribbon in the **Report** view. You will then see the **View as roles** window shown in Figure 2-20.

FIGURE 2-20 View as roles

You can view as several roles simultaneously. This is because you can allocate a single user or a security group to multiple roles in the Power BI service; in this case, the security rules of the roles will complement each other. For example, if you select both the Plains and the Southeast roles, you'll see data for both territories. For this reason, you should always have clear names for your RLS roles.

EXAM TIP

You should know the effect of combining multiple security roles for a single user based on the description of security filters of each role.

When viewing data as roles, you'll see the bar at the top, as shown in Figure 2-21.

Now viewing report as: Plains, Southeast   Stop viewing

FIGURE 2-21 Now viewing report as

> **IMPORTANT   APPLICATION OF ROW-LEVEL SECURITY**
>
> It is important to understand that the filters applied by row-level security are only applied at query time and not at processing time. The implication of this is that the filters won't change the values of calculated columns and calculated tables.

Another option in the View as roles window is Other user. With this option, you can test dynamic row-level security, which we cover next.

Dynamic row-level security

The roles you have created so far have been static, which means that all users within a role will see the same data. If you have several rules that specify how you should secure your data, this approach may mean you have to create many roles, as well as update the data model every time you introduce a new role or remove an old one.

There is an alternative approach, called dynamic row-level security, which allows you to show different data to different users within the same role.

> **REAL WORLD   DYNAMIC ROW-LEVEL SECURITY**
>
> Because dynamic row-level security can use a single role, this approach is preferable in large-scale implementations of Power BI where there are many users who need to see different data.

For this approach, your data model must contain the usernames of people who should have access to the relevant rows of data. You will also need to pass the active username as a filter condition. Power BI has two functions that allow you to get the username of the current user:

- **USERNAME** This function returns the domain and login of the user in the domain\login format.
- **USERPRINCIPALNAME** Depending on how the Active Directory was set up, this function usually returns the email address of the user.

> **NOTE   USING USERNAME AND USERPRINCIPALNAME**
>
> If your computer is not part of an Active Directory domain, both functions will return the same result—domain\login. Once you publish your dataset to Power BI service, both functions will return the email address of the user.
>
> These functions can be used only in measures or table filter DAX expressions; if you try to use either of them in a calculated column or a calculated table, you will get an error.

To see how dynamic row-level security works in the Wide World Importers data model, create a new security role first:

1. Select **Manage roles** on the **Modeling** ribbon.
2. Create a new security role and call it **Dynamic RLS**.
3. For the **Dynamic RLS** role, specify the following table filter DAX expression for the **Employee** table:

```
[Email] = USERPRINCIPALNAME()
```

4. Select **Save**.

Now you can test the new role:

1. Select **View as** on the **Modeling** ribbon.
2. Select both the **Other user** and **Dynamic RLS** check boxes.
3. Enter **jack.potter@wideworldimporters.com** in the **Other user** box.
4. Select **OK**.
5. Go to the **Data** view.
6. Select the **Employee** table.

Note that the Employee table is now filtered to just Jack Potter's row, as shown in Figure 2-22.

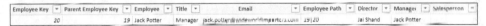

Employee Key	▼	Parent Employee Key	▼	Employee	▼	Title	▼	Email		▼	Employee Path	▼	Director	▼	Manager	▼	Salesperson	▼
20		19		Jack Potter		Manager		jack.potter@wideworldimporters.com			19|20		Jai Shand		Jack Potter			

FIGURE 2-22 Employee table viewed as Jack Potter

Although this approach may be good enough in certain cases, it's a common requirement for managers to see the data of those who report to them. Since Jack is a Manager, he should be able to see data of the salespersons who report to him. For that, you should modify the table filter DAX expression of the Dynamic RLS role as follows:

```
PATHCONTAINS(
    [Employee Path],
    LOOKUPVALUE(
        Employee[Employee Key],
        Employee[Email],
        USERPRINCIPALNAME()
    )
)
```

This table filter DAX expression keeps those rows where Jack is part of the hierarchy path. You are leveraging the same calculated column you created earlier when you flattened the parent-child hierarchy of employees.

After you make this change, the Employee table will display four rows: Jack's row and three rows of the salespersons who report to Jack, as seen in Figure 2-23.

Employee Key	Parent Employee Key	Employee	Title	Email	Employee Path	Director	Manager	Salesperson
20	19	Jack Potter	Manager	jack.potter@wideworldimporters.com	19|20	Jai Shand	Jack Potter	
16	20	Archer Lamble	Salesperson	archer.lamble@wideworldimporters.com	19|20|16	Jai Shand	Jack Potter	Archer Lamble
15	20	Taj Shand	Salesperson	taj.shand@wideworldimporters.com	19|20|15	Jai Shand	Jack Potter	Taj Shand
14	20	Lily Code	Salesperson	lily.code@wideworldimporters.com	19|20|14	Jai Shand	Jack Potter	Lily Code

FIGURE 2-23 Employee table viewed as Jack Potter

So far, you've created the roles in Power BI Desktop. Once you publish the report, you'll need to assign users or security groups to roles in Power BI service separately. We review these skills in Chapter 5.

NEED MORE REVIEW? ROW-LEVEL SECURITY

For more examples of implementing row-level security in Power BI, see "Row-level security (RLS) guidance in Power BI Desktop" at *https://docs.microsoft.com/en-us/power-bi/guidance/rls-guidance*.

Set up the Q&A feature

Both Power BI Desktop and the Power BI service allow you to create visualizations that provide answers to specific questions. This capability gives you great control over formatting, but it will not work if you have RLS set up and users only have read access to content.

Another way to explore data in Power BI is to use the Q&A feature, also known as natural language queries. This feature enables you to get answers to your questions by typing them in natural language. Even users with read-only access can query datasets in a natural language.

To start using Q&A in Power BI Desktop, you must be in the Report view. To insert the Q&A visual, double-click the empty space on the report canvas. Alternatively, you can select **Q&A** on the **Insert** ribbon. Either way, you'll see a visual, as shown in Figure 2-24.

Although the suggestions may not be immediately useful, you can ask your own questions. For example, you can enter **profit by sales territory as column chart**, and the result will be as shown in Figure 2-25.

Note that the Q&A visual updates its result as you type. In Figure 2-25, before we typed "as column chart," the Q&A visual was showing a bar chart.

FIGURE 2-24 Q&A visual

FIGURE 2-25 Q&A showing profit by sales territory

If desired, you can turn the Q&A result into a standard visual by selecting the button between the question and the cog wheel in the upper-right corner of the Q&A visual.

The Q&A visual depends on the field names as they are defined in the data model. For example, entering **revenue by sales territory** in the Q&A visual won't provide any meaningful results, as seen in Figure 2-26.

FIGURE 2-26 Q&A visual showing revenue by sales territory

This issue can be fixed by teaching Q&A, as outlined next.

Teach Q&A

The Q&A visual didn't understand the term *revenue* because it doesn't appear in the Wide World Importers data model. The Q&A visual underlines the terms it doesn't understand with red. If you select *revenue* in the Q&A visual, you'll be given suggestions to replace *revenue* with another term (such as *profit* in our example), or you can define the term. Selecting **define revenue** allows you to teach Q&A, as seen in Figure 2-27.

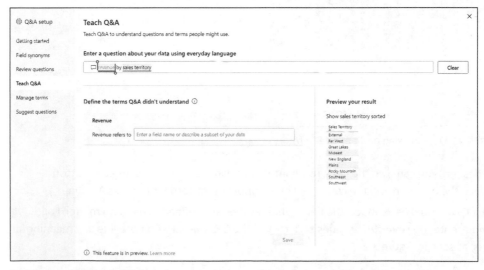

FIGURE 2-27 The Teach Q&A window

In the **Define the terms Q&A didn't understand** section, you can teach Q&A that *revenue* refers to a certain field—for example, *Total Including Tax*:

1. Enter **total including tax** next to Revenue refers to.

2. Select **Save**.

3. Close the **Q&A setup** window.

The Q&A visual now understands the term *revenue*, as you can see in Figure 2-28.

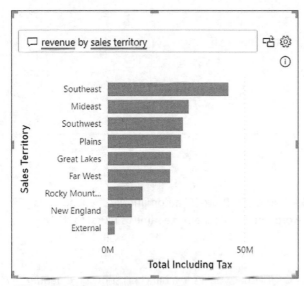

FIGURE 2-28 Q&A showing revenue by sales territory

Since teaching Q&A can be time-consuming, you can also add synonyms to your data model if you know them in advance, as covered next. Additionally, this is another example where naming columns in Power Query Editor with friendly names will make this process easier.

Synonyms

Separately from teaching Q&A, you can introduce your own Q&A keywords and make Power BI recognize them. This technique is especially useful if your business users use acronyms or unique terminology such as substituting *units* for *quantity*; in that case, you can create a synonym for the Quantity field that will reduce confusion for your report users.

1. In the **Report** view, select **Q&A setup** on the **Modeling** ribbon.

2. Select **Field synonyms** on the left.

3. Expand the **Sale** section. You should see a list of fields in the Sale table, as shown in Figure 2-29.

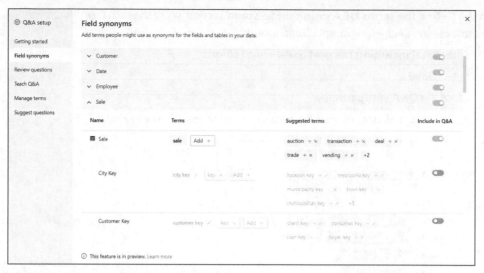

FIGURE 2-29 Field synonyms for the Sale table

4. Next to **Quantity**, select **Add**.

5. Enter **units** and press the **Enter** key. Note that Power BI automatically changed *units* to *unit* because it stores singular words and treats them the same as plural for Q&A purposes.

6. Close the **Q&A setup** window.

If you now enter **units by color** in the Q&A visual, you'll see a bar chart showing Quantity by Color, despite not using the term *quantity* explicitly.

Additionally, in the **Field synonyms** section of **Q&A setup**, you can exclude specific tables and fields from Q&A if you don't want Q&A to use the table or field. Hidden objects are excluded by default. This behavior is useful if you need to include staff data in your data model but don't want users to query this data.

> **NOTE COMPANION FILE**
>
> You can see the implemented synonyms in the 2.2.6 Set up the Q&A feature.pbix file in the companion files folder.

> **NEED MORE REVIEW? Q&A BEST PRACTICES**
>
> Q&A, when set up correctly, can be a powerful tool that enables data exploration by report consumers. For Q&A best practices, see "Best practices to optimize Q&A in Power BI" at *https://docs.microsoft.com/en-us/power-bi/natural-language/q-and-a-best-practices*.

Skill 2.3: Create measures by using DAX

You used some DAX earlier in the chapter to create quick measures, calculated tables, and calculated columns, as well as to configure row-level security. In practice, DAX is most often used to create measures in Power BI.

Writing your own formulas is an important skill that allows you to perform much more sophisticated analysis based on your data compared to not using DAX.

In this section, we start by reviewing DAX fundamentals; then we look at CALCULATE, one of the most important functions in DAX, specifically in Time Intelligence or time-related calculations, which we review separately.

DAX can help you replace some columns with measures, allowing you to reduce the data model size. Not all DAX formulas have to be complex, and we review some basic statistical functions in this section as well.

> **This skill covers how to:**
> - Use DAX to build complex measures
> - Use CALCULATE to manipulate filters
> - Implement Time Intelligence using DAX
> - Replace numeric columns with measures
> - Use basic statistical functions to enhance data
> - Create semi-additive measures

Use DAX to build complex measures

Many things can be computed by using calculated columns, but in most cases it's preferable to write measures, because they don't increase the model size. Additionally, some calculations are simply not possible with calculated columns. For example, to calculate a ratio dynamically, you'd need to write a measure.

As you saw earlier, quick measures already allow you to perform basic calculations without writing DAX. In this section, you start using DAX to build complex measures.

It is important to understand that Power BI allows you to aggregate columns in visuals without using measures; this practice is sometimes called *implicit measures*. Implicit measures can be useful when you want to quickly test how a visual might look or perform a quick analysis on a column. However, it's always best practice to create *explicit measures* by using DAX—even in case of trivial calculations such as SUM. Here are some of the reasons why it's preferable to create measures yourself:

- Implicit measures may provide unexpected results in some cases due to the Summarize by column property. For example, if you have a column that contains product prices and Power BI sets the summarization to Sum, then dragging the column in a visual will not produce meaningful results. Though you can change the summarization in the visual, following this approach means that you need to pay attention to this property every time you use implicit measures.

- Explicit measures can be reused in other measures. This is beneficial because you can write less code, which saves time and improves the maintainability of your data model.

- If you connect to your Power BI dataset from Excel, you cannot use implicit measures.

- Implicit measures cannot leverage inactive relationships.

- Implicit measures are not supported by calculation groups.

> **MORE INFO CALCULATION GROUPS**
>
> While calculation groups are outside of scope of the exam, they can be extremely useful in practice. For more information, see "Calculation groups" at *https://docs.microsoft.com/en-us/ analysis-services/tabular-models/calculation-groups*.

> **NOTE LEARNING DAX**
>
> Teaching DAX is not the purpose of this book. If you want to learn DAX, *The Definitive Guide to DAX* by Marco Russo and Alberto Ferrari (Microsoft Press, 2019) is a great explanation of DAX and its use.

Measures are different from calculated columns in a few ways. The main difference is that you can see the results of a calculated column immediately after defining the calculation, whereas the results of a measure aren't shown until you use it in a visual. This behavior allows measures to return different results depending on filters and where they're used.

Another difference between calculated columns and measures is that calculated column formulas apply to each row of a table, whereas measures work on columns and tables, not specific rows. Therefore, measures most often use aggregation functions in DAX.

There are a few ways to create a measure in Power BI Desktop. One way is as follows:

1. Go to the **Report** view.
2. In the **Fields** pane, right-click a table in which you want to create a new measure.
3. Select **New measure**.
4. Enter the measure formula and press **Enter**.

You can also create a measure by selecting **New measure** on the **Home** ribbon, but make sure you have the right table selected in the **Fields** pane; otherwise, your measure may not be created in the correct table. If you created a measure in the wrong table, instead of re-creating the measure, you can move it by performing these steps:

1. Go to the **Report** view.
2. In the **Fields** pane, select the measure you want to move.
3. On the **Measure tools** ribbon, select the table your measure should be stored in from the **Home table** drop-down list.

For example, to compute the total profit of Wide World Importers, use the following measure formula:

```
Total Profit = SUM(Sale[Profit])
```

You can compute total sales excluding tax by using the following measure formula:

```
Total Sales Excluding Tax = SUM(Sale[Total Excluding Tax])
```

If you want to compute the profit margin percentage, there are two ways of doing it. One is as follows:

```
Profit % =
DIVIDE(
    SUM(Sale[Profit]),
    SUM(Sale[Total Excluding Tax])
)
```

> **NOTE USING DIVIDE**
>
> We're using DIVIDE in the formula to avoid division by zero. DIVIDE also has an optional third parameter, which is the value to return in case you divide by zero.

However, this involves repeating your own code, which is undesirable because formulas become more difficult to maintain. You can avoid this by referencing the measures you created previously:

```
Profit % =
DIVIDE(
    [Total Profit],
    [Total Sales Excluding Tax]
)
```

> **NOTE FORMATTING MEASURES**
>
> Even though the Profit % measure has a percentage sign in its name, Power BI will format the measure as a decimal number by default. You can change the measure format on the **Measure tools** ribbon in the **Formatting** grouping. Formatting a measure after it has been created is a great habit to learn.

When you're referencing measures, it's best practice to not use table names in front of them. Unlike column names, measure names are unique; different tables may have the same column names, but it's not possible to have measures that share the same name.

Another feature of DAX that allows you to avoid repeating yourself is variables. Think of a variable as a calculation within a measure. For instance, if you want to avoid showing zeros in your visuals, you can write a measure as follows:

```
Total Dry Items Units Sold =
IF(
    SUM(Sale[Total Dry Items]) <> 0,
    SUM(Sale[Total Dry Items])
)
```

By using a variable, you can avoid calling SUM twice:

```
Total Dry Items Units Sold =
VAR TotalDryItems = SUM(Sale[Total Dry Items])
VAR Result =
    IF(
        TotalDryItems <> 0,
        TotalDryItems
    )
RETURN
    Result
```

Variables are especially useful when you want to store computationally expensive values, because variables are evaluated no more than once. As you'll see later in this chapter, we can use many variables within the same formula.

> **NOTE COMPANION FILE**
>
> You can see the measures above in the 2.3.1 Use DAX to build complex measures.pbix file in the companion files folder.

Use CALCULATE to manipulate filters

Earlier in this chapter, you saw that the CALCULATE function can be used to alter relationships when paired with other DAX measures; the USERELATIONSHIP function with CALCULATE can activate inactive relationships, and CROSSFILTER with CALCULATE can change the filter direction.

The CALCULATE function also allows you to alter the filter context under which measures are evaluated: you can add, remove, or update filters, or you can trigger context transition. We cover row context, filter context, and context transition in more detail later in this chapter.

CALCULATE accepts a scalar expression as its first parameter, and subsequent parameters are filter arguments. Using CALCULATE with no filter arguments is only useful for context transition.

Adding filters

CALCULATE allows you to add filters in several formats. To calculate profit for the New England sales territory, you can write a measure that you can read as "Calculate the Total Profit where the Sales Territory is New England":

```
New England Profit =
CALCULATE(
    [Total Profit],
    City[Sales Territory] = "New England"
)
```

Importantly, you're not limited to using one value per filter. You can calculate profit for New England, Far West, and Plains:

```
New England, Far West, and Plains Profit =
CALCULATE(
    [Total Profit],
    City[Sales Territory] IN {"New England", "Far West", "Plains"}
)
```

You can specify filters for different columns at once, too, which you combine by using the AND DAX function. For example, you can calculate profit in New England in 2020 like so:

```
New England Profit 2020 =
CALCULATE(
    [Total Profit],
    City[Sales Territory] = "New England",
    'Date'[Year] = 2020
)
```

Translated into plain English, this measure formula can be read as "Calculate Total Profit where the Sales Territory is New England and the Year is 2020."

Removing filters

There are several DAX functions that you can use as CALCULATE modifiers to ignore filters, one of which is ALL. ALL can remove filters from:

- One or more columns from the same table
- An entire table
- The whole data model (when ALL is used with no parameters)

> **IMPORTANT   SORT BY COLUMN AND ALL**
>
> If you're removing filters from a column that is sorted by another column, you should remove filters from both columns. Otherwise, you may get unexpected results.

For example, you can show profit for all sales territories regardless of any filters on the City[Sales Territory] column:

```
Profit All Sales Territories =
CALCULATE(
    [Total Profit],
    ALL(City[Sales Territory])
)
```

If you create a table that shows the new measure alongside Total Profit by Sales Territory, you'll get the result shown in Figure 2-30.

Sales Territory	Total Profit	Profit All Sales Territories
External	1,093,669.85	85,729,180.90
Far West	9,923,891.70	85,729,180.90
Great Lakes	10,046,782.10	85,729,180.90
Mideast	12,843,350.00	85,729,180.90
New England	3,813,022.75	85,729,180.90
Plains	11,596,968.65	85,729,180.90
Rocky Mountain	5,493,609.45	85,729,180.90
Southeast	18,994,984.65	85,729,180.90
Southwest	11,922,901.75	85,729,180.90
Total	**85,729,180.90**	**85,729,180.90**

FIGURE 2-30 Total Profit and Profit All Sales Territories by Sales Territory

Note that the new measure displays the same value for any sales territory, which is the total of all sales territories combined regardless of sales territory.

> **NEED MORE REVIEW?** **FILTER FUNCTIONS IN DAX**
>
> In addition to ALL, there are several other DAX functions that remove filters, such as ALL-EXCEPT and ALLSELECTED. Full details of each function are outside of the scope of this book. For an overview, see "Filter functions" at *https://docs.microsoft.com/en-us/dax/filter-functions-dax*.

Updating filters

When you specify a filter such as City[Sales Territory] = "New England", it's an abbreviated way that corresponds to the following filter:

```
FILTER(
    ALL(City[Sales Territory]),
    City[Sales Territory] = "New England"
)
```

By adding this filter, you are both ignoring a filter by using ALL, and you're adding a filter at the same time. This technique allows you to filter for New England regardless of the selected sales territory.

If you create a table that shows Total Profit and New England Profit by Sales Territory, the result should look like Figure 2-31.

Sales Territory	Total Profit	New England Profit
External	1,093,669.85	3,813,022.75
Far West	9,923,891.70	3,813,022.75
Great Lakes	10,046,782.10	3,813,022.75
Mideast	12,843,350.00	3,813,022.75
New England	3,813,022.75	3,813,022.75
Plains	11,596,968.65	3,813,022.75
Rocky Mountain	5,493,609.45	3,813,022.75
Southeast	18,994,984.65	3,813,022.75
Southwest	11,922,901.75	3,813,022.75
Total	**85,729,180.90**	**3,813,022.75**

FIGURE 2-31 Total Profit and New England Profit by Sales Territory

When you have Sales Territory on rows, each row from the Total Profit column is filtered for a single sales territory and the Total row shows values for all sales territories. In contrast, by using the measure above in the New England Profit column, you are filtering regardless of the current sales territory, showing only the New England Profit.

Context transition

Another important function of CALCULATE is context transition, which refers to transitioning from row context to filter context.

In DAX, there are two evaluation contexts:

- **Row context** This context can be understood as "the current row." Row context is present in calculated columns and iterators. Iterators are functions that take a table and go row by row, evaluating an expression for each row. For example, FILTER is an iterator; it takes a table, and for each row, it evaluates a filter condition. Those rows that satisfy the condition are included in the result of FILTER.

- **Filter context** This context can be understood as "all applied filters." Filters can come from slicers, from the Filter pane, or by selecting a visual element. Filters can also be applied programmatically by using DAX.

To review context transition, let's create a sample table in the data model:

1. On the **Home** ribbon, select **Enter data**.
2. Enter **Sample** in the **Name** box.
3. Enter the data shown in Figure 2-32.
4. Select **Load**.

FIGURE 2-32 Entering data

Now that you have the table, you can add two calculated columns to it to see the effect of context transition:

1. Go to the **Data** view.

2. Select the **Sample** table in the **Fields** pane.

3. Create a calculated column with the following formula:

```
Sum Number = SUM('Sample'[Number])
```

4. Create another calculated column with the following formula:

```
Calculate Sum Number = CALCULATE(SUM('Sample'[Number]))
```

The result should look like Figure 2-33.

Letter	Number	Sum Number	Calculate Sum Number
A	1	6	1
B	2	6	2
C	3	6	3

FIGURE 2-33 Calculated columns in the Sample table

SUM, as an aggregation function, uses filter context. Because there are no filters in the data model—there are no visuals, and you're not adding any filters by using DAX—SUM aggregates the Whole Number column, so the result in the Sum Number column is 6 regardless of the row.

On the other hand, the Calculate Sum Number column uses the same formula as Sum Number but has been wrapped in CALCULATE. CALCULATE automatically performs context transition, so the result is different than using the SUM function alone. Context transition takes all values from all other columns and uses them as filters. Therefore, for the first row, you aggregate the Number column, where

- **Sample[Letter]** is **A**
- **Sample[Number]** is **1**
- **Sample[Sum Number]** is **6**

Where the sum of 1 is equal to 1, since there's only one such row that meets these filters, you get 1. Separately for row 2, the sum of 2 equals 2, and for row 3, the sum of 3 equals 3. You can make context transition even clearer by modifying the Sample table slightly:

1. On the **Home** ribbon, select **Transform Data**.

2. Select the **Sample** query.

3. Select the cog wheel in the **Source** step.

4. Change the third row to be the same as the second row, as shown in Figure 2-34.

	Letter	Number	*
1	A	1	
2	B	2	
3	B	2	
*			

Create Table

OK   Cancel

FIGURE 2-34 Modified Sample table

5. Select **OK**.

6. On the **Home** ribbon of Power Query Editor, select **Close & Apply**.

If you now look at the Sample table in the **Data** view, the result will look like Figure 2-35.

Letter	Number	Sum Number	Calculate Sum Number
A	1	5	1
B	2	5	4
B	2	5	4

FIGURE 2-35 Sample table after update

Although the first row is calculated as you saw in the previous example, the second and third row are now both showing 4. Intuitively, you could expect to see 2 and 2 in each row, though you're getting 4 and 4. This is because for each row, due to context transition triggered by CALCULATE, you're summing the Number column, where

- **Sample[Letter]** is **B**
- **Sample[Number]** is **2**
- **Sample[Sum Number]** is **5**

Because there are two such rows, you get 2 + 2 = 4 in both rows.

Implement Time Intelligence using DAX

It is common for business users to want to aggregate metrics—for example, revenue—across time, such as year-to-date revenue for a certain date, or prior-year revenue for the comparable period. Fortunately, DAX has a family of functions that facilitate such calculations, referred to as Time Intelligence.

All Time Intelligence functions require a calendar table that has a date type column with unique values. If the date column is not part of a relationship, the calendar table must be marked as a date table, which can be done as follows:

1. Go to the **Report** or **Data** view.
2. Select the calendar table in the **Fields** pane.
3. On the **Table tools** ribbon, select **Mark as date table** > **Mark as date table**.
4. Select the date column from the **Date column** drop-down list.
5. Select **OK**.

Most Time Intelligence functions return tables that can be used as filters in CALCULATE. For example, the DATESYTD function can be used to calculate a year-to-date amount as follows:

```
Profit YTD =
CALCULATE(
    [Total Profit],
    DATESYTD('Date'[Date])
)
```

You can also combine Time Intelligence functions. For example, to calculate year-to-date profit for the previous year, use the following formula:

```
Profit PYTD =
CALCULATE(
    [Profit YTD],
    DATEADD('Date'[Date], -1, YEAR)
)
```

Some Time Intelligence functions, such as DATESYTD, can accommodate fiscal years. For example, if you had a fiscal year ending on June 30, you could calculate profit year-to-date for the fiscal year as follows:

```
Profit FYTD =
CALCULATE(
    [Total Profit],
    DATESYTD('Date'[Date], "30-6")
)
```

The Total Profit, Profit YTD, Profit PYTD, and Profit FYTD measures can be seen together in Figure 2-36.

Year	Total Profit	Profit YTD	Profit PYTD	Profit FYTD
⊟ 2017	14,208,987.05	14,208,987.05		11,913,804.30
May	505,502.90	505,502.90		505,502.90
June	1,789,679.85	2,295,182.75		2,295,182.75
July	1,635,407.10	3,930,589.85		1,635,407.10
August	1,865,778.55	5,796,368.40		3,501,185.65
September	2,024,158.20	7,820,526.60		5,525,343.85
October	2,184,080.85	10,004,607.45		7,709,424.70
November	1,980,397.50	11,985,004.95		9,689,822.20
December	2,223,982.10	14,208,987.05		11,913,804.30
⊟ 2018	23,666,819.70	23,666,819.70	14,208,987.05	12,593,760.10
January	1,637,255.50	1,637,255.50		13,551,059.80
February	1,754,601.40	3,391,856.90		15,306,061.20
March	2,015,527.80	5,407,304.70		17,321,189.00
April	1,785,869.10	7,193,253.80		19,107,058.10
May	1,899,343.10	9,092,596.90	505,502.90	21,006,401.20
June	1,980,462.70	11,073,059.60	2,295,182.75	22,986,863.90
July	1,805,425.30	12,878,484.90	3,930,589.85	1,805,425.30
August	1,944,448.15	14,822,933.05	5,796,368.40	3,749,873.45
September	2,082,198.40	16,905,131.45	7,820,526.60	5,832,071.85
October	2,293,561.45	19,198,692.90	10,004,607.45	8,125,633.30
November	2,117,718.90	21,316,411.80	11,985,004.95	10,243,352.20
December	2,350,407.90	23,666,819.70	14,208,987.05	12,593,760.10
⊞ 2019	26,322,158.20	26,322,158.20	23,666,819.70	13,937,615.90
⊞ 2020	21,531,215.95	21,531,215.95	26,322,158.20	8,426,299.50
⊞ 2021			21,531,215.95	
Total	85,729,180.90		21,531,215.95	

FIGURE 2-36 Time Intelligence calculations

Notice how the Profit YTD measure shows the cumulative total profit within each year. The Profit PYTD measure shows the same values as Profit YTD one year before. Profit FYTD shows the cumulative total profit for fiscal years, resetting on July 1 of each year.

> **NOTE COMPANION FILE**
>
> You can see the measures above in the 2.3.3 Implement Time Intelligence using DAX.pbix file in the companion files folder.

Replace numeric columns with measures

It is sometimes possible to replace some numeric columns with measures, which can reduce the size of the data model. In the Wide World Importers example, several columns can be replaced with measures.

For example, the *Total Chiller Items* and *Total Dry Items* columns in the *Sale* table show quantity of chiller and dry items, respectively. Essentially, these columns show filtered quantities depending on whether an item is a chiller or a dry item.

Before you replace the two columns with measures, create the following measure, which you'll reference and build upon later:

```
Total Quantity = SUM(Sale[Quantity])
```

You can now create the following two measures and use them instead of columns:

```
Total Chiller Items (Measure) =
CALCULATE(
    [Total Quantity],
    'Stock Item'[Is Chiller Stock] = TRUE
)

Total Dry Items (Measure) =
CALCULATE(
    [Total Quantity],
    'Stock Item'[Is Chiller Stock] = FALSE
)
```

If you remove the *Total Chiller Items* and *Total Dry Items* columns from the model, you'll make it smaller and more efficient.

Another example of a column that can be replaced by a measure is *Total Including Tax* from the Sale table. Since *Total Excluding Tax* and *Tax Amount* added together equals Total Including Tax, you can use the following measure instead:

```
Total Including Tax (Measure) =
SUMX(
    Sale,
    Sale[Total Excluding Tax] + Sale[Tax Amount]
)
```

Again, once you have the measure, removing the *Total Including Tax* column reduces the size of the data model.

Use basic statistical functions to enhance data

As mentioned previously, it's best practice to create explicit measures even for basic calculations such as SUM, because you can build on these to create more complex measures. Here are several basic statistical measures that are frequently used:

- SUM
- AVERAGE
- MEDIAN
- COUNT
- DISTINCTCOUNT
- MIN
- MAX

As you'll recall, we have frequently used SUM in our previous examples. All these functions take a column as a reference and produce a scalar value. In addition to this, every function except for DISTINCTCOUNT has an equivalent iterator function with the X suffix—for instance, SUMX is the iterator counterpart of SUM. Iterators take two parameters: a table to iterate through and an expression to evaluate for each row. The evaluated results are then aggregated according to the base function; for example, SUMX will sum up the results. When you're learning the difference, it can be helpful to create sample tables similar to the examples shown in this book to visually compare the nuances of the different functions.

Create semi-additive measures

In general, there are three kinds of measures:

- **Additive** These measures are aggregated by using the SUM function across any dimensions. A typical example is revenue, which can be added across different product categories, cities, and dates, as well as other dimensions. Revenue of all months within a year, when added together, equals the total year revenue.

- **Semi-additive** These measures can be added across some but not all dimensions. For example, inventory counts can be added across different product categories and cities, but not dates; if you had five units yesterday and two units today, that doesn't mean you'll have seven units tomorrow. On the other hand, if you have five units in Sydney and two units in Melbourne, this means you've got seven units in the two cities in total.
- **Non-additive** These measures cannot be added across any dimensions. For instance, you cannot add up the average price across any dimension, because the result would not make any practical sense. If the average sale price in Sydney was $4.50 and it was $3.50 in Melbourne, you cannot say that across both cities, the average price was $8.00 or even $4.00 because the number of units sold could be very different.

In this section, we're focusing on semi-additive measures. There are several ways to write a semi-additive measure, and the correct way to do so depends on business requirements. Let's say your business is interested in inventory counts, and you have the data model shown in Figure 2-37.

FIGURE 2-37 Inventory data model

If you have inventory figures for all dates of interest in your data, you can write the following measure:

```
Inventory Balance =
CALCULATE(
    SUM(Inventory[Balance]),
    LASTDATE('Date'[Date])
)
```

In addition to LASTDATE and its sister function FIRSTDATE, there are some DAX functions that can help you retrieve the opening or closing balance for different time periods:

- OPENINGBALANCEMONTH
- OPENINGBALANCEQUARTER
- OPENINGBALANCEYEAR
- CLOSINGBALANCEMONTH
- CLOSINGBALANCEQUARTER
- CLOSINGBALANCEYEAR

The functions that start with *CLOSING* evaluate an expression for the last date in the period, and the functions that start with *OPENING* evaluate an expression for one day before the first date in the period. This means that the opening balance for February 1 is the same as closing balance for January 31.

For example, you can calculate the opening month balance for inventory as follows:

```
Inventory Opening Balance Month =
OPENINGBALANCEMONTH(
    SUM(Inventory[Balance]),
    'Date'[Date]
)
```

The date-based functions listed here work only if you have data for all dates of interest. If you'd chosen to use CLOSINGBALANCEMONTH but your data ends on May 23, 2020, as is the case for sample data, you'll get a blank value for May 2020. For cases such as this, you can use LASTNONBLANKVALUE or FIRSTNONBLANKVALUE, as shown next:

```
Inventory Last Nonblank =
LASTNONBLANKVALUE(
    'Date'[Date],
    SUM(Inventory[Balance])
)
```

This measure will show the latest available balance in the current context.

The *Inventory Balance*, *Inventory Opening Balance Month*, and *Inventory Last Nonblank* measures can be seen in Figure 2-38.

Year	Inventory Balance	Inventory Opening Balance Month	Inventory Last Nonblank
⊟ 2020			4
⊟ Qtr 1	8		8
⊞ January	4		4
⊞ February	11	4	11
⊞ March	8	11	8
⊟ Qtr 2		8	4
⊞ April	10	8	10
⊞ May		10	4
Total			4

FIGURE 2-38 Inventory measures

Determining which calculation should be used strongly depends on the business requirements since there is no single correct answer that applies to all scenarios. Missing data may mean there's no inventory, or it may mean that data isn't captured frequently enough. The data modeler should understand the underlying data before writing the calculations to ensure that the data isn't represented incorrectly.

Skill 2.4: Optimize model performance

Sometimes after you create the first version of your data model, you may realize that it doesn't perform well enough. Because of the way Power BI stores data, it may mean that your data model isn't performing as efficiently as it can. In this section, we review the skills necessary to optimize a model's performance and show you how to identify measures, visuals, and relationships that are slow. Finally, we review aggregations in Power BI, which can dramatically speed up data models that use DirectQuery.

When working with imported data in Power BI, keep in mind that it's a columnstore database, which means that the number of distinct values in a column—also known as cardinality—usually plays a more important role than the number of rows. Therefore, one way to address poor performance is to reduce cardinality levels, which you can do by changing data types or summarizing data.

> **This skill covers how to:**
> - Remove unnecessary rows and columns
> - Identify poorly performing measures, relationships, and visuals
> - Improve cardinality levels by changing data types
> - Improve cardinality levels through summarization
> - Create and manage aggregations

Remove unnecessary rows and columns

In Power BI, it's preferable to load only data that is needed for reporting and add more data later as required. In practice, you should disable loading of queries that aren't required for reporting and filter the data to only the required rows and columns before loading into the model.

Removing unnecessary rows

Reducing the number of rows requires some filtering criteria, which can be based on attributes or dates. For example, instead of loading all Wide World Importers data, you could load data only for a specific sales territory if you're only interested in analyzing that sales territory. You can use parameters when filtering to make the process more manageable; this approach will also make it possible to change filters once the dataset is published to Power BI service.

You can also filter by dates and load only some recent data in case you're not interested in historical data. In addition to parameters, you can apply relative date filters, such as "is in the previous 2 years."

Filtering rows after you create reports won't break any visuals in the existing reports.

Removing unnecessary columns

Columns in a data model usually serve at least one of two purposes: they can be used to support visuals or calculations, or both. It's preferable to not load columns that aren't used for any purpose, especially if they have a high number of distinct values.

Some data warehouses include primary keys for fact tables. Although doing so may be useful for data audit purposes, you should remove primary keys from Power BI data models because they have a unique value for every row, and fact tables can be long. Primary keys of fact tables can occupy over 50 percent of data model size without bringing any benefit. In the Wide World Importers example, removing the Sale Key column from the Sale table reduces the file size by 43 percent.

If you need to count the number of rows in a fact table, using COUNTROWS rather than DISTINCTCOUNT of the primary key column is more efficient.

Removing columns that are used in visuals or calculations is going to break existing reports or even the dataset. You can use the Remove Other Columns functionality in Power Query Editor to have a step to refer to if you need to add a column to your model later. This step will also prevent columns added to the dataset being automatically brought into your model, such as a new column added to a SQL table by a database administrator.

Identify poorly performing measures, relationships, and visuals

Sometimes you may notice that the report performance is not optimal. Power BI Desktop has a feature called Performance Analyzer, which you can use to trace the slow-performing visuals and see the DAX queries behind them.

To turn on Performance Analyzer, go to the **Report** view and select **View** > **Performance analyzer**. This opens the Performance Analyzer pane shown in Figure 2-39.

Performance Analyzer works by recording traces, and it then shows you how long each visual took to render. To start recording traces, select **Start recording**. After that, you need to perform some actions, such as applying filters, that will recalculate the visuals, or you can select **Refresh visuals** to refresh the visuals as they are. You'll then see the rendering duration for each visual.

To identify the slowest visuals, you can sort visuals in the Performance Analyzer pane by selecting the arrow next to **Duration (ms)**.

Each visual that contains data has a DAX query behind it, which you can copy by expanding the line of the visual in the Performance Analyzer pane and selecting **Copy query**. You can analyze the query further in DAX Studio, for example. It's also possible to export all traces by selecting **Export**.

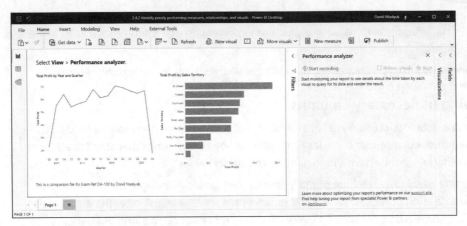

FIGURE 2-39 Performance Analyzer

To clear the Performance Analyzer pane, select **Clear**. Once you've finished recording traces, select **Stop**.

> **NOTE COMPANION FILE**
>
> You can see these visuals in the 2.4.2 Identify poorly performing measures, relationships, and visuals.pbix file in the companion files folder.

Improve cardinality levels by changing data types

Power BI employs several compression mechanisms to reduce the size of data, the details of which are outside the scope of this book. However, one way to decrease the data size is by reducing the cardinality of columns, which can be achieved by changing data types.

In Power BI, two data types can be used for decimal numbers:

- **Decimal number** Can store more than four decimal places
- **Fixed decimal number** Can store up to four decimal places only

If your data contains more than four decimal places for some values and you don't need that level of precision, you should change the data type to Fixed Decimal Number to save space.

Another way to change the cardinality levels is to split decimal number columns into pairs of whole numbers and decimal numbers, which should be done as close to the data source as possible. Whole numbers can be of any range, whereas decimal numbers should be between 0 and 1. These two columns can then be aggregated by using SUMX in the following fashion:

```
Full number =
SUMX(
    'Fact table',
    'Fact table'[Whole number] + 'Fact table'[Decimal number]
)
```

Although you'll get two columns instead of one, in many cases you'll see improvements in cardinality levels and, as a result, a decrease in the data model size. For the same reasons, in Power BI it's best practice to split Date/Time columns with Time components into two: Date and Time. This is because you are increasing the number of duplicates in each column, and therefore the column is more efficiently stored in memory.

Some text columns, such as invoice numbers that are stored as text, can also sometimes be reduced in size. For example, if your fact table contains a column for invoice numbers, which always have the INV prefix and eight numbers that follow it, such as INV01234567, you can remove the INV prefix and change the data type of numbers from Text to Whole Number. If the prefix is inconsistent, you can split it and move it to a different column. This is because storing whole numbers is usually more efficient than storing text.

EXAM TIP

You should be able to recognize models that would benefit from splitting columns and selecting different data types.

Improve cardinality levels through summarization

If your source data provides the level of detail that's not required by reporting, then you may want to consider summarizing your data to reduce cardinality. For example, if the source data contains daily sales information but you only report monthly values, you may want to summarize your sales data to be at the month level instead of the day level. This approach will reduce the size of your model dramatically, though it will make the reporting of daily data impossible.

It's preferable to summarize your data as close to the data source as possible. Power Query also allows you to summarize data by using the **Group by** functionality on the **Transform** ribbon.

Data summarization involves a trade-off between data model size and the available level of detail; whether you should summarize data depends on business requirements. When working in DirectQuery mode, you can also use aggregations, covered in the next section.

> **NEED MORE REVIEW? DATA REDUCTION TECHNIQUES**
>
> All possible data reduction techniques are outside the scope of this book. For more examples of reducing your data when working with imported data, see "Data reduction techniques for Import modeling" at *https://docs.microsoft.com/en-us/power-bi/guidance/import-modeling-data-reduction*.

Create and manage aggregations

By using composite models, you can optimize the performance of data sources that use the DirectQuery mode by using aggregations. For instance, if you're using DirectQuery with a fact table containing data for each customer and you report on values for all customers combined, you can create an aggregation at the total customers level. For cases when you need to report data on individual customers, you can still use the original table, and Power BI will automatically determine whether it should use the aggregation or the original table.

> **NOTE REPRODUCING THE STEPS**
>
> Working in DirectQuery mode requires a database, so there's no corresponding companion file. Setting up a database is not tested in the exam; if you have access to a database, the steps to create and manage aggregations are going to be similar, as described in this section.

An aggregation table can be a table created in a variety of ways:

- Imported M query
- Calculated table in DAX
- Another table in DirectQuery mode

Once you have a suitable table, you can turn it into an aggregation table, as described next. The aggregation table should contain at least some of the same keys and columns you want to aggregate, and it does not have to come from the same source as the detail table.

For example, let's say you're using the *Sale* table in DirectQuery mode, and you have an aggregation table called *SaleAllCustomers*, which is the same as *Sale*, except it doesn't have detailed information on each customer. Managing aggregations involves the following steps:

1. Right-click the **Sale** table in the **Fields** pane.

2. Select **Manage aggregations**.

3. In the Aggregation table drop-down list, select **SaleAllCustomers**. You'll see the options presented in Figure 2-40.

4. For each column, you can select the appropriate summarization and the corresponding detail table and column, if relevant:

   - **Count** This can only be used for count, not for distinct count.
   - **GroupBy** This is used for relationship keys.
   - **Max** This corresponds to the maximum value.
   - **Min** This corresponds to the minimum value.
   - **Sum** This corresponds to sum.
   - **Count table rows** This counts rows in a table.

5. After you make your selections, select **Apply all**, and Power BI will hide the aggregation table.

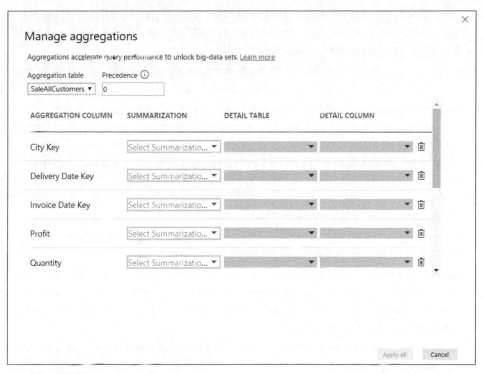

FIGURE 2-40 Manage aggregations

Queries that can be resolved by using the aggregation table will use the aggregation table. In case the aggregation is insufficient—as in our example that involved reporting values for individual customers—the detail table will be used automatically.

> **NEED MORE REVIEW?** **USE AND MANAGE AGGREGATIONS**
>
> For more advanced discussion of aggregations, including different patterns and other considerations, see "Use aggregations in Power BI Desktop" at *https://docs.microsoft.com/en-us/power-bi/transform-model/desktop-aggregations*.

Chapter summary

- Power BI supports various types of schemas: flat (fully denormalized), star, and snow-flake. The preferred schema for Power BI is the star schema.
- You can configure various column and table properties in the Model view.
- Power BI has a feature called quick measures, which allows you to define calculations without writing any DAX code.

- Power BI requires that self-referencing hierarchies (parent-child) are flattened before they can be used in visuals. You can use parent-child functions in DAX to flatten parent-child hierarchies, such as PATH and PATHITEM.

- In some cases, it may be preferable to define role-playing dimensions, which allow you to use a single dimension to filter one fact table by using different keys in the table.

- Power BI supports the following three cardinality types for relationships: one-to-one, one-to-many, and many-to-many. For one-to-one relationships, the cross-filter direction is always Both (each table filters the other). One-to-many dimensions can have their cross-filter direction set to either Single (the one side filters the many side) or Both. The cross-filter direction of many-to-many relationships is chosen by the data modeler depending on business requirements. Relationships whose cross-filter direction is set to Both are also known as bidirectional relationships.

- For bidirectional relationships, security filters won't flow in both directions automatically, though you can configure that in the relationship properties.

- For best performance, the data model should look carefully at the storage mode of each table, cardinality and cross-filter direction of relationships, and cardinality of columns (number of distinct values). Aggregations can be helpful to improve the performance when using the DirectQuery mode.

- Power BI supports both direct many-to-many relationships and many-to-many relationships via a bridge table.

- You can create a common date table in Power BI by using Power Query or DAX, or you can load your table from a data source.

- When measures don't support a certain level of granularity, you should make them return blank so that you don't confuse your users.

- In addition to using measures, you can use DAX to create calculated tables and calculated columns in Power BI.

- Power BI supports the creation of hierarchies, which can be useful to make models more user-friendly, though they have no technical advantages over several fields being used together in a visual without being combined in a hierarchy.

- You can secure your data model by using row-level security, which can use static DAX filters on one or more tables, or dynamic row-level security that considers which user is viewing the report.

- Power BI allows you to use natural language queries by using the Q&A visual. You can add synonyms to your data model to make Q&A work better.

- CALCULATE is one of the most important functions in DAX, and it can be used to manipulate filters. More specifically, you can add, ignore, and update filters. CALCULATE is also used for context transition.

- The Time Intelligence family of DAX functions allows you to aggregate values across time; for instance, you can use DATESYTD to calculate year-to-date values, or you can use DATEADD to calculate a value during the same period last year. There are also functions, such as OPENINGBALANCEMONTH, that allow you to create semi-additive measures.

- In some cases, it may be preferable to replace numeric columns with measures to reduce the size of the data model.

- In general, you should load only data that is necessary for analysis by removing columns or filtering rows in Power Query, especially for primary keys of fact tables.

- Performance Analyzer in Power BI can help you identify performance bottlenecks.

- You can improve the cardinality of columns by selecting appropriate data types as well as summarizing data.

Thought experiment

In this thought experiment, demonstrate your skills and knowledge of the topics covered in this chapter. You can find the answers in the section that follows.

You are a data analyst at Contoso responsible for creating Power BI reports. Management has requested a report based on the historical data available. Based on background information and business requirements, answer the following questions:

1. A data model has a fact table that has over 15 million rows. There is a date/time column called DateTime, which contains both date and time. You need to reduce the size of the data model. Your solution must preserve as much of the original data as possible. Which solution should you implement?

    A. Change the data type of the DateTime column to Text.

    B. Clean the DateTime column.

    C. Split the DateTime column into two separate columns: one column that contains dates, and one column that contains the time portion.

    D. Change the data type of the DateTime column to date.

2. You create a visual that is supposed to show revenue by year. You use the Year column from the Calendar table and the Revenue measure from the Sale table. The formula of the Revenue measure is as follows:

    ```
    Revenue = SUM(Sale[Total Including Tax])
    ```

    The result is shown in Figure 2-41. After checking data, you can see that in 2019, revenue was $50 million. How can you fix the visual? The solution must use minimum amount of DAX and ensure that the Calendar table can be used with other fact tables. The solution must also take into account that you may be interested in analyzing other measures based on the Sale table.

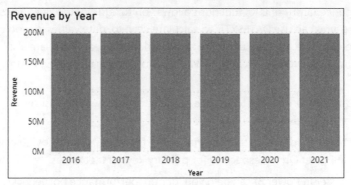

FIGURE 2-41 Revenue by Year

    A. Use the TREATAS function in DAX.

    B. Create a relationship between the Calendar and the Sale tables.

    C. Merge the Sale and Calendar tables.

    D. Create a calculated table that calculates revenue for each year.

3. There are two roles in a data model: CentralRegion, which filters the Region table to only show the Central region, and AppliancesDepartment, which filters the Department table to only show the Appliances department. A user is a member of both roles. What will they see in a sales report?

    A. Sales from the Central region or the Appliances department: They will see all departments in the Central region and all regions in the Appliances department.

    B. Sales from the Central region and the Appliances department: They will only see the Appliances department within the Central region.

    C. Only one role will be applied, whichever was configured first.

    D. The user will see an error message.

4. Your Date table currently consists only of one column called Date, which contains dates. You need to add a column to the Date table that shows month and year in the MMMM YYYY format, such as May 2021. What should you do? Your solution must require the minimum amount of effort and storage, and the solution must ensure that the values are sorted chronologically.

    A. Create a calculated column that uses the FORMAT function.

    B. Create a calculated column that uses the EOMONTH function format as MMMM YYYY.

    C. Duplicate the Date column and apply a custom format string.

    D. Create a new calculated table called "Date – MMMM YYYY" and format as MMMM YYYY.

5. You need to write a measure that calculates the monthly balance. Which formula should you use?

   A. CALCULATE(SUM(Inventory[Balance]), ENDOFMONTH('Date'[Date]))

   B. CALCULATE(SUM(Inventory[Balance]), MAX(Inventory[Date]))

   C. CALCULATE(SUM(Inventory[Balance]), DATESMTD(Inventory[Date]))

   D. CALCULATE(MAX(Inventory[Balance]), LASTDATE(Inventory[Date]))

6. You connect to a table in a database that has 900 million rows and that contains sales data for each line item. Importing all data resulted in a 15 GB PBIX file, and your company can only publish files that are up to 10 GB, so you opted for DirectQuery. Among the available dimensions are Date, Region, and Product. Most of the time, users view sales by Date and Region, though they still view data by Product in some cases. Users complain about report performance when they view summarized reports by Date and Region. What should you do? Your solution must minimize the amount of changes to the data model and ensure that users can still view sales data by product.

   A. Use DirectQuery and connect to an aggregated view in the database.

   B. Create an aggregation table.

   C. Set the Storage mode of the Sales table to Dual.

   D. Use the Group by functionality in Power Query to group the sales data by Date and Region.

7. You inherit a Power BI data model that contains several tables, one of which has many calculated columns that all use the RELATED function. You would like to reduce the size of the model. What should you do?

   A. Append tables.

   B. Merge tables.

   C. Separate tables into several data models.

   D. Hide unused columns.

8. You created a sales report and enabled row-level security on it. There are multiple roles, each filtering the dataset to one department. Each role has a corresponding Active Directory group. The report is primarily used by sales managers, each of whom can view their department only. One sales manager has recently moved from one department to another. What should you do?

   A. Update role membership in Power BI service.

   B. Change roles in Power BI Desktop.

   C. Raise a request to remove the user from their old Active Directory group and add them to the new one.

Thought experiment answers

1. The answer is **C**. Splitting a date/time column into a date and a time column will keep the original data and reduce the number of distinct values in columns, resulting in a smaller data model. Changing the data type to Text, as option A suggests, won't change the number of distinct values and therefore won't reduce the size of the file. Option B, cleaning a column, removes nonprintable characters, which does not reduce the number of distinct values when applied to a column of type Date/Time. If you change the data type of the DateTime column to Date in accordance to option D, you'll see a reduction in the size of the model, and you'll lose the time portion, which goes against the requirements.

2. The answer is **B**. Creating a physical relationship is the best solution because it requires no DAX, it allows the Calendar table to be used with tables other than Sale, and you can use other measures from the Sale table together with fields from the Calendar table. Although using the TREATAS function that option A suggests may work, it requires using unnecessarily complex DAX, especially considering that you may be interested in analyzing measures other than Revenue. The merged table from option C will prevent the Calendar table from being used with other tables or it will duplicate data from the Calendar table unnecessarily. Option D would fix the graph, but it won't solve the problem when other measures are analyzed by year.

3. The answer is **A**. Power BI supports multiple roles for a single user, and they are combined by using the union logic, so the user will see all departments within the Central region and all regions within the Appliances department.

4. The answer is **B**. If you use the EOMONTH function, you'll get a calculated column that contains the end-of-month dates, and you can then apply a custom format string to show the values in the desirable format. Since the values will still be of type Date, they will be automatically sorted in the correct order. If you use the FORMAT function, you'll get the values in the format that you want, though they will be text values that require a sorting column—otherwise, the values will be sorted alphabetically. A sorting column will use extra storage. If you apply a custom format string to a duplicated Date column, the values will look as desired, though underneath they will still be dates, so there will be more than one value for each month-year combination. By creating a new calculated table as in option D, you are increasing the data model size and introducing unnecessary complexity.

5. The answer is **A**. SUM will correctly aggregate inventory balances for all dimensions except Date, since ENDOFMONTH will pick the last date of month to show the monthly balance. In option B, MAX is used as a filter in CALCULATE, and it won't work because it returns a scalar value instead of a table. Option C will provide incorrect values in cases where you have daily or weekly inventory balances. Option D won't aggregate the balances correctly—it will pick the maximum balance across the available values.

6. The answer is **B**. Creating an aggregation table will require minimum changes to the data model, since Power BI will decide automatically whether to use an aggregated table or retrieve data by using DirectQuery. If you use DirectQuery to connect to an aggregated view that option A suggests, you'll have to introduce new measures or change the existing ones to use the correct table. Setting the Storage mode to Dual, as in option C, will import data and result in a file that is too big to be published. Grouping data according to option D will prevent users from browsing sales data by product.

7. The answer is **B**. Using the RELATED function in a calculated column often means duplicating data. If columns need to be in the same table—for example, to build a hierarchy—then it may be preferable to merge tables into one. Appending tables, as in option A, would stack them vertically and wouldn't provide the desired output. Separating tables in several data models, as option C suggests, will reduce the size of the model, though it won't allow us to have the same data. Hiding unused columns as suggested in option D doesn't reduce the size of the model.

8. The answer is **C**. Since the security is managed by Active Directory groups, the user should be removed from their old department security group and added to their new department security group. If you add them to a new role in the Power BI service without affecting their group membership, as in option A, they'll see sales of both old and new departments. Changing roles in Power BI Desktop in option B won't help because role membership is managed outside of Power BI Desktop.

CHAPTER 3

Visualize the data

So far, we've reviewed the skills necessary to prepare and model the data to lay the foundation you need before visualizing the data, the topic of this chapter. Data visualization is a key element of Power BI, and you need effective data visualization to create effective reports. This step becomes the foundation for data analysis, the topic of Chapter 4, "Analyze the data."

In Power BI, you can create reports and dashboards to visualize data. One of the things that sets Power BI apart from other visualization tools is that you can create interactive reports—that is, the visuals that can interact with each other by cross-filtering the underlying data.

We start this chapter by reviewing the skills necessary to create reports in Power BI. We then cover how to design and configure a report for accessibility and how to set up page refresh options. We then review how to set up and create dashboards—visuals from multiple reports that can be pinned to a dashboard to create a single screen with the most important visual elements. Finally, we cover the rich set of features designed to improve report usability.

Skills covered in this chapter:

- 3.1: Create reports
- 3.2: Create dashboards
- 3.3: Enrich reports for usability

Skill 3.1: Create reports

A Power BI report can be based on only one dataset, and a report may have several pages. Reports can be authored both in Power BI Desktop and the Power BI service.

We start this section by reviewing various visualization items and formatting options available for Power BI reports. We also cover configuring the layout of pages and making reports accessible to users.

This skill covers how to:

- Add visualization items to reports
- Choose an appropriate visualization type
- Format and configure visualizations
- Import a custom visual
- Configure conditional formatting
- Apply slicing and filtering
- Add an R or Python visual
- Configure the report page
- Design and configure for accessibility
- Configure automatic page refresh
- Create a paginated report

Add visualization items to reports

Power BI provides several ways to add a visual to a report page:

- Select a visual icon from the **Visualizations** pane.
- Select the check box next to a field in the **Fields** pane.
- Drag a field from the **Fields** pane onto the canvas.
- Select **New visual** on the **Insert** ribbon.
- Turn a Q&A result into a standard visual.

We describe how to choose an appropriate visualization type in the next section. You can also import nonstandard visuals known as *custom visuals*, which we review later in this chapter.

In addition to visuals, there are a few other options in Power BI that visualize data, provide information, and improve the usability of your report available on the Insert ribbon:

- **Text box** Can hold formatted text, including hyperlinks
- **Buttons** Can be formatted differently for various states, such as on hover or on press
- **Shapes** Similar to buttons, except the look and formatting options are different
- **Image** A shape that contains an image

Buttons, shapes, and images can be set to perform the following actions:

- **Back** Takes a user back to the previous page; especially relevant after performing drill-through
- **Bookmark** Takes a user to a bookmark you specify
- **Page navigation** Takes a user to a specific report page

- **Q&A** Launches a Q&A pop-up that can only process natural language queries without any extra functionality provided by the Q&A visual

- **Web URL** Takes a user to the specified web URL

Buttons can also perform *drill-through*, which takes a user to a specific page while carrying the applied filters from the original page. We review the drill-through functionality toward the end of this chapter.

Choose an appropriate visualization type

Besides the Table and Matrix visuals, which we used earlier in the book, Power BI offers over 30 built-in visuals. You can see a fragment of the Visualizations pane in Figure 3-1,

FIGURE 3-1 Standard visuals in Power BI

In this section, we review the visuals and show you how to choose an appropriate visual based on your objectives.

EXAM TIP

You should be able to select the right visual for comparing parts to whole, across categories and time, and spatially.

NOTE **COMPANION FILE**

You can find all visuals from this section in the 3.1.2 Choose an appropriate visualization type. pbix file in the companion files folder.

Bar charts

Power BI has six variations of bar charts:

- Stacked bar chart
- Stacked column chart
- Clustered bar chart
- Clustered column chart
- 100% stacked bar chart
- 100% stacked column chart

All six charts have the same four field wells:

- **Axis**   Columns to be placed on the horizontal or vertical axis. When using more than one column, users can drill down to the next field.
- **Legend**   The categorical column used to color items.
- **Values**   One or more numerical fields to be plotted; if you use a legend, you can put only one field into this field well.
- **Tooltips**   Additional fields that users can see in the tooltip when they hover over a bar or a column. The default tooltips will be shown when you hover over the bars or columns.

You can see the various bar charts in Figure 3-2.

FIGURE 3-2 Bar charts

It is best to use bar or column charts when you are comparing values across categories. This is because you can directly compare the values against each other. If you want to compare values across time, use a line or area chart, covered next.

Line and area charts

Power BI has a line chart and two types of area charts:

- Line chart
- Area chart
- Stacked area chart

These charts have the following common field wells:

- **Axis**   Columns to be placed on the horizontal axis. When using more than one column, users can drill down.
- **Legend**   The categorical column used to color items.
- **Values**   One or more numerical fields to be plotted; if the chart has a legend, you can use only one field for values.
- **Tooltips**   Additional fields that users can see in the tooltip when they hover over a bar or column.

Area charts are similar to the line chart but have a shaded area under the lines. Additionally, the line and area charts have the Secondary values field well, which allows you to use a secondary y-axis if you're not using the Legend field well.

The three visuals are shown in Figure 3-3.

FIGURE 3-3 Line and area charts

Line and area charts are best used when you want to show historical trends or compare values across time. If you use a secondary y-axis, you should make it clear which line belongs to which axis by including axis titles to avoid confusion.

Combo charts

There are two combo charts in Power BI:

- Line and stacked column chart
- Line and clustered column chart

Both have the same five field wells:

- **Shared axis**   Columns to be placed on the horizontal axis. When using more than one column, you can drill down.
- **Column series**   Similar to a legend; one column may be used.

- **Column values** One or more numerical fields to be plotted; if you have a column series, you can use only one field.

- **Line values** One or more numerical fields to be plotted as lines.

- **Tooltips** Additional fields that users can see in the tooltip when they hover over a bar or column.

You can see both charts in Figure 3-4.

FIGURE 3-4 Combo charts

Combo charts can be the appropriate choice when you plot two fields that have different value ranges and you want to use a legend for one of them. For instance, you could plot Profit and Quantity by Year, as shown in Figure 3-4.

By default, the column values appear on the right and the line values appear on the left. In the Format settings, you can switch the axes, as well as hide one or the other, which will align the axes.

Combo charts allow you to show line markers and set the line width to zero, which makes them suitable for comparing values across categories and time, and not only time.

Ribbon chart

The ribbon chart is like a column chart with ribbons between the columns used to highlight changes in the relative ranking of categorical items. The item with the highest ranking will be displayed on top.

The chart has four field wells:

- **Axis** Columns to be placed on the horizontal axis. When using more than one column, you can drill down.

- **Legend** The categorical column used to color items.

- **Values** One or more numerical fields to be plotted; if you use a legend, you can use one field only.

- **Tooltips** Additional fields that users can see in the tooltip when they hover over a bar or column.

Tooltips in ribbon visuals will show additional information compared to the visuals we have covered thus far. When you hover over the ribbons between columns, you'll see how the values changed between two columns. Figure 3-5 shows the ribbon chart and the tooltips when you hover over a ribbon.

FIGURE 3-5 Ribbon chart

The ribbon chart is suitable when you want to show the progression of ranking changes between different categories across time.

Waterfall chart

The waterfall chart shows color-coded values in a running total fashion. By default, positive values are green and negative values red. This visual has four field wells:

- **Category** Columns to be placed on the horizontal axis, where each item is a stage. When using more than one column, you can drill down.
- **Breakdown** You can use one column here to show changes between categories.
- **Values** One numerical field to be plotted.
- **Tooltips** Additional fields that users can see in the tooltip when they hover over a bar or column.

When you're using the breakdown field well, hovering over a breakdown item will show the change between two categorical items. Figure 3-6 shows the waterfall chart and the tooltips when you hover over a breakdown item.

FIGURE 3-6 Waterfall charts

When you use the breakdown field well, only the top five items are shown by default, with the rest grouped into Other. The Other group is yellow by default because it may contain both Increase and Decrease items. You can change the colors, as well as the number of breakdown items, in the Format pane.

A waterfall chart is a good choice when you want to show what caused the most significant changes between time periods. The chart may also be appropriate to illustrate what the total amount is made of while showing the total at the same time for comparison.

Funnel

The funnel chart is like a bar chart with bars centered, and it has three field wells:

- **Group** For one or more categorical columns, where each item is a stage. When using more than one column, you can drill down.
- **Values** One numerical field to be plotted.
- **Tooltips** Additional fields that users can see in the tooltip when they hover over a bar or column.

When you hover over a categorical item in a funnel chart, you see a tooltip with the proportion that category makes up of the first and previous items. It also shows the size of the last item relative to the first one. You can see the chart used in Figure 3-7 with tooltips showing.

FIGURE 3-7 Funnel chart

Because of this additional information in the tooltips, a funnel chart can be a proper choice for showing values by stages. This visual can also be used for revealing bottlenecks in a process or to track workflow.

Scatter chart

The scatter chart can visualize two or more metrics for categorical items. Each item will be plotted according to the x- and y-coordinates, which will be taken from the metrics. When you use a third metric for size, the chart can be called a bubble chart. You can also create a dot plot by using a categorical column on the x-axis.

The visual has the following field wells:

- **Details** You can use one or more categorical columns in this field well to plot points. When using more than one column, you can drill down.
- **Legend** A categorical column used to color items.
- **X-axis** One field to be placed on the horizontal axis.
- **Y-axis** One numerical field to be placed on the vertical axis.
- **Size** For one numerical field to be used for relative bubble sizing.
- **Play axis** You can use a column here, which is usually a time-series column such as Year or Date.
- **Tooltips** Additional fields that users can see in the tooltip when they hover over a bar or column.

An example of a scatter chart is shown in Figure 3-8.

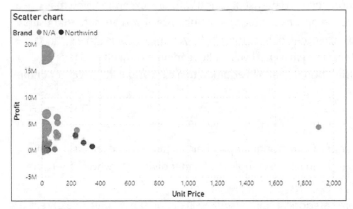

FIGURE 3-8 Scatter chart

A scatter chart can be an effective way to show a relationship between two metrics or to highlight outliers.

Pie and donut charts

The pie and donut charts are the same except the latter has empty space in the middle. Both charts have the same four field wells:

- **Legend** For one or more categorical columns used to color items. When using more than one column, you can drill down.
- **Details** Each slice may be split by a categorical column used here.

- **Values** You may use one or more numerical fields here; if you show Details, you are limited to one field only.
- **Tooltips** Additional fields that users can see in the tooltip when they hover over a bar or column.

When hovering over a slice, you'll see the proportion it makes up. You can see both pie and donut charts in Figure 3-9, with a tooltip showing for an item in the donut chart.

FIGURE 3-9 Pie and donut charts

You can use either of these charts to show the relationships of parts to the whole. Both charts are not considered best practice in data visualization with one exception: you may use a pie or a donut chart when there are only two categories. Otherwise, if you are sure that users will not be comparing parts to each other, only to the whole, you may also use these charts. Be aware that having too many items in such a chart will make reading it difficult and take up a lot of real estate in your report. Using donut charts in addition to a card visual in the center of the donut may be helpful.

Treemap

The treemap chart can be thought of as rectangular pie chart because it also shows the relationship of parts to the whole. You can nest rectangles to further divide the whole. There are four field wells:

- **Group** For one or more categorical columns that will define the relative size of rectangles. When using more than one column, you can drill down.
- **Details** Each rectangle can be split by the categorical column used here.
- **Values** One or more numerical fields to be plotted; if you show Details, you are limited to one field only.
- **Tooltips** Additional fields that users can see in the tooltip when they hover over a bar or column.

Unlike the pie and donut charts, the treemap chart does not show percentages in tooltips by default. You can see a treemap chart in Figure 3-10.

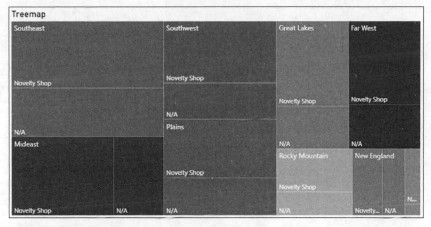

FIGURE 3-10 Treemap chart

The rectangles in a treemap chart are arranged top to bottom and left to right based on numerical values in descending order.

A treemap visual can be a good choice when you want to show proportions between each part and the whole, as well as highlight the most important contributors and outliers.

Maps

Power BI has several options when it comes to visualizing geospatial data. In this section, we review two map visuals: Map and Filled map (also known as a choropleth map). Each of these visuals has the following field wells:

- **Location**   One or more categorical columns that contain locations to be plotted; you can drill down when you use two or more columns.
- **Legend**   You can use a column here to color items.
- **Latitude**   One field can be used here.
- **Longitude**   One field can be used here.
- **Tooltips**   Additional fields that users can see in the tooltip when they hover over a bar or column.

Additionally, the Map visual can use the Size field well for different bubble sizes based on a numerical field. If you are using the legend with the Map visual, your bubbles will be turned into pie charts.

> **NOTE   MAPPING ACCURACY**
>
> To improve the accuracy of maps, you can geocode your fields by selecting an appropriate data category in field properties.

You can see the Map and Filled map visuals in Figure 3-11.

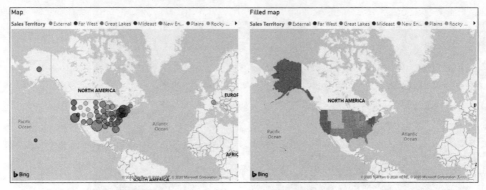

FIGURE 3-11 Map and Filled map

Maps are effective when you're working with spatial data and showing the geographical distribution of values. Power BI will automatically zoom to show the most data based on the size of the visual. You should ensure that users are able to see all fields by using color coding and by choosing between a Map and a Filled map. For example, in Figure 3-11 the External category is easily seen in the Map visual but virtually impossible to notice in the Filled map.

Gauge

The gauge chart can be thought of as one half of a donut chart that compares a value to a target or a maximum value. The gauge chart has five field wells:

- **Value**   For a numerical field; displayed in the center.
- **Minimum value**   A numerical field may be used as the start of the scale.
- **Maximum value**   A numerical field may be used as the end of the scale.
- **Target value**   You can use one numerical field here, which is displayed as a line/needle on the gauge.
- **Tooltips**   Additional fields that users can see in the tooltip when they hover over a bar or column.

You can see an example of a gauge chart in Figure 3-12.

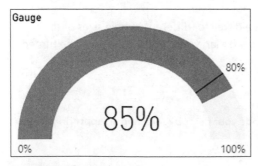

FIGURE 3-12 Gauge chart

Although the gauge visual will be displayed with any of the field wells filled, it should at least have a field in the Value field well. By default, the visual sets the minimum at 0 and the maximum at double the amount of Value, so it will be half-filled.

The gauge is best used to track KPIs or targets, especially those with known maximum values, such as proportions. Other visuals can be used to track KPIs, which we cover next.

Card, multi-row card, and KPI

Besides the gauge visual, there are three other related visuals that can be used to display KPIs. The card visual has a single field well that accepts one field of any type, and it only displays one value.

The multi-row card visual also has a single field well, but it can accept multiple fields. If at least one of the fields is of type Text, then values are divided into rows, with one row per category.

The KPI visual has three field wells:

- **Indicator**   For a numerical field; displayed in the center
- **Trend axis**   For a column, preferably one that contains time-series data like year or date
- **Target goals**   For one or two numerical fields against which the indicator is compared

The KPI visual displays its values for the last item on the trend axis, which is different from the total value across the whole trend axis.

You can see all three visuals in Figure 3-13.

FIGURE 3-13 Card, multi-row card, and KPI visuals

The card visual is best used when there's only one value to display.

If you want to compare a value against one or two targets, it's best to use the KPI visual, which can also display a trend in the background. The trend itself contains limited information and is only useful for high-level analysis.

When you want to display several metrics across a category, you may want to use the multi-row card. It's also a good choice for displaying several unrelated metrics at once.

Artificial intelligence visuals

As of this writing, Power BI has the following generally available artificial intelligence visuals:

- **Key influencers** Helps users understand the main drivers behind a metric and compare the importance of the drivers
- **Decomposition tree** Allows users to perform the root cause analysis or interactive drill-down
- **Q&A** Answers natural language queries visually

We review the key influencers and decomposition tree visuals separately in Skill 4.2: Perform advanced analysis. For the Q&A visual, refer to Skill 2.2: Develop a data model.

Format and configure visualizations

Power BI allows you to format all visuals in various ways so that you can design an effective report. To see the formatting options of a visual, select the visual and then select **Format** (paintbrush icon) on the **Visualizations** pane.

Many visuals have some formatting options that are unique to them, but there are common options that most visuals have:

- **General** In this section, you can specify x-position, y-position, width, height, and alt text (a description that will be read by a screen reader on selecting the visual).
- **Title** Title text, word wrap, font color, background color, alignment, text size, and font family.
- **Background** Background color and transparency.
- **Lock aspect** If enabled, when you adjust the size of a visual manually, its aspect will be locked.
- **Border** Border color and radius.
- **Shadow** Shadow color, position, and preset.
- **Tooltips** In this section you can choose to use the default tooltip type or to use a specific report page as a tooltip. For default tooltips, you can format the label and value colors, text size, font family, background color, and transparency.
- **Visual header** This section allows you to hide the whole visual header or some of its elements. Additionally, you can format its background, border, and icon colors, as well as transparency. You can also add a visual header tooltip icon here.

Some properties can be formatted conditionally, which we review later in this chapter.

Import a custom visual

In addition to built-in visuals, Power BI offers a way to use custom visuals, also known as visuals created by using the Power BI SDK. There are two main ways to import a custom visual in Power BI Desktop:

- AppSource
- From a file

AppSource

First, you may import a visual from AppSource, which you can do in one of two ways:

- In the **Report** view, select **Insert** > **More visuals** > **From AppSource**.
- Select the ellipsis on the **Visualizations** pane, then select **Get more visuals**.

Either way, you will see the options shown in Figure 3-14.

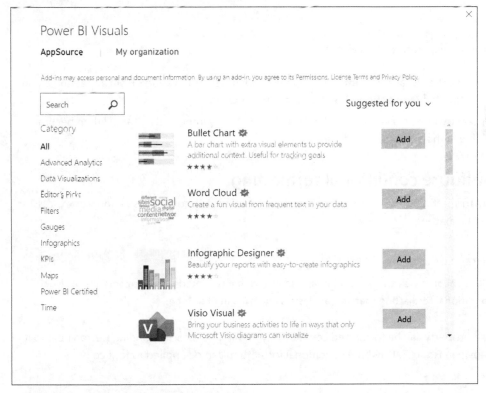

FIGURE 3-14 Power BI visuals from AppSource

In addition to AppSource, which offers publicly available visuals, the Power BI administrator of your organization may also add some organizational visuals, which you can select from the **My organization** section.

From a file

As an alternative to AppSource, you can import a visual from a PBIVIZ file in one of two ways:

- In the **Report** view, select **Insert** > **More visuals** > **From my files**.
- Select the ellipsis on the **Visualizations** pane, then select **Import visual from a file**.

Either way, before you can import a visual, you may see the caution shown in Figure 3-15.

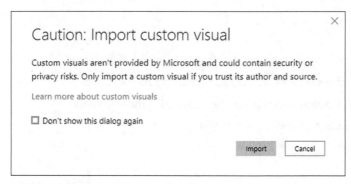

FIGURE 3-15 Import custom visual caution

To import a visual, select **Import**. You may also prevent this caution from appearing again by selecting the **Don't show this dialog again** check box.

After you import a visual from AppSource or a file, the imported visual will then become available in the Visualizations pane.

Configure conditional formatting

Some formatting properties can be formatted based on a condition, also known as expression-based formatting.

> **NOTE CONDITIONAL FORMATTING**
>
> In this chapter, we review conditional formatting that is related to the appearance of visuals. Conditional formatting that aids analysis is reviewed in Chapter 4.

If a property can be formatted conditionally, it will have a corresponding button next to it, as shown in Figure 3-16, where conditional formatting can be applied to font color.

FIGURE 3-16 Conditional formatting button

If you select the button, you'll see options like those shown in Figure 3-17.

FIGURE 3-17 Conditional formatting options

You may see different options depending on the property you're formatting. For instance, when you're configuring the color, you'll see the following options in the **Format by** drop-down list:

- **Color scale** Suitable for continuous color gradients. You can select a field based on which you want to set the color. You can enter the minimum and maximum values for the field and set the corresponding colors. If you want a center color, you can select the **Diverging** check box, and you can specify the corresponding value, too.

- **Rules** This option is suitable for discrete colors with no gradients between them. As with the color scale, you can select a field on which you want to base your color. You can then assign colors to value ranges, specific numbers, or blank values.

- **Field value** When you have a field that returns a color code, you can use this option. A color value can be in any of the following formats:
  - 3-, 6-, or 8-digit hex code, like #ABC123
  - RGB or RGBA value, like RGB(10, 20, 30)
  - HSL or HSLA value, like HSLA(10, 50%, 50%, 0.75)
  - Color name, like *red* or *green*

When formatting a property other than color, make sure that the field you select returns values in the expected format.

Some formatting properties won't support all Format by options. For example, for Title text, you can only use the Field value option, because a title text can only be a text string.

If you want to remove conditional formatting of a property, you can select the eraser button next to it.

Apply slicing and filtering

One of the core features of Power BI is allowing report users to apply filters and see the values change in an instant. Filters can be applied in the following two ways:

- Slicers
- Filters pane

Slicers

Slicers are visuals that can apply filters to other visuals. Importantly, slicers accept only columns as fields to filter by. You can configure slicers in various ways depending on the data type of the column or columns you use.

Any slicer can be displayed as List or Dropdown. You can add a search bar to a List or Dropdown slicer by hovering over it and selecting **More options** (the ellipsis) > **Search**. This is especially useful when you have a number of options within the slicer. Additionally, in the **Selection controls** section of the **Format** pane, you can do the following:

- Force a single selection.
- Select whether the Ctrl key is required for multiple selections.
- Show the Select all option.

You can create a Hierarchy slicer by using multiple columns from one or more related tables. Non-hierarchical List slicers specifically can have a vertical (default) or horizontal orientation as well.

Additionally, a slicer that uses a numeric column can also be displayed as:

- **Between**   Applies the lower and upper limits for values, inclusive
- **Less than or equal to**   Sets the upper limit for values, inclusive
- **Greater than or equal to**   Sets the lower limit for values, inclusive

A slicer that uses a date/time column can also be displayed as:

- **Between**   Sets the start and end date/time values, inclusive.
- **Before**   Sets the end date/time value, inclusive.
- **After**   Sets the start date/time value, inclusive.
- **Relative Date**   This option can filter for one or more periods, such as days or months, before or after today's date. It can also filter for the current period.
- **Relative Time**   Same as the Relative Date option but for time periods such as minutes or hours.

You can see examples of various slicers in Figure 3-18.

FIGURE 3-18 Slicers

> **NOTE   IGNORING FILTERS FROM SLICERS**
>
> If you want some visuals to ignore a certain slicer, you can configure the interaction between them. This is covered later in this chapter in Skill 3.3: Enrich reports for usability.

To clear a slicer selection, select the **Clear selections** (eraser) button on the slicer header that becomes visible when you hover over the slicer.

It's possible to filter the values in a slicer. For this, you need to apply a visual-level filter in the Filters pane, which is covered next.

Filters pane

Besides slicers, you can apply filters by using the Filters pane on the right-hand side of the report, which has three sections:

- **Filters on this visual**   These filters apply to a specific visual you select, and this section is visible only when you select a visual. You can use both measures and columns to filter on. Fields that are used in field wells of a visual will automatically appear here.

- **Filters on this page**   These filters apply to all visuals on the currently selected page. It's not possible to make certain visuals ignore these filters, and you can only use columns to filter on.

- **Filters on all pages**   These filters apply to all visuals in the report across all pages. You can't make specific visuals ignore these filters, and you can only use columns to filter on.

You can see the Filters pane in Figure 3-19.

Filters in the Filters pane are shown as filter cards. Cards with applied filters are shaded. In Figure 3-19, the Sales Territory filter card is shaded because it's filtered to one value: Far West. There are no filters on Color in Figure 3-19, so the card is not shaded.

FIGURE 3-19 Filters pane

You can add a field to the Filters pane in one of two ways:

- Drag a field from the **Fields** pane into a section in the **Filters** pane.
- Right-click a field in the **Fields** pane and select **Add to filters**, and then select the section you want to add the field to.

You can apply Basic filtering to any column, which corresponds to the List option in slicers. You can also select the **Require single selection** check box if you want users to select only one value.

Depending on the data type of the field you're adding, you'll see different Advanced filtering options you can apply. For example, for Date/Time type columns, you have the option of filtering in a relative or a static time period, such as filtering for the last two calendar weeks. For Text type columns, you can filter when a column contains a certain value.

As with slicers, selections in a filter card can be cleared by selecting the **Clear filter** button that becomes visible when you hover over the filter card. Other buttons that become visible when you hover over a filter card include:

- **Lock filter** This locks the filter selections, preventing report viewers from changing them. To unlock the filter, select the **Filter locked** button.
- **Hide filter** This will hide the filter card from report viewers.
- **Remove filter** This removes a filter card; not available for fields that are used in visuals.

You can search for filters in the Filters pane in the same way you search in the Fields pane. You can also sort and reorder the filter cards.

You can always check which filters affect a certain visual by hovering over its filter button on the visual header, as shown in Figure 3-20.

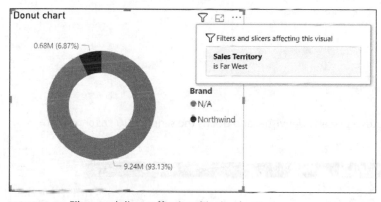

FIGURE 3-20 Filters and slicers affecting this visual

Add an R or Python visual

Incorporating an R or Python visual can be a powerful addition to the standard visuals in Power BI. You can create an R or Python visual only in Power BI Desktop, and for that you'll need to have one of them installed on your machine first.

When you select **R script visual** or **Python visual** from the **Visualizations** pane for the first time in a report, you'll see a prompt like the one in Figure 3-21.

FIGURE 3-21 Enable script visuals

Selecting **Enable** creates a placeholder visual and opens the script editor, as shown in Figure 3-22.

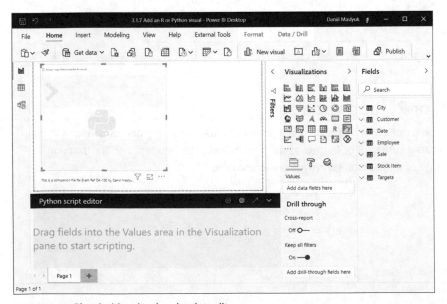

FIGURE 3-22 Placeholder visual and script editor

To create a visualization, you must first add fields. In the Wide World Importers example, let's create a Python visual by adding the following fields:

- *Buying Group* from the *Customer* table
- *Profit* from the *Sale* table
- *Quantity* from the *Sale* table
- *Unit Price* from the *Sale* table

Once you've added the fields, paste the following code below the placeholder text in the Python script editor:

```
import matplotlib.pyplot as plt
import seaborn as sns

dataset = dataset.fillna("Other")

p = sns.pairplot(dataset, hue="Buying Group", palette="husl")
p._legend.remove()
plt.legend(loc="best", title="Buying Group")
plt.tight_layout()
plt.show()
```

Doing so produces a visual, as shown in Figure 3-23.

FIGURE 3-23 Python plot

The Python code must output an image to produce a visual; it can't work with other forms of output such as data frames.

One aspect in which R and Python visuals are significantly different from other visuals is that they can't cross-filter other visuals. Although you can cross-filter an R or Python visual by another visual, you can't select elements in an R or Python visual to cross-filter another visual.

Configure the report page

You can change various page properties by selecting the Format pane after making sure that no visual is selected. You will then see the following sections:

- **Page information** You can change the page name here, as well as allow the page to be used as a tooltip or a Q&A answer, or both. If you choose to use the page as a Q&A answer, you can add alternate names for it, similar to adding synonyms for fields.

- **Page size** Here you can select one of the preset sizes or specify a custom size in pixels. The preset sizes are as follows:

  - **16:9** (1280 by 720 pixels)

  - **4:3** (960 by 720 pixels)

  - **Letter** (816 by 1056 pixels)

  - **Tooltip** (320 by 240 pixels)

- **Page background** You can select a background color and specify the transparency, or you can choose a background image, specify the transparency, and select how to scale it:
  - **Normal** Displays the image in its original size
  - **Fit** Stretches the image to canvas size without keeping proportions
  - **Fill** Stretches the image to touch the canvas from inside, keeping proportions
- **Page alignment** You can set the vertical alignment of the page to Top or Middle.
- **Wallpaper** This is similar to a page background, except that it also covers the area outside of the page. Wallpaper comes into play when you embed a report and its size does not match the embed area, so you'll see the wallpaper outside of the report area.
- **Filter pane** You can format the Filter pane here by selecting various colors and sizes.
- **Filter cards** In addition to the Filter pane, you can format filter cards. You can format the available and applied filter cards separately.

If you usually format your pages in certain ways, you may want to format a page once and then duplicate it to create new pages instead of formatting new pages. In corporate environments, you may also want to use a selected company background image so that reports across an organization are consistent.

Design and configure for accessibility

When you're designing a report, it's always best to know what business users want out of the reports you create, because it may be different from what you have in mind. Therefore, it's a good idea to gather feedback from end users in the initial stages of building the report so that you don't have to make as many edits in the future. Adopting techniques such as human-centered design can be useful to embed a feedback loop during this process.

Acknowledging that not all users will have the same technical skill level, you should strive for consistency across pages in your reports. For example, if you have the same slicers on different pages, place them in the same position to make them more user-friendly. In the same way, it's best to use the same font size and font face for visual titles.

Avoid putting too much information into too few visuals. If you have a few very complex visuals, consider splitting your visuals into several simpler visuals and then grouping them among common themes and relevance.

You want to aim for the key insights to be immediately shown to your users. If key information becomes visible only after interaction with the report, consider making the information easier to access by moving it to a more obvious location. Additionally, important information should not be exclusively presented in tooltips, because accessing them will be difficult for users who don't use a mouse.

Including a home page with information about the report, when it was last refreshed, and navigation tips may be useful for users to refer to. By regularly reviewing your report for readability and updating formatting options as new data becomes available, you ensure that users are able to clearly understand your report.

You can make your Power BI reports accessible to more users, including those who may have visual or physical impairments. There are a number of ways to make your reports more accessible, without the need for specialized design:

- Page names, titles, and labels
- Markers
- Alternative text (Alt text)
- Tab order
- Report theme and color selection

Page names, titles, and labels

Titles of visuals and report page names help users navigate the report. As much as possible, avoid using jargon or acronyms in titles of visuals and page names, because new or external users may not be familiar with the terminology you use. For example, instead of "PY," consider spelling out "Prior Year," and instead of "Amount," consider using the exact metric name that's familiar to business users.

You should ensure that visuals are easy to understand by including data labels and axis titles where relevant. If you're using data labels and each data point has a label, consider decluttering your visual by removing the value axis. Because each point is labeled, displaying the axis in this case does not add any value.

When formatting data labels, you can choose to show them only for some measures by customizing them in the **Format** pane. You can also position data labels below or above data points to improve readability—for example, in cases where you have multiple lines on a chart.

Markers

If you use colors to distinguish different series of values, consider using markers of different shapes, because not all people see colors in the same way. You can turn markers on for line, area, combo, and scatter charts. In the **Shapes** section of the **Format** pane, you can enable markers and select their color, shape, and size. You can also customize markers for each series.

Alt text

As we discussed previously, you can set alt text for visuals in the **General** section of the **Format** pane when a visual is selected. Alt text will be read out to users of screen readers.

It's advisable to add alt text for all nondecorative visualization items, thus ensuring that report users can understand what you are showing even if they can't see the visuals.

A visual's alt text should contain the information you want the report user to take away from it. Calling out a specific data point may be risky because users can apply filters to Power BI reports. Conditional formatting is appropriate when you want to call out some insights dynamically.

Tab order

Some users may navigate your reports by using their keyboard. The default order in which they will navigate visuals may not match the perceived order. To change the tab order, in the **Report** view select **View** > **Selection** > **Tab order**.

You can change the tab order of visuals in the **Selection** pane in two ways:

- Drag and drop the items within the list
- Select an item and use the up and down arrows

It's advisable to hide decorative elements, such as shapes, from the tab order. To do so, select the number to the left of the visual in the tab order list. Figure 3-24 shows the **Selection** pane where a shape is hidden from the tab order.

FIGURE 3-24 Tab order in the Selection pane

When you hide decorative elements from tab order, they aren't available for selection by keyboard users, and this improves the navigation experience.

Report theme and color selection

In general, the colors you choose should have sufficient contrast between text and background to make text legible and easy to read.

Some color combinations may be difficult to discriminate for users who have color vision deficiencies. For example, avoid green and red on the same page if you want to make your reports accessible. There are other undesirable color combinations, and it's always best to check whether your colors are accessible by using a color accessibility tool.

Power BI includes several predefined color themes, which you can see in the **Themes** grouping of the **View** ribbon. You can also create and import your own theme to facilitate the process of building reports.

> **NEED MORE REVIEW?** **ACCESSIBILITY IN POWER BI**
>
> If you'd like to read further about creating accessible reports in Power BI, including more examples and illustrations, see "Design Power BI reports for accessibility" at *https:// docs.microsoft.com/en-us/power-bi/create-reports/desktop-accessibility-creating-reports*.

Configure automatic page refresh

When you're using DirectQuery, it's often desirable to have your report refreshed automatically to reflect the latest data. This capability is especially important when you monitor near-real-time data, such as data coming from sensors or streaming data.

You can set up automatic page refresh by enabling the **Page refresh** section in the **Format** pane of a report page. The toggle of the **Page refresh** section needs to be set to **On**. Power BI will then refresh all visuals on a page at the rate that depends on the refresh type you select. Power BI supports two types of automatic page refresh: fixed interval and change detection.

> **IMPORTANT** **AUTOMATIC PAGE REFRESH IN POWER BI SERVICE**
>
> For automatic page refresh to work in the Power BI service, the feature must be enabled by the tenant administrator. Change detection also requires Premium capacity.

Fixed interval

In some scenarios, you may want to refresh your visuals at a constant rate—for example, 30 seconds. For this, you need to select **Auto page refresh** from the **Refresh type** drop-down list and set the refresh interval, which can be in multiples of seconds, minutes, hours, or days. This type of page refresh is suitable for some scenarios, but it may put unnecessary strain on the server because it will refresh data even if there are no changes.

You can also select **Show details** to see the actual refresh rate and when data was last refreshed. When logged into your Power BI account, you can see whether the feature is enabled by your Power BI tenant administrator and the minimum interval allowed by your administrator.

Fixed interval automatic page refresh is configured for each page individually. Figure 3-25 shows a page set to refresh every 10 seconds.

FIGURE 3-25 Page refresh set to 10 seconds

Change detection

The change detection type of refresh can be more efficient than the fixed interval automatic page refresh because visuals are refreshed only when there's a change in data. Change detection uses a measure you define to check whether there are changes in the data—if the value of a measure is different from last time, then the visuals will be refreshed.

You can select one measure per model that will be used to detect changes. Unlike fixed interval automatic page refresh, which can be configured for each page separately, you can define only one change detection measure per model, though you can use change detection for some pages and fixed interval refresh for other pages.

To set up change detection as the preferred refresh type for a page, select **Change detection** from the **Refresh type** drop-down list in the **Page refresh** section of the **Format** pane of the page.

Next, to configure the change detection measure, select **Add change detection** from the **Page refresh** section. Alternatively, you can select **Change detection** on the **Modeling** ribbon, or right-click a field in the **Fields** pane and select **Change detection**. Figure 3-26 shows the available options.

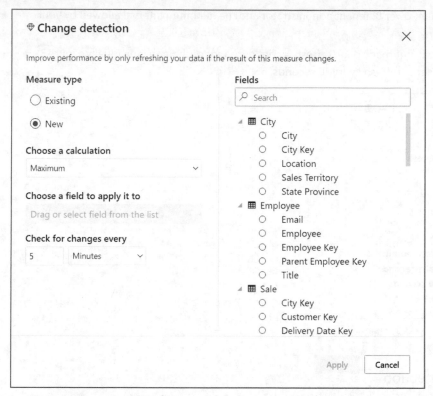

FIGURE 3-26 Change detection

When selecting the change detection measure, you can select an existing measure or a new one by defining your own calculation. For new calculations, you can select a column and use one of the following aggregations, depending on the data type:

- Count
- Count (Distinct)
- Minimum
- Maximum
- Sum

In addition to the measure, you must select how often Power BI should check for changes, which can be multiples of seconds, minutes, or hours.

After you select the measure and check frequency, select **Apply**.

Create a paginated report

Although the reports you create in Power BI Desktop can be printed, they're primarily meant to be used online in the Power BI service or mobile apps. Usually, the reports are formatted to fit well on a computer or mobile phone screen, and different report pages often serve different purposes.

There are valid use cases for printing reports and sharing them offline. For example, someone may want to print a sales performance report that shows each region on a different page and distribute the report before a meeting. For cases like this, a *paginated report* would be a good fit. You can create paginated reports by using Power BI Report Builder.

NOTE **INSTALLING POWER BI REPORT BUILDER**

You can download the Power BI Report Builder installer from the Microsoft Download Center at *https://aka.ms/pbireportbuilder*.

As with normal Power BI reports, you create paginated reports by using data from various data sources, and you can even use a Power BI service dataset as a data source.

NOTE **DOWNLOADING REPORT DEFINITION LANGUAGE (RDL) FILES**

To download an RDL file from the Power BI service, you must have a dataset already published. Publishing to the Power BI service is covered in more detail in Chapter 5.

To start creating a paginated report based on a Power BI dataset, go to a workspace, hover over a dataset, and select **More options** > **Download the .rdl**. When you open the RDL file, you should see a blank canvas with placeholder text, as shown in Figure 3-27.

FIGURE 3-27 Power BI Report Builder

The RDL file will already contain a data source—the Power BI dataset you downloaded the RDL file from. To create a report, you'll need to add one or more datasets to your paginated report. Once you're finished, you can select **Publish** on the **Home** ribbon and select a workspace to publish to. Note that you can only publish to Premium workspaces.

> **NEED MORE REVIEW?**   **CREATING PAGINATED REPORTS**
>
> Specific steps required to complete a paginated report are out of the scope of this book. For a step-by-step tutorial, see "Tutorial: Create a paginated report and upload it to the Power BI service" at *https://docs.microsoft.com/en-us/power-bi/paginated-reports/paginated-reports-quickstart-aw.*

Skill 3.2: Create dashboards

For much of this book so far, we've worked on building a Power BI report from a single dataset. This in itself can be one of the limitations of a report—it can contain data only from one dataset. There may be a number of scenarios when you want to show users visuals from multiple datasets side by side. To do so, you can display them in a dashboard.

A Power BI dashboard has only one screen, and it can include visuals from a variety of reports based on data from different datasets. Dashboards can be created only in the Power BI service, and they contain features that are not available in reports, such as data alerts. The visuals within a dashboard are called *tiles*.

> **This skill covers how to:**
> - Manage tiles on a dashboard
> - Set mobile view
> - Configure data alerts
> - Use the Q&A feature
> - Add a dashboard theme
> - Pin a live report page to a dashboard

Manage tiles on a dashboard

A dashboard tile can show a pinned visual or a variety of other content, such as text, videos, or hyperlinks, to other reports to make navigation and insights easier for users.

You can pin tiles from a variety of sources:

- A report
- Another dashboard

- Excel workbook
- Quick insights
- Q&A result
- Paginated report

To pin a report visual, hover over it when viewing a report and select **Pin visual** from the visual header. Power BI prompts you to select a dashboard to pin the visual to—you can select an existing dashboard or create a new one, as shown in Figure 3-28.

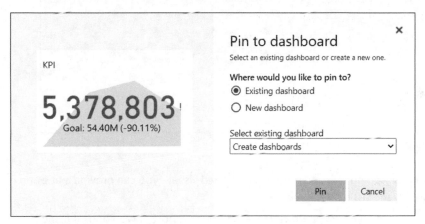

FIGURE 3-28 Pin to dashboard options

To pin the visual, select **Pin**.

NOTE **THEMES**

If your report uses a theme, you'll have the option to keep the report theme or use the dashboard theme. We cover dashboard themes later in this chapter.

In addition to pinning visuals, from the dashboard you can select **Edit** > **Add tile** to add a tile that contains one of the following:

- **Web content**   Supports any HTML for content embedding.
- **Image**   For publicly accessible images. Access that requires authentication and uploading images aren't supported.
- **Text box**   For entering static text, which can be formatted.
- **Video**   For videos hosted on YouTube or Vimeo. Videos can be played on the dashboard without leaving the page.
- **Custom Streaming Data**   You can add streaming data sourced from an API, Azure Stream, or PubNub.

To edit a dashboard tile, hover over it and select **More options** > **Edit details**. Figure 3-29 shows the details of a pinned tile.

FIGURE 3-29 Tile details

For any tile, you can set the title and subtitle. For pinned visuals, you can provide a title and also choose to display the last refresh time.

Selecting a pinned tile on a dashboard can take you to the report or workbook it came from. Additionally, for most tiles, you can set a custom link, which can be any external link, a dashboard, or a report in the same workspace as the dashboard.

It's important to understand that visuals in tiles aren't as interactive as report visuals; although you may see tooltips, you can't cross-filter one tile by selecting an item in another tile. Furthermore, if you make changes to a visual that you previously pinned on a dashboard, the changes aren't going to be reflected in the corresponding dashboard tile, and you'll need to pin the visuals again to update the tile.

To have interactivity in a tile, you must pin a live report page, which is covered later in this chapter.

Set mobile view

A Power BI report has a desktop and mobile layout to cater for different screen sizes. Similarly, a dashboard has a web and a mobile view (also known as a phone view). Figure 3-30 shows an example of a dashboard in web view.

Because this view may not work well on a phone, you can create a phone view to optimize the consumption on a mobile device if you have edit rights to a dashboard. Note that the web view doesn't change when you create a mobile view. To start creating a phone view, select **Edit** > **Mobile view**. Figure 3-31 shows the phone view editor.

FIGURE 3-30 Dashboard in web view

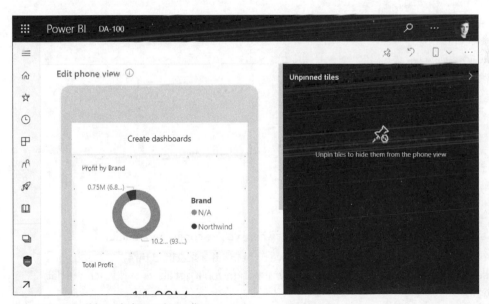

FIGURE 3-31 Dashboard phone view editor

In the phone view editor, you can reorder tiles by dragging them around the screen as well as resize tiles by dragging from the lower-right corner. You can also hide a tile from the phone view by hovering over a tile and selecting **Hide tile**. To add back a tile from the **Unpinned tiles** pane, hover over a tile and select **Add tile**.

If your dashboard contains several tiles, you may want to show only a few key tiles for users to refer to quickly. You may want to hide all tiles first by selecting **Unpin all tiles** in the top menu; then you can readd the desired tiles one by one. To reset the phone view to its original state, select **Reset tiles**.

To go back to the web view, select **Web view** from the **Phone view** drop-down list in the upper-right corner.

Configure data alerts

Dashboards in Power BI allow you to configure data-driven alert notifications on cards, KPIs, and gauges pinned from report visuals. To start configuring an alert, hover over a tile and select **More options** > **Manage alerts** > **Add alert rule**. Figure 3-32 shows the alert options.

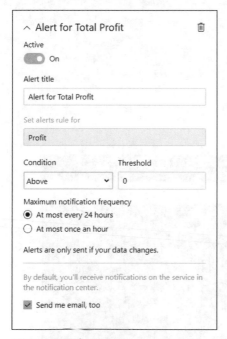

FIGURE 3-32 Alert options

Setting the alert title is useful in scenarios where you've configured multiple alerts.

You can set the alert condition to be above or below the specified threshold, and you can set the maximum notification frequency, although you'll get alerts only when the data changes.

Only the user who configures the alert will see it, and alerts are synchronized between the Power BI service and Power BI mobile apps. By default, in addition to a notification in Power BI service or a mobile app, you'll get an email, but you can turn off this option by clearing the **Send me email, too** check box in the alert options.

To delete an alert, you can select **Delete alert rule** (trash can icon) in the upper-right corner. If you want to disable an alert without deleting it, switch the **Active** toggle to **Off**.

You can see a list of all configured alerts in Power BI service settings by selecting **Settings** > **Settings** > **Settings** > **Alerts**.

Use the Q&A feature

As you saw in Chapter 2, "Model the data," Power BI has a feature called Q&A, which allows you to ask questions about your data by using natural language queries. Q&A is available in both reports and dashboards.

To start using Q&A in a dashboard, select **Ask a question about your data** on the dashboard and enter a question. Figure 3-33 shows a sample Q&A result. From there, you can go back to the dashboard by selecting **Exit Q&A**, or you can save the result to the dashboard by selecting **Pin visual**.

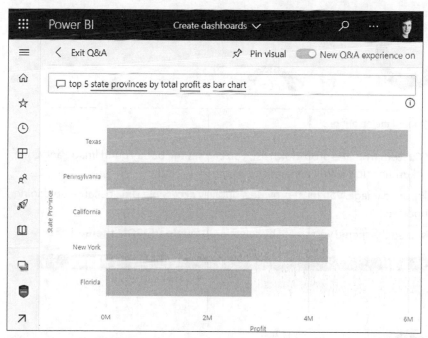

FIGURE 3-33 Sample Q&A result

If you want to edit a Q&A result that you pinned, hover over its tile and select **Go to Q&A**, where you can change the question and pin the new result.

> **NOTE   IMPROVING Q&A RESULTS**
>
> If you want to improve the results of Q&A, you'll need to do it in the dataset. Refer to Skill 2.2: Develop a data model for more information.

Add a dashboard theme

You can apply a theme to a dashboard similar to how you apply a theme to a report. This technique can be especially beneficial if you want to apply a uniform theme to a dashboard that has visuals from reports with different themes.

To configure the dashboard theme, select **Edit** > **Dashboard theme**. From the drop-down list, you can select a preconfigured theme or create a custom theme. For example, Figure 3-34 shows the color-blind friendly theme.

FIGURE 3-34 Dashboard theme options

If you select **Custom** from the drop-down list, you can set the background image and color, as well as tile background, font color, and opacity, as shown in Figure 3-35.

To set a background image, you must provide a publicly accessible URL, because uploading images isn't supported.

You can download the theme you create by selecting **Download JSON theme**.

FIGURE 3-35 Custom theme options

To add a more sophisticated theme, you can upload your own JSON theme by selecting **Upload JSON theme**.

> **NOTE** **JSON THEMES**
>
> The structure of a dashboard JSON theme is the same as that of a report theme. The technical details of JSON theme files are out of the scope of this book.
>
> You can download various themes from the Power BI Themes Gallery at *https://community.powerbi.com/t5/Themes-Gallery/bd-p/ThemesGallery*.

Pin a live report page to a dashboard

There are a couple of limitations of pinned visuals: they can't cross-filter and interact with each other, and you can pin only one visual at a time.

Pinning a live report page to a dashboard overcomes both limitations. You can simultaneously pin multiple visuals on a dashboard, and the visuals then become interactive.

To pin a live page to a dashboard, go to the desired report page in the Power BI service and select **Pin to a dashboard** from the top menu. Power BI asks you to select a dashboard to pin the page to, as shown in Figure 3-36.

FIGURE 3-36 Pin live page

Selecting **Pin live** will pin the report page to a dashboard as a tile. You can then edit, move, and resize the tile as needed. Note that visuals within the tile are interactive; as with reports, you can use slicers and filter visuals by selecting other visuals.

Skill 3.3: Enrich reports for usability

Power BI reports can be made more user-friendly by adding bookmarks, tooltips, navigation, and interactivity, all of which we review in this section. Taking time to consider usability of your reports when gathering feedback from users can help differentiate between good and great dashboards.

There are several ways to make insights clearer, such as sorting visuals, configuring the interactions between visuals, and setting up drill-through and drilldown.

As you saw with dashboards, reports can also be designed for mobile devices, and we finish the chapter by showing how you can adjust reports for consumption on the go.

> **This skill covers how to:**
> - Configure bookmarks
> - Create custom tooltips
> - Edit and configure interactions between visuals
> - Configure navigation for a report
> - Apply sorting
> - Configure Sync slicers
> - Use the Selection pane
> - Use drill-through and cross-filter
> - Drill down into data using interactive visuals
> - Export report data
> - Design reports for mobile devices

Configure bookmarks

By using bookmarks in Power BI, you can create compelling data stories and enhance the user experience by creating a step-by-step presentation of key insight, or by hiding and showing certain visuals through the click of a button.

Though one of the defining features of Power BI is its interactivity, in some cases you may prefer to draw the attention of users to specific aspects of your reports. For example, you might want to highlight a certain visual with applied filters that show an interesting insight.

Bookmarks in Power BI allow you to do exactly that: they let you save the states of your pages and switch between them in presentation mode or by linking to them. Bookmarks can save the following:

- Filters, including cross-filtering and selections in slicers
- Current page

- Objects visibility
- Sort order
- Drill-down level

To create a bookmark, open the Bookmarks pane by selecting **View** > **Bookmarks**. Once you apply filters or otherwise achieve the desired state of the page you are on, select **Add** in the Bookmarks pane. The bookmark will then appear in the Bookmarks pane with a default name of *Bookmark 1*. You can rename a bookmark by double-clicking it or by selecting **More options** (the ellipsis next to a bookmark) and selecting **Rename**. The More options menu also contains the following items:

- **Update**   If you decide to change the state of a bookmark, you can update an existing bookmark instead of creating a new one.
- **Delete**   This option deletes the bookmark.
- **Group**   You can group bookmarks to tidy up the Bookmarks pane—for example, by moving bookmarks from each page into a separate group. This feature is especially useful when you have many bookmarks.
- **Data**   This option determines whether the filter, sort, and drill state of the page is saved in the bookmark. By default, this option is selected. Deselecting it can be useful when you only want to save the visibility of visuals, which is controlled by the Display option.
- **Display**   This option, which is selected by default, determines whether the bookmark saves the visibility of visuals. This setting can be useful when you only want to change filters with your bookmark without changing the visibility of visuals.
- **Current page**   By default, this option is selected; it determines whether selecting the bookmark takes you to the page where it was created. Deselecting the option can be useful when you want to change a report-level filter without switching to a different page.
- **All visuals**   This option determines whether the bookmark is applied to all visuals or selected visuals only. By default, a bookmark is applied to all visuals.
- **Selected visuals**   You can create a bookmark and only apply it to the visuals that were selected at the time you created the bookmark. You can select visuals in the canvas pane or in the Selection pane. It is important to note that you cannot use the Selected visuals option to bookmarks that have already been created.

The visibility of visuals, captured by the **Display** option of bookmarks, can be configured in the **Selection** pane, which we review later in this chapter.

In a bookmark, you can highlight a single visual by selecting **More options** (the ellipsis in the visual header) and selecting **Spotlight**. Once you do this, the visual will be highlighted with a shade around it, and the rest of the report canvas will be tinted. You can see this effect in Figure 3-37.

At this stage, you can create a bookmark by selecting **Add** in the **Bookmarks** pane. If you created one bookmark before, the new bookmark would be called Bookmark 2, and so on.

To undo the Spotlight effect, you can select any other area on the report canvas or select another visual in the Selection pane.

FIGURE 3-37 Spotlight

After you have created some bookmarks, you can change their order by dragging and dropping them in the Bookmarks pane. When creating multiple bookmarks, make sure that you name each bookmark appropriately and group them where relevant. Note that the Bookmarks pane contains bookmarks from the whole report, not just the current page.

You can navigate between bookmarks by selecting them in the Bookmarks pane, or you can select the **View** button, which will replace the pages bar at the bottom with the bookmark title bar. Ideally the order of bookmarks should make sense because some users may navigate the bookmarks by using their keyboard.

When you are in the View mode, also known as presentation mode, you can close or collapse all panes to have more room for your report. Figure 3-38 shows the bookmark title bar in the View mode.

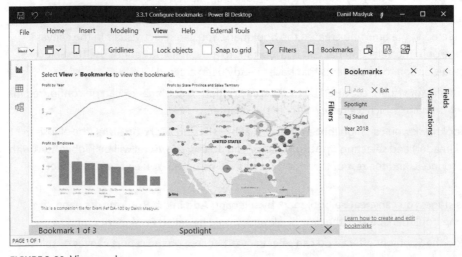

FIGURE 3-38 View mode

To exit from the View mode, select **Exit** in the Bookmarks pane, or select **Close** (the cross icon) in the bookmark title bar.

> **NOTE** **COMPANION FILE**
>
> You can see examples of bookmarks in the 3.3.1 Configure bookmarks.pbix file in the companion files folder.

You can also use bookmarks for navigation within a report. Configuring navigation for a report is reviewed later in this chapter.

Create custom tooltips

Most Power BI visuals have default tooltips that show the values for a selected data point. In addition to this, Power BI allows you to set custom tooltips for each visual, which can be useful to provide additional context for a data point and allow you to use your page real estate more effectively.

Custom tooltips are report pages that you configure to show instead of the default tooltips. They will then dynamically filter to show data relevant to the data point you have hovered over.

Before you can set custom tooltips, you must create a tooltip page in the following way:

1. In the **Report** view, create a new report page by selecting **New page** (the plus sign) on the page navigation bar.
2. Right-click the new page on the navigation bar and select **Rename page**.
3. Enter a new name, such as **Trend tooltip**, and press **Enter**.
4. Go to the **Format** pane of the page, expand **Page information**, and switch the **Tooltip** toggle to **On**.
5. Still in the **Format** pane, expand **Page size**, and select **Tooltip** from the **Type** drop-down list. You can also set a custom page size.
6. Add a visual you want to show in the tooltip. In the Wide World Importers example, you can add a line chart that shows **Profit** by **Year**.
7. Right-click the **Trend tooltip** page in the page navigation bar and select **Hide page**.

You now have a tooltip page, as shown in Figure 3-39.

You can now assign the custom tooltip to a visual of your choice by performing the following steps:

1. On a different page, create a bar chart that shows **Profit** by **Employee**.
2. In the **Format** pane for the new visual, expand the **Tooltip** section.
3. Ensure **Report page** is selected from the **Type** drop-down list.
4. Select **Trend tooltip** from the **Page** drop-down list.

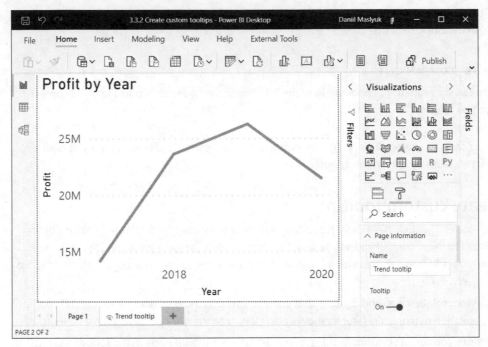

FIGURE 3-39 Trend tooltip

At this stage, you can hover over a bar to see the custom tooltip from the **Trend tooltip** page. Figure 3-40 shows the custom tooltip when you hover over the bar of *Archer Lamble*.

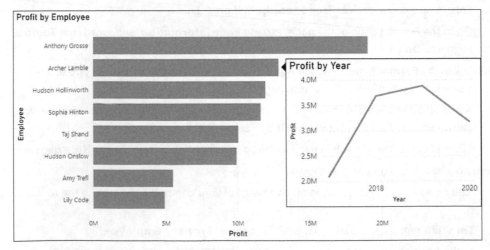

FIGURE 3-40 Trend tooltip shown as report page tooltip

Note that the tooltip shows the **Trend tooltip** page that is filtered to show data only for *Archer Lamble*.

When creating a tooltip page, you don't have to show the same values in the tooltip as you show in the main visual—the tooltip can contain any arbitrary information. You can also use any page size for the tooltip page, and you can have more than one visual on it, too. Text may become harder to read when in a tooltip, so be conscious about user experience when creating these.

> **NOTE** **COMPANION FILE**
>
> You can see an example of a page tooltip in the 3.3.2 Create custom tooltips.pbix file in the companion files folder.

Edit and configure interactions between visuals

One of the defining features of Power BI is the interaction of visuals with each other. For example, you can select an item in a bar chart, and it will cross-highlight a column chart. This behavior is illustrated in Figure 3-41.

FIGURE 3-41 Cross-highlighting in action

In Figure 3-41, we selected a bar that displays *Profit* for *Tailspin Toys*. The other bars in this graph then became dimmed, and portions of columns in the other visual became highlighted. These highlighted portions represent Quantity values in each Color that relate to *Tailspin Toys*. This behavior is called *cross-highlighting*: selecting a data point in a visual will highlight portions of other visuals.

To change this behavior, you can select the bar chart, after which the **Format** ribbon becomes visible. Select **Format** > **Edit interactions**. If you have more charts on the page, you'll see new buttons appear in the top-right corner of other charts:

- **Filter**   Only shows values that relate to the selected data point
- **Highlight**   Highlights portions of visuals that relate to the selected data point
- **None**   Ignores any selections

You can see the interaction buttons and the effect of each interaction option in Figure 3-42.

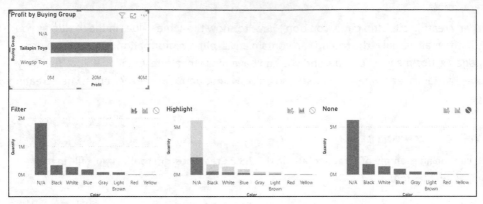

FIGURE 3-42 Three interaction options

To hide the interaction buttons, select **Format** > **Edit interactions** again.

Not every visual type has all three interaction options; some only have two, such as Filter and None. For example, it is not possible to highlight part of a slicer or a card. In these cases, the default behavior will be Filter instead of Highlight.

NOTE **DEFAULT INTERACTION**

Highlight is the default interaction, which you can change to Filter in report settings: **File > Options and settings > Options > Current file > Report settings > Change default visual interaction from cross highlighting to cross filtering.**

Configure navigation for a report

Besides using the page bar for navigation in the report, you can configure buttons, shapes, and images to link to specific report pages or bookmarks. As we covered earlier in the chapter, speaking with your users early in the report building process will help improve the overall experience of your report. You can configure report navigation by performing the following steps:

1. Select an existing visualization item or insert a new one from the **Insert** ribbon.

2. With the item selected, in the **Visualization** pane set the **Action** toggle to **On**.

3. Expand the **Action** section in the **Visualization** pane.

4. Select **Page navigation** or **Bookmark** from the **Type** drop-down list to go to a page or bookmark, respectively. Depending on your selection, the **Destination** or **Bookmark** drop-down list will then appear in the **Action** section.

5. Select the desired page or bookmark from the **Destination** or **Bookmark** drop-down list, respectively.

At this stage, if you hold the **Ctrl** key on your keyboard and select the visualization item, you will be taken to the page or bookmark you linked the item to. You can create more links to other pages or bookmarks for more interactive navigation using the same technique.

> **NOTE COMPANION FILE**
>
> You can find an example of a navigation button in the 3.3.4 Configure navigation for a report. pbix file in the companion files folder.

> **NOTE POWER BI SERVICE**
>
> When you are in reading view in the Power BI service, you do not need to hold the **Ctrl** key for navigation by using buttons, shapes, or images.

Apply sorting

When you create a visual, Power BI will try to sort the data in the most appropriate way. For example, column charts are usually sorted in descending order of values. You can apply different sorting according to business requirements.

To change sorting of a visual, hover over it, select **More options** > **Sort by**, and select the field you want to sort by. To sort in descending or ascending order, hover over the visual, and select **More options** > **Sort descending** or **Sort ascending**, respectively.

The Table visual supports sorting by multiple columns at the same time. In the Wide World Importers example, you can sort a table by two columns in the following way:

1. Create a table with the following fields:

   A. **Year** from the **Date** table (set summarization to **Don't summarize**)

   B. **Employee** from the **Employee** table

   C. **Profit** from the **Sale** table (set summarization to **Sum**)

2. In the visual, select the header of the **Year** column. Ensure that the arrow in the header points up for ascending order. If it points down, select the header again.

3. Press and hold the **Shift** key.

4. Select the header of the **Profit** column. Ensure that the arrow in the header points down for descending order. If it points up, select the header again.

The result should be as shown in Figure 3-43.

Year	Employee	Profit
2017	Anthony Grosse	3,226,119.90
2017	Archer Lamble	2,095,143.15
2017	Hudson Hollinworth	2,030,810.35
2017	Sophia Hinton	1,932,312.80
2017	Taj Shand	1,670,251.95
2017	Hudson Onslow	1,618,314.95
2017	Amy Trefl	821,910.75
2017	Lily Code	814,123.20
2018	Anthony Grosse	5,171,057.00
2018	Archer Lamble	3,683,691.45
Total		**85,729,180.90**

FIGURE 3-43 Table sorted by two fields

NOTE **COMPANION FILE**

The table sorted by multiple fields can be found in the 3.3.5 Apply sorting.pbix file in the companion files folder.

NOTE **SORT BY COLUMN**

As discussed in Skill 2.1: Design a data model, you can also apply different sorting to columns in the data model—this feature is called Sort by column. When you use a sorted column on an axis in a visual, Power BI will usually sort the visual by this column instead of sorting by values.

Configure Sync slicers

Report-level filters, which we reviewed earlier in this chapter, can be useful when a filter is applicable to every page, whereas page-level filters are appropriate for page-specific filters. Sometimes there are filters that apply to more than one page, but not to all pages. Although the Filters pane does not offer a way to synchronize filters between only some pages, you can sync slicers between pages to address this scenario.

When you sync slicers, selections on one page are reflected on another page or pages. One way to synchronize slicers between pages is by copying a slicer on a different page:

1. Select a slicer and press **Ctrl+C**.
2. Go to a different report page and press **Ctrl+V**.

3. When prompted as shown in Figure 3-44, select **Sync**.

FIGURE 3-44 Sync visuals

Alternatively, you can select **View** > **Sync slicers** and the slicer you want to sync, as shown in Figure 3-45.

FIGURE 3-45 Sync slicers pane

If you don't have this slicer on other pages, you can select **Add and sync with all pages** or select specific pages to add the slicer to. Selecting a check box under the Sync column adds the slicer; selecting a check box under the Visible column also makes it visible.

> **NOTE HIDDEN SLICERS**
>
> If you add a slicer without making it visible, it will be hidden, and it will still affect the visuals on the page. Visual visibility is configured in the Selection pane, reviewed in the next section.

Typically, you sync slicers that use the same columns. It's also possible to sync slicers that are based on different columns by using sync groups. For this, in **Advanced options** of **Sync slicers**, you need to enter the same group name for each slicer, and they'll sync even if they're based on different columns, like *Invoice Date* and *Delivery Date*.

Finally, you can select **Sync field changes to other slicers** if you want slicers to be updated in case you change a column in one of them. For example, if you have a slicer on *Color*, and later you swap the field for *Month*, then synced slicers will all be updated to have *Month* as a column.

> **NOTE COMPANION FILE**
>
> You can find an example of Sync slicers usage in the 3.3.6 Configure Sync slicers.pbix file in the companion files folder.

Use the Selection pane

The Selection pane allows you to control the visibility of visuals. To open the pane, select **View** > **Selection**. In the pane, you will see a list of visuals on the current page, which will all be visible by default.

The default names of the visuals correspond to their titles, and if a visual has no title, the visual will have the same name as the chart type. You will also see all visuals that have been hidden in the same pane. As a result, you may see multiple visuals with the same name. In this case, you can give your visuals meaningful names by adding appropriate titles.

To rename a visual in the Selection pane, double-click the visual in the Selection pane and enter a new name. Note that if your visual has a visible title, the title will be updated after you rename the visual in the Selection pane.

The Selection pane allows you to hide visuals by selecting **Hide this visual** (the eye icon) next to a visual. Note that hiding a visual does not remove it from the page; instead, the visual becomes invisible, but it is still part of the page. One of the implications of this is that hidden slicers can still filter other visuals. However, hidden visuals aren't evaluated, which results in improved performance. You can see the **Layer order** section of the **Selection** pane with one visual hidden in Figure 3-46.

FIGURE 3-46 Selection pane

In the Selection pane, you can show or hide all visuals at once by selecting **Show** or **Hide**, respectively. You can change the layer order of visuals, also known as z-index or z-order, by selecting a visual and then the up or down arrows at the top of the pane. The layer order of a visual determines which visual gets selected when you click in an area where two visuals overlap.

You can also group, ungroup, and merge groups within the Selection pane. Grouping visuals is useful for some scenarios, such as hiding visuals for bookmarks, moving around the report, or copying a number of visuals to other pages. Merging allows you to merge several groups into a single group without creating nested groups. To group visuals, you need to perform the following actions:

1. Select several visuals by holding the **Ctrl** key.
2. Right-click one of the selected visuals.
3. Select **Group** > **Group**.

Ungrouping and merging are performed in a similar way. You can also rename groups in the same way as you rename a visual.

EXAM TIP

You should know the difference between the layer order and tab order, and how each of them contributes to the accessibility of a report.

Use drill-through and cross-filter

It is common for business users to want to see the details that make up aggregated values. For example, if a user looks at a column chart and notices an unexpected number, they may want to see the data behind the value. For this, you can set up a details page to which users will drill through.

To enable report users to drill through to a specific page, you need to place one or more fields in the **Drill through** section of the **Visualizations** pane of the page shown in Figure 3-47.

FIGURE 3-47 Drill through

In the **Drill through** section, there are two toggles:

- **Cross-report** With this option, you can allow this page to be used as a drill-through page from other reports.

- **Keep all filters** This option controls whether all filters from the initial page are applied or only filters on the fields in the **Add drill-through fields here** field well.

> **NOTE** **CROSS-REPORT DRILL-THROUGH**
>
> When you're configuring cross-report drill-through, data models of the reports don't need to match, but the drill-through field names must match exactly, including table names of the fields—otherwise, cross-report drill-through won't work.

When you add a column to the **Add drill-through fields here** field well, you can select whether drill-through will be allowed when it's used as category or summarized. For measures, you can't select this because measures can't be used as category.

To set up drill-through in the Wide World Importers example, complete these steps:

1. Name a blank page **Sales Summary**.
2. Create a column chart that shows **Profit** by **Employee**.
3. Create a new page and rename it to **Sales Details**.
4. On the Sales Details page, add a table visual that shows the following fields:
   A. Date
   B. Customer
   C. Stock Item
   D. Profit
5. Add **Profit** to the **Drill through** section of the **Sales Details** list and ensure **Allow drill through when** is set to **Summarized**.

> **NOTE** **BACK BUTTON**
>
> When you add a field to the Drill through section, a Back button will be added automatically in the upper-left corner. Note that this button won't work in case of cross-report drill-through.

Once the steps above are completed, you can right-click a column on the **Sales Summary** page and select **Drill through** > **Sales Details**, which will take you to the **Sales Details** page filtered to the Employee whose column you right-clicked.

An alternative to right-clicking is setting the action of a button to Drill through. The steps you need to take in this case are similar to what we covered earlier in this skill, in "Configure navigation for a report."

A drill-through button will be formatted differently depending on whether you can drill through. By default, it will be shaded when drill-through won't be performed upon selecting the button.

For a button drill-through to work, the same requirements apply as to a right-click drill-through. You'll need to select one or more data points from any visual on the initial page where the drill-through field is summarized or used as category, depending on your selection for the field in the Drill through section.

Drill down into data using interactive visuals

Many visuals allow you to explore data interactively when you use several levels of fields—for example, *Year*, *Quarter*, and *Month* columns on the x-axis in a line chart. Whether you use a hierarchy defined in the data model or several individual columns together has no difference. When you right-click a data point in a visual that uses a hierarchy, depending on the current hierarchy level, you may see the following extra options:

- **Drill down**   Goes to the next level of the hierarchy within the selected point. For example, drilling down to Quarter from Year 2020 will show quarters for the year 2020 only.

- **Show next level**   Goes to the next level with no filter on the previous level. For example, selecting this option to go from Year to Quarter will show all quarters for all years without showing years.

- **Expand to next level**   This option combines the current and next levels. For example, when you select this option to go from Year to Quarter, you'll see quarters for each year separately.

- **Drill up**   Goes back up one level.

When a visual uses a hierarchy, the visual header will have extra buttons that correspond to these options. Figure 3-48 shows the buttons and the effect of each drill-down option.

FIGURE 3-48 Visual header extra buttons and various drill-down effects

By default, when you drill down, the corresponding filters may be applied to other visuals on the page. To disable this behavior, perform the following steps:

1. Select a visual that performs drill-down.
2. Select the **Format** ribbon.
3. Select **Selected visual** from the **Apply drill down filters to** drop-down list.

Export report data

Power BI allows you to export data from each visual individually. To export data from a visual, follow these steps:

1. Hover over the visual you want to export data from.
2. In the visual header, select **More options** > **Export data**.
3. Select the folder you want to export data to.
4. Enter a new file name and select **Save**.

This saves data to a CSV file that you can further manipulate in Excel, for example.

Design reports for mobile devices

We reviewed mobile views for dashboards earlier in the chapter. Similar to how you work with dashboards, you can create separate views of your report to optimize the experience for smaller screens. In this section, we review mobile views of reports.

To start creating a mobile view for a page, select **View** > **Mobile layout**. This opens the mobile layout editor, as shown in Figure 3-49.

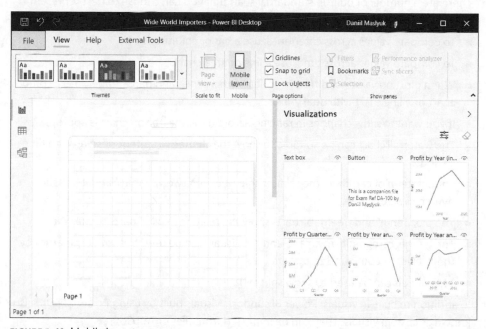

FIGURE 3-49 Mobile layout

The experience of creating mobile layouts for report pages is similar to that of creating a mobile view of a dashboard. Because not all visuals may be equally important, you can select which visuals appear on mobile view.

To add a visual to the canvas, drag it from the **Visualizations** pane onto the canvas. You can then move around and resize the visual as needed. You can also remove a visual from the canvas by selecting the cross icon in the upper-right corner of the visual.

To remove all visuals from the canvas, select **Remove all visualizations** (the eraser icon) in the **Visualizations** pane.

When you design a mobile view for a page, the original view remains untouched. To exit from the mobile layout editor, select **View** > **Mobile layout**.

If you don't design a mobile layout, the report will automatically appear horizontally in the mobile app.

Chapter summary

- There are multiple ways to add a visual to a report page, one of which is to select a visual icon from the Visualizations pane. Besides visuals, you can add other elements from the Insert ribbon: Text box, Buttons, Shapes, and Image. You can set various actions for these elements such as bookmarks, page navigation, or hyperlinks.

- There are a number of built-in standard visuals that you can choose to best represent data:
  - To compare values across categories, use a bar or column chart.
  - To compare values across time, use a line or area chart.
  - When plotting values of different scales, such as units and percentages, use a combo chart or a line chart with dual y-axes.
  - If you want to show changes in ranking across time, the ribbon chart is appropriate.
  - The waterfall chart can be suitable to show the changes in categories between time periods.
  - The scatter plot can show the relationship between two variables, and it can show dynamics across time.
  - The pie, donut, and treemap charts show the relationships of parts to the whole.
  - The gauge, card, multi-row card, and KPI visuals can be used to show key metrics by themselves or compared to targets.
  - Map visuals can be used to show spatial data.

- In addition to built-in visuals, Power BI supports visuals built by using Power BI SDK, also known as custom visuals. They can be imported from files or AppSource.

- Power BI visuals can be formatted in different ways in the Format pane. Some formatting options can be tied to measures—this is known as expression-based or conditional formatting.

- To apply filters to visuals, you can use slicers, the Filters pane, or both. Slicers can be used to filter by a single column, or you can build hierarchical slicers. Filters in the Filters pane can be applied to a visual, a page, or the whole report.

- Power BI supports R and Python visuals, which must be installed separately. R and Python visuals can only be used to display graphs.

- For each page, you can configure its size, background, alignment, and wallpaper, as well as format the Filters pane. You can also set a page to be a tooltip page or a Q&A result.

- You can make your Power BI more accessible by carefully selecting page names, titles, and labels. You should use different markers for different categories and not rely on color as the only way to discriminate categories. For each visual, you can set alternative text and its tab order. You should use colors that provide sufficient contrast between font and background, and you can use report themes to make working with colors easier during the development.

- When using DirectQuery, you can configure automatic page refresh for each page separately. Power BI supports two types of automatic page refresh: fixed interval and change detection. Change detection works by checking for changes in the value of a measure you define.

- You can create paginated reports by using Power BI Report Builder and publish them to the Power BI service. Paginated reports are a great fit for reports meant to be printed and shared offline.

- A dashboard can have pinned visuals from a variety of sources, including Power BI reports. Additionally, you can add tiles that aren't backed by datasets—for example, videos and web content.

- Pinned visuals become dashboard tiles that aren't fully interactive. To have visuals interact with each other, you can pin a live report page to a dashboard.

- Dashboards support the Q&A feature that is also available in reports. Q&A results can be pinned to dashboards.

- Users can individually set alerts for cards, KPIs, and gauges pinned from reports from a dashboard. These alerts can display notifications and send emails when a value goes above or below the specified threshold. Data alerts are only visible to users who configure them.

- You can add a theme to a dashboard by selecting one of the preset themes or defining your own. Alternatively, you can upload a JSON theme, which uses the same format as report themes.

- Dashboards can have mobile views to optimize the viewing experience for different screen sizes. You can reorder, resize, and hide tiles when creating a mobile view, and the web view remains intact.

- Bookmarks can help create data stories or highlight specific insights in the report. A bookmark can be configured to save the state of a page, including filters and the visibility of visuals.

- You can override the standard tooltips by configuring a page tooltip for a visual.

- Selecting a data point on a visual can cross-highlight, cross-filter, or have no effect on other visuals on the same page depending on how you configure visual interactions.

- In addition to using the page navigation bar, you can employ buttons to configure navigation for a report by using the Page navigation or Bookmark actions.

- Most visuals can be sorted by the fields they use in ascending or descending order. The Table visual supports sorting by multiple fields simultaneously by holding the Shift key.

- Sync slicers is useful when you want to synchronize filters between several but not all pages of a report. You can also sync filters between different fields by using the advanced options of Sync slicers.

- In the Selection pane, you can hide, rename, and group visuals together. You can also change the layer and tab order of visuals or grouped visuals.

- Power BI reports support drill-through to different pages of the same report or other reports, called cross-report drill-through.
- When a visual uses a hierarchy, you can drill down to explore the data points of the visual in more detail.
- Power BI reports can be optimized for smaller screens by configuring mobile layouts.

Thought experiment

In this thought experiment, demonstrate your skills and knowledge of the topics covered in this chapter. You can find the answers in the section that follows.

You are a data analyst at Contoso responsible for creating Power BI reports. The management requested you to visualize data coming from a Power BI dataset built by your colleague.

Based on background information and business requirements, answer the following questions:

1. Your department wants to see a single visual that explains the factors that contribute to revenue growth the most. Which visualization should you use?

   A. Decomposition tree

   B. Funnel chart

   C. Key influencers

   D. Stacked column chart

2. You'd like to create a navigation page in your report that will take users to different pages depending on their choice. Your solution must involve minimal effort, and you must be able to test it in Power BI Desktop. Which element(s) should you use?

   A. Buttons with the Bookmark action

   B. Buttons with the Page navigation action

   C. Table

   D. Text box with hyperlinks

3. You need to ensure that users can effectively navigate your reports by using the keyboard. Which property should you configure?

   A. Bookmarks

   B. Layer order

   C. Mobile layout

   D. Tab order

4. Your colleague already designed a report page that includes two visuals: a bar chart showing sales by client, and a column chart showing sales by product category. You need to ensure that whenever a user selects a client or product category, the other chart shows only the corresponding sales without showing overall sales. How should you configure interactions?

    A. Filter

    B. Highlight

    C. None

5. You've created a bar chart that shows sales by client. You want users to see profit figures when they hover over a client. Which options would work in this case? Each answer presents a complete solution.

    A. Add Profit as a visual-level filter.

    B. Add Profit to drill-through fields.

    C. Add Profit to tooltips.

    D. Create a report page that shows Profit and add it as a tooltip.

6. You'd like to add a welcome video that is hosted on YouTube to a dashboard. Users have to be able to play the video without leaving the dashboard page, and your solution must involve the least amount of code. Which kind of tile should you use?

    A. Custom streaming data

    B. Text box with the video URL

    C. Video

    D. Web content

Thought experiment answers

1. The answer is **C**. The Key influencers visual shows the most important factors based on the fields you provide. Though it may be possible to get some insight into success factors by using a decomposition tree—option A—doing so would involve significant time and effort. Neither the funnel nor the stacked column chart from options B and D, respectively, will highlight the most important factors out of many.

2. The answer is **B**. Using the Page navigation action allows you to select the pages you want to navigate to without creating bookmarks, as in option A. Though it's possible to use a table to drill through to a specific page—option C—doing so would involve considerably more effort than buttons. Option D, text boxes with hyperlinks, would require you to know the URL of each page, and it wouldn't work in Power BI Desktop.

3. The answer is **D**. Tab order determines the order in which users switch between visuals when using the keyboard. Bookmarks—option A—aren't helpful for navigating within each page. Layer order—option B—determines the order in which visuals are layered

and may be different from Tab order. Mobile layout—option C—is used to create mobile reports.

4. The answer is **A**. The Filter interaction filters a chart, and it's not showing the overall values as Highlight from option B does. If you select None—option C—there will be no interaction between charts.

5. The answer is **C** or **D**. If you add Profit to tooltips, you'll see the corresponding value when hovering over a bar. Similarly, a report page that shows Profit and that's configured to be the tooltip page will also show a client's Profit when you hover over a bar. Adding Profit to visual-level filters, as in option A, won't show Profit anywhere. Similarly, adding Profit to drill-through fields won't show Profit when hovering over bars in the visual.

6. The answer is **C**. Using the Video type of Tile allows you to embed a video that can be played without leaving the page, and you only need a video URL. Custom streaming data—option A—is meant for data, not videos. Though you can put a video URL in a text box as option B suggests, a user will have to leave the page to view the video. Although you can use the Web content tile to embed a video by using embed code, doing so requires pasting several lines of code, and the video may have scroll bars in case its aspect ratio is different from that of a tile.

CHAPTER 4

Analyze the data

In the previous chapter, we reviewed the skills necessary to visualize the data in Power BI. In this chapter we look at ways you can enhance your reports to expose insights from data—for example, by applying extra formatting or setting filters. We also discuss the Quick Insights feature and show how you can use its results in your reports.

Power BI is equipped with artificial intelligence that can run algorithms on your data to mine it for further insights. In the second half of the chapter, we review the AI visuals and AI Insights, as well as show how you can group values, identify outliers, and conduct time-series analysis.

> **NOTE   COMPANION FILE**
>
> Visuals from the figure files are available in the 4 Analyze the data.pbix file from the companion files folder.

Skills covered in this chapter:

- Skill 4.1: Enhance reports to expose insights
- Skill 4.2: Perform advanced analysis

Skill 4.1: Enhance reports to expose insights

When you visualize data, you'll often need to apply some enhancements to your visuals or reports to highlight insights in your data. In this section, we explore techniques that don't involve artificial intelligence.

> **This skill covers how to:**
>
> - Apply conditional formatting
> - Perform top N analysis
> - Explore statistical summary
> - Add a Quick Insights result to a dashboard

- Create reference lines by using the Analytics pane
- Use the Play Axis feature of a visualization and conduct time-series analysis
- Personalize visuals

Apply conditional formatting

One way to highlight specific data points that you find interesting is to use conditional formatting, and there are several ways to use it in Power BI. The way in which you apply conditional formatting depends on the type of visual.

Tables and matrixes

The Table and Matrix visuals offer the most options to conditionally format values:

- **Background color**   Changes the background color of cells
- **Font color**   Changes the font color of values
- **Data bars**   Displays bars in cells
- **Icons**   Displays icons in cells
- **Web URL**   Underlines values and turns cells into hyperlinks; otherwise doesn't change the appearance of values

You can configure conditional formatting in the following way:

1. Select a Table or Matrix visual.
2. In the **Visualizations** pane, select **Format** > **Conditional formatting**.
3. From the drop-down list, select the field you want to format conditionally.
4. Set the relevant conditional formatting toggle to **On**.

Unless you're using the Web URL conditional formatting, you'll see your values formatted immediately by using default settings, which you can change by selecting **Advanced controls** below the **On** toggle. You can combine several types of conditional formatting for a single field.

To remove conditional formatting, switch the **On** toggle to **Off**.

BACKGROUND COLOR AND FONT COLOR

The background color and font color advanced controls are the same. For example, Figure 4-1 shows the advanced controls when you are applying conditional formatting to the background color.

FIGURE 4-1 Conditional formatting advanced controls

When configuring conditional formatting for background color or font color, you can select what you want to format by:

- **Color scale**   You can set the minimum and maximum color, which can be the lowest and highest field values in the current state of the visual, respectively, or the values you enter manually by selecting **Custom** from the corresponding drop down list. You can also select the **Diverging** check box and set the center color. Furthermore, you can select how you want to format blank values in the **Default formatting** drop-down list; you can choose 0, which means don't format, or use a specific color.

- **Rules**   You can assign a color to a single value, to a range of values, or to a blank value. When entering values, you can enter numbers or percentages. If a value meets criteria for more than one rule, the last applicable rule is applied. You can reverse the order of rules by selecting **Reverse color order**.

- **Field value**   You must use a field that returns a color code as a hex code, RGB code, HSL code, or color name.

You can also select the detail level the conditional formatting should apply to:

- Values only
- Values and totals
- Totals only

Additionally, conditional formatting of one field can be based on a different field. For instance, you can conditionally format revenue amounts based on profit margin.

> **NOTE EXISTING FORMATTING**
>
> If you applied formatting to cell background or font color, conditional formatting would override it.

DATA BARS

The data bars conditional formatting allows you to format cells with bars based on their values. Figure 4-2 shows the available advanced controls.

FIGURE 4-2 Data bars advanced controls

For the minimum and maximum bar lengths, you can use the default values, which will be determined based on the lowest and highest field values in the visual. Alternatively, you can enter custom values by selecting Custom from the corresponding drop-down list. Setting custom minimum and maximum values can be particularly useful when you are dealing with measures that have known value ranges, such as proportions.

You can customize the positive and negative bar colors, as well as the axis color.

The **Bar direction** drop-down list allows you to make bars go from left to right or from right to left, and the **Show bar only** check box will hide values and leave only data bars visible.

Effective use of conditional formatting can be extremely beneficial to users, allowing them to quickly identify significant data points when analyzing the report.

ICONS

Advanced controls for icons are similar to those for background and font color. Figure 4-3 shows the available options.

FIGURE 4-3 Icons advanced controls

Unlike with background and font color conditional formatting, you can only format by rules and field value. Although there are many icon styles to choose from when you format by rules, you can use your own images when you format by field value.

Additionally, you can set the icon layout (left of data, right of data, or icon only) and icon alignment (top, middle, or bottom).

Figure 4-4 shows four types of conditional formatting in a matrix.

Category	Background color	Font color	Data bars	Icons
Black	1,101,101	$30,209,672	$26,269,280 ▲	$14,390,527
Blue	605,738	$41,289,464	$35,903,882 ▲	$17,713,073
Gray	309,847	$6,823,755	$5,933,696 ▲	$1,475,749
Light Brown	274,500		$4,941,000 ◆	($274,500)
N/A	5,745,694	$89,523,436	$77,896,013 ●	$40,792,234
Red	29,033		$4,726,465 ▲	$2,179,948
White	873,153	$17,365,861	$15,100,749 ▲	$8,882,849
Yellow	11,562		$1,490,145 △	$569,303
Total	**8,950,628**	**$198,043,439**	**$172,261,230**	**$85,729,181**

FIGURE 4-4 Matrix conditional formatting

Other visuals

Besides the Table and Matrix visuals, many visuals support conditional formatting for data colors. It can be configured in the **Format** section of the **Visualization** pane similarly to the way you configure background color or font color conditional formatting for a table or matrix. For more information, refer to Skill 3.1: Create reports.

Perform top N analysis

In Skill 3.3, Enrich reports for usability, we reviewed how you can sort visuals, which can already draw your attention to the most significant items. If there are many items and you only want to show the top ones, you have several options:

- Visual-level filter
- Q&A
- DAX

Visual-level filter

One way to show the top items is to use a visual-level filter of type Top N. You can set a Top N filter on a visual in the following way:

1. Select the visual you want to filter.
2. In the **Filters on this visual** section of the **Filters** pane, expand the card of the categorical field you want to filter.
3. Select **Top N** from the **Filter type** drop-down list.
4. Select **Top** or **Bottom** under **Show items** and enter the number of items you want to keep.
5. Under **By value**, add a data field by which you want to rank the categorical items. Note that the field need not be part of the visual.
6. Select **Apply filter**.

For example, Figure 4-5 shows a bar chart that displays top 10 stock items by profit.

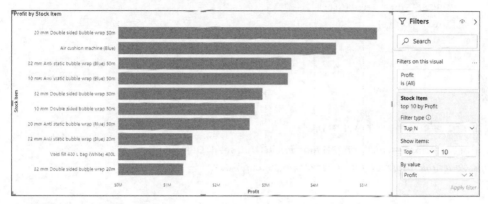

FIGURE 4-5 Top N filter

Q&A

To get the same result as in Figure 4-5, you can use the following query in the Q&A visual:

```
top 10 stock items by profit
```

For more details on the Q&A feature, refer to Skill 2.2: Develop a data model.

DAX

In some scenarios, Q&A or a visual-level filter won't work—for example, when you want to show the percentage of profit generated by top 10 stock items. In cases like this, you can write a measure that only considers profit of the top 10 stock items.

Let's say you already have the following measure:

```
Total Profit = SUM(Sale[Profit])
```

Then the following measure will only show Profit for top 10 stock items:

```
Top 10 Stock Items Profit =
CALCULATE(
    [Total Profit],
    TOPN(
        10,
        VALUES('Stock Item'[Stock Item]),
        [Total Profit],
        DESC
    )
)
```

NEED MORE REVIEW? TOPN IN DAX

For more information on the TOPN function in DAX, see "TOPN" at
https://docs.microsoft.com/en-us/dax/topn-function-dax.

And then you can use the following measure to display the proportion of the top 10 stock items in overall profit:

```
Top 10 Stock Items Profit % =
DIVIDE(
    [Top 10 Stock Items Profit],
    [Total Profit]
)
```

Using DAX is essential when you're using measures with and without the Top N filter in the same visual.

EXAM TIP

You should know which Top N analysis method—visual-level filter, Q&A, or DAX—to select based on the business requirements.

Explore statistical summary

In Skill 1.2, Profile the data, you saw how Power Query can be used to display the statistics for each column in your tables; for example, you can see the minimum, maximum, and average value for a numeric column along with a value distribution chart. Although the charts can already provide you with good understanding of your data, you can't add more charts to further explore data.

In Skill 2.3, Create measures by using DAX, we reviewed the basic statistical functions available in DAX that you can use to enhance your data model. By using DAX, you can create your own value distribution charts in Power BI.

> **NOTE   IMPLICIT AND EXPLICIT MEASURES**
>
> Although you don't always need to write DAX, it's best practice to do so instead of using implicit measures. Refer to Skill 2.3 for a discussion on implicit versus explicit measures.

Let's say you're interested in the value distribution of *Unit Price* from the *Sale* table, and you've created the following explicit measure:

```
Sale Rows = COUNTROWS(Sale)
```

You can then build a chart as follows:

1. Select **Stacked column chart** from the **Visualizations** pane.
2. Add the Unit Price field from the Sale table to the **Axis** field well.
3. Add the Sale Rows measure to the **Values** field well.
4. In the **Visualizations** pane, select **Format** and expand the **X axis** section.
5. Select **Categorical** from the **Type** drop-down list.

The result appears in Figure 4-6.

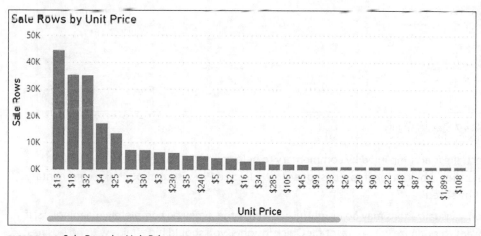

FIGURE 4-6 Sale Rows by Unit Price

If instead of showing the count of each value you want to build a histogram with value ranges, you must bin values, as detailed later in this chapter in Skill 4.2: Perform advanced analysis.

Add a Quick Insights result to a dashboard

If you aren't sure what to show in your reports or you want to check if you may have missed some insights, you can use the Quick Insights feature in the Power BI service. Power BI will try to build some interesting visualizations from your data automatically, and you can then pin a visual you like to a dashboard.

You can run Quick Insights on a dataset in the following way:

1. In the Power BI service, go to the workspace that contains the dataset you want to get Quick Insights from.

2. Next to the dataset, select **More options** > **Get quick insights**. If you've used the feature on the dataset before, you'll see the **View insights** option.

3. Wait for the algorithms to finish running and select **View insights**.

An example of Quick Insights is shown in Figure 4-7.

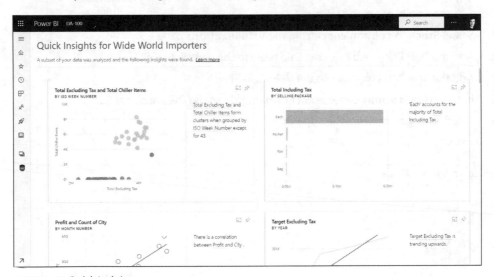

FIGURE 4-7 Quick Insights

Each tile is accompanied by commentary to help you make sense of data. If you like a visualization, you can pin it to a dashboard by selecting **Pin visual**, though the commentary won't be saved.

Some visualizations may be insightful, whereas others may be completely meaningless. If you want to optimize your dataset for Quick Insights, you should hide fields with no business meaning, such as keys, so that Quick Insights doesn't include them. You should also hide fields that contain duplicate information, such as product codes and product names, because duplicate information may lead to repetitive insights.

When you hover over a Quick Insights result, you can select **Focus mode** to apply filters or find related insights by selecting **Get Insights**. Getting Quick Insights from Quick Insights results is called *scoped insights*. Figure 4-8 shows an example of related insights.

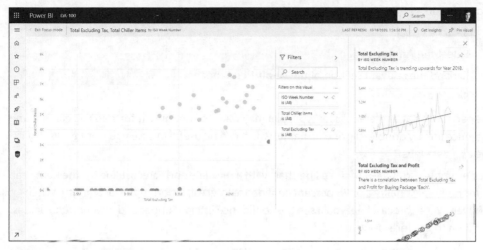

FIGURE 4-8 Scoped insights

From here, you can review the related insights and pin a visual you find useful. To go back to the initial Quick Insights results, select **Exit Focus mode**.

Create reference lines by using the Analytics pane

Reference lines can be a useful addition to charts to make it easier for users to draw insights. In Power BI, you can add one or more reference lines to a visual from the **Analytics** pane inside the **Visualizations** pane. The Analytics pane shows the number of reference lines of each type that were added to a visual.

Depending on the visual and data types used in the visual, you may be able to add some of the following reference lines:

- **Trend line**   Fitted straight trend line
- **X-axis constant line**   Static vertical line
- **Y-axis constant line**   Static horizontal line
- **Min line**   Dynamic minimum line
- **Max line**   Dynamic maximum line
- **Average line**   Dynamic average (mean) line
- **Median line**   Dynamic median line
- **Percentile line**   Dynamic line for which you need to enter the percentile value
- **Forecast**   Forecast line of a set length
- **Symmetry shading**   Shades the regions across the symmetry line
- **Ratio line**   Ratio of total for all points of Y values over X values

You can add a new reference line to a visual in the following way:

1. Select a visual.

2. Select the **Analytics** pane.

3. Expand the relevant section of the **Analytics** pane.

4. Select **Add.**

Depending on the reference line type, you may want to configure it further. You can rename a reference line by double-clicking its name, which can be useful in case you want to display its name as a data label.

For example, Figure 4-9 shows a line chart with a max line and forecast line for the next year with monthly seasonality and 75 percent confidence interval, ignoring the last month. When you hover over a forecast line, you'll see the confidence interval upper and lower bound values in addition to the forecast value.

FIGURE 4-9 Profit forecast and max line

To remove a reference line from a visual, select the cross icon next to its name in the **Analytics** pane.

Use the Play Axis feature of a visualization and conduct time-series analysis

In virtually all organizations, dates—and time in general—are an important dimension. Data that is indexed in time order is often called *time series*. As discussed in Skill 3.1: Create reports, you usually analyze time-series data by using a line, area, stacked area, or ribbon chart.

In some cases, you may want to analyze data by more than a couple dimensions, making it difficult to visualize by using one of the popular visuals. For example, you may want to build a visual that shows the following information:

- Sales Territory

- Profit %

- Quantity

- Month

If you only wanted to visualize three out of the four fields, you could build a line chart or a bar chart, for instance, depending on the combination of the fields. If you want to visualize all four fields, you may want to consider showing the information for one month at a time.

In this scenario, you don't want to make the viewer flip through months manually. Instead, to make your report user-friendly, use the Play axis of the scatter chart that will automatically go through months after a user selects the Play button. Figure 4-10 shows the chart before a user interacts with it.

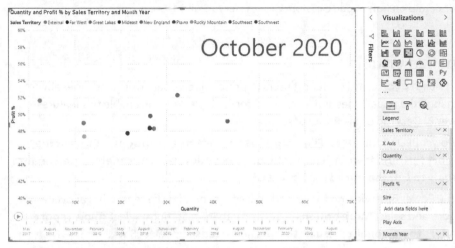

FIGURE 4-10 Scatter chart with Play axis

By default, the chart will show data for the last available month. Once a user selects the Play button, the shapes—in this case, State Territories—will be moving from month to month.

A user can select a specific shape to track its progress with a line. The line will connect the various positions of the shape across time. At the same time, other shapes will be dimmed. This behavior is shown in Figure 4-11.

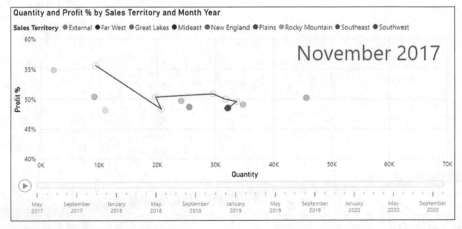

FIGURE 4-11 Shape path across time

When you're using a scatter chart with a Play axis, it's best to educate viewers on how to use the chart. You can do so by using internal presentations or by adding text to a report page.

> **NOTE   USING THE PLAY AXIS FOR MULTIPLE VISUALS**
>
> A limitation of the scatter chart with a Play axis is that the Play axis affects only the scatter chart itself. If you want to show multiple visuals across time progressively, you can use the Play Axis (Dynamic Slicer) custom visual. Using specific custom visuals is outside the scope of this book. For details on how to add a custom visual, refer to Skill 3.1: Create reports.

Personalize visuals

As a report builder, you can allow report users to personalize visuals, which means enabling them to change the visual types and fields used, for example. You can enable this feature in either Power BI Desktop or the Power BI service:

- In Power BI Desktop, select **File** > **Options and settings** > **Options** > **Current file** > **Report settings**; then, in Report Settings, select **Allow report readers to personalize visuals to suit their needs** and select **OK**.

- In the Power BI service, go to the workspace that contains the report, hover over a report, and select **More options** > **Settings**; then, in Settings, select **Allow report readers to personalize visuals to suit their needs** and select **Save**.

With the feature enabled, report readers in Power BI service can hover over a visual and select **Personalize this visual**, which spotlights a visual and allows a user to change it, as shown in Figure 4-12.

FIGURE 4-12 Personalizing visuals

When users personalize visuals, only they can see the changes. They can then save the changes as bookmarks and retrieve them later.

> **IMPORTANT VISUAL HEADERS**
>
> If you want your users to personalize visuals, visual headers must be visible. The report setting that controls this is called **Hide the visual header in reading view**.

Skill 4.2: Perform advanced analysis

You can enhance your analysis by employing advanced algorithms built into Power BI. In this section, we review the skills necessary to identify the outliers in your data, group, and bin data. We also explore using AI visuals and applying AI Insights.

> **This skill covers how to:**
> - Identify outliers
> - Use groupings and binnings
> - Use the Key influencers to explore dimensional variances
> - Use the Decomposition tree visual to break down a measure
> - Apply AI Insights

Identify outliers

When a data point is not in the expected range, it's called an *outlier*. Identifying outliers can be useful because they may happen for a variety of reasons, which you may often want to investigate. For example, a negative product unit price may mean a product return, or it may mean there's a bug in the transactional database, which must be reported and corrected as soon as possible.

When detecting outliers, you need to decide on the business logic behind the outlier—that is, what an outlier would constitute in your case. The logic will allow you to divide all data points into two groups—outliers and data points in the expected range.

You can detect outliers in a variety of ways. Besides data profiling and Quick Insights, which we reviewed earlier in the book, one of the most useful charts for detecting data anomalies is the scatter chart.

One way to use the scatter chart to identify outliers is to use the Details, X Axis, and Y Axis field wells. For example, the scatter chart in Figure 4-13 uses the Wide World Importers data and has *Stock Item* on Details, *Quantity* on X Axis, and *Profit* on Y Axis. You can immediately see some points standing out. You can hover over the points you're interested in to get more details and investigate further by cross-filtering other visuals or performing drill-through.

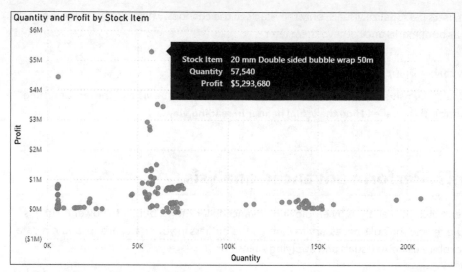

FIGURE 4-13 Quantity and Profit by Stock Item

The scatter chart can also be used to cluster data points, which can often group some outliers together. You can perform clustering in a scatter chart as follows:

1. Hover over a scatter chart and select **More options** > **Automatically find clusters**. Note that this option will be disabled if you use a field in the Legend field well.

2. If desired, change the name, description, and number of clusters.

3. Select **OK**.

Once finished, you'll see a new field in your model and the Legend field well. In the Wide World Importers example, if you wanted to see five clusters, you'd see the Stock Item (clusters) shown in Figure 4-14.

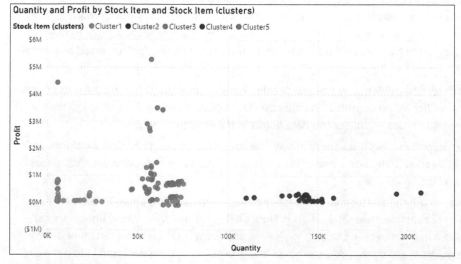

FIGURE 4-14 Stock Item clusters

You can now see two clusters of outliers: Cluster2 has outliers in terms of Quantity, whereas Cluster5 has outliers in terms of Profit. Note that you can use the new Stock Item (clusters) field in other visuals and filters.

If you want to edit the clusters, right-click the clusters field in the **Fields** pane and select **Edit clusters**. A quick way to change a cluster name is by double-clicking it to highlight it and typing the new name.

Use groupings and binnings

In addition to data clustering, you can perform grouping and binning of columns in Power BI to bring together data with business logic and higher-level data analysis.

Grouping

Grouping allows you to manually group values in a column by leveraging a user interface instead of having to write DAX. For instance, you can group Sales Territory values into regions by following these steps:

1. In the **Fields** pane, right-click the **State Territory** column in the **City** table and select **New group**.
2. In the **Name** text box, enter **Sales Region**.
3. Holding the **Ctrl** key, select **Southeast** and **Southwest**, and select **Group**.
4. Enter **South** as the new group name.
5. Repeat steps 3 and 4 for the following two groups:
   - **West**—Far West, Plains, and Rocky Mountain
   - **East**—Great Lakes, Mideast, and New England
6. Select the **Include Other group** check box. At this stage, the configuration should look like Figure 4-15.
7. Select **OK**.

After you finish, Power BI creates a new column in the City table that you can use in visualizations and calculations, if needed. For example, you can use the new Sales Region column as the legend in a Filled map, as shown in Figure 4-16.

You can also create groups by selecting data points in a visual. For example, let's say you have a scatter chart like the one shown in Figure 4-13. You can group values as follows:

1. Holding the **Ctrl** key, select a few data points on the scatter chart.
2. Right-click one of the selected data points.
3. Select **Group data**.

This will create a column with two data groups that you can use as the chart legend.

The default group names are often not very user-friendly; to edit a group, right-click the column in the **Fields** pane and select **Edit groups**.

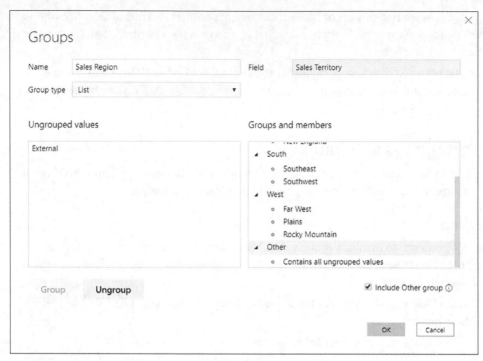

FIGURE 4-15 Sales Region group

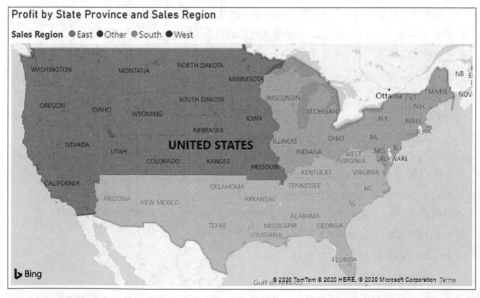

FIGURE 4-16 Sales Region on map

Binning

When you work with categorical values, you can only create groups of type List. When you work with numeric or date/time columns, you can also create *bins*, which may be more appropriate when there are too many values to group manually.

Binning splits numeric and date/time data into groups of equal size. You can specify the number or size of bins. The default size or count is calculated automatically.

In the Wide World Importers example, you can bin the Profit column in the following way:

1. Right-click the **Profit** column in the **Fields** pane and select **New group**.
2. Ensure **Bin** is selected in the **Group type** drop-down list.
3. Select **Number of bins** from the **Bin type** drop-down list
4. Enter **10** as **Bin count**.
5. Select **OK**.

This creates the Profit (bins) column, which you can use in a column chart to create a histogram, as shown in Figure 4-17. The histogram uses the count of Sale rows as values.

```
Sale Rows = COUNTROWS(Sale)
```

FIGURE 4-17 Profit histogram

You can edit bins by right-clicking the corresponding column in the **Fields** pane and selecting **Edit groups**. If you want to change the group type from Bin to List, you'll need to re-create the group.

Use the Key influencers to explore dimensional variances

The Key influencers visual helps you understand the variables that drive a metric. For example, you may want to understand what influences profit to increase, and you may be looking at factors such as location, buying package, and time of the year. The Key influencers visual will analyze the data you provide and rank each factor in terms of importance.

The Key influencers visual has the following field wells:

- **Analyze**   The metric you want to analyze. It can be continuous or categorical.
- **Explain by**   The factors you want to check in terms of influence.
- **Expand by**   When analyzing a measure or a summarized field, you can increase the detail level without considering these factors as influencers.

In the Wide World Importers example, you can build a Key influencers visual as follows:

1.   Select the Key influencers visual from the **Visualizations** pane.

2.   Add **Profit** from the **Sale** table to the **Analyze** field well and ensure that summarization is set to **Sum**.

3.   Add the following fields to the **Explain by** field well:

- **State Province** from the **City** table
- **Buying Group** from the **Customer** table
- **Buying Package** from the **Stock Item** table

4.   Add **Year** and **Month** from the **Date** table to the **Expand by** field well.

The result is shown in Figure 4-18.

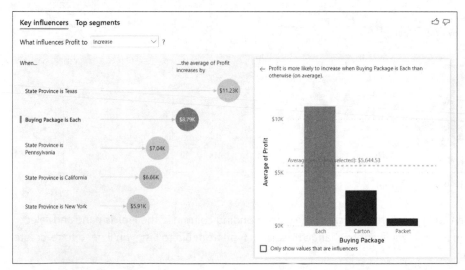

FIGURE 4-18 Key influencers

You can select each bubble to see how it influences Profit. For instance, the right half of Figure 4-18 shows that when *Buying Package* is *Each*, Profit is more likely to increase. Also note that Buying Group is not a major influence on Profit, since it's not shown in the visual.

Whereas the Key influencers tab in the Key influencers visual shows how each factor individually affects a metric, the Top segments tab shows how a combination of factors influences a measure. The Top segments tab is shown in Figure 4-19.

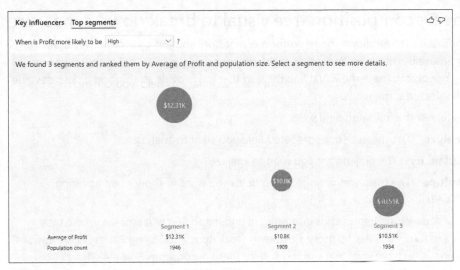

FIGURE 4-19 Top segments

Below each segment, you can see the average profit in the segment and the population count, or the number of records you have for the segment. Note that in this case average does not mean the average of the Profit column but instead the average of the aggregated Profit value, which in this case is sum.

You can select a segment to see what it consists of and how it compares to the overall population. Figure 4-20 shows an example of a segment.

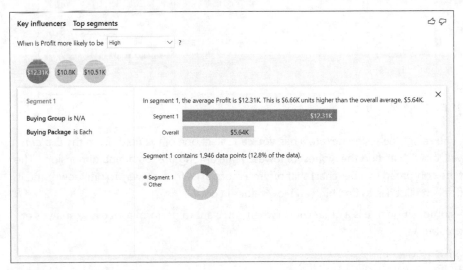

FIGURE 4-20 Top segment example

The Key influencers visual is appropriate to use when you want to find out the most important factors that affect a metric you select. You can also compare the relative significance of each factor.

Use the Decomposition tree visual to break down a measure

The Decomposition tree allows you to perform exploratory analysis by successively breaking down a measure by multiple dimensions. In the process, you can select a dimension you want to slice by, or you can make the visual find the split that will provide the highest or lowest value among all selected dimensions.

The visual has the following field wells:

- **Analyze**   The measure or aggregated field you want to analyze
- **Explain by**   The dimensions you want to analyze by
- **Tooltips**   The measures or aggregated fields you want to show when hovering over a bar

Let's say Wide World Importers is interested in understanding what makes up the total Profit figure in terms of Sales Territory, Customer, Stock Item, and Selling Package. You can see the Decomposition tree visual that can be used for these purposes in Figure 4-21.

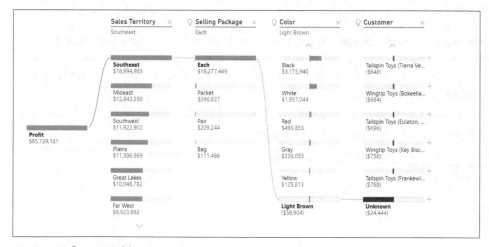

FIGURE 4-21 Decomposition tree

When you select the **+** sign next to a bar, you can select one of the fields from the *Explain by* field well, or you can find the highest or lowest value among the remaining dimensions. The visual can be compared to a bar chart that offers a more user-friendly way to drill down, and it uses artificial intelligence to find high and low values in data.

The Decomposition tree is a great choice when you want to perform root cause analysis or ad hoc exploration.

EXAM TIP

You should know when the AI visuals in Power BI—Q&A, Key influencers, and Decomposition tree—are appropriate to use depending on the problem at hand. For Q&A, refer to Skill 2.2: Develop a data model.

Apply AI Insights

In Power BI, you can leverage AI to enhance your data during the data preparation stage by connecting to certain pretrained machine learning models. You can find the following AI Insights on the **Home** or **Add column** ribbon in Power Query Editor:

- **Text Analytics**   Can detect the language, extract key phrases, or score sentiment in a text column
- **Vision**   Analyzes images to generate tags based on what they contain
- **Azure Machine Learning**   Applies an Azure Machine Learning model to your data

> *NOTE*   **AI INSIGHTS REQUIREMENTS**
>
> The Text Analytics and Vision options require access to a Power BI Premium capacity. For Azure Machine Learning, you need to have access to an Azure ML model. Details on how to grant access to an Azure ML model are outside the scope of this book. For more details, see "Use AI Insights in Power BI Desktop" at *https://docs.microsoft.com/en-us/power-bi/transform-model/desktop-ai-insights*.

For example, you can extract key phrases from the Stock Item names in the following way:

1. In Power Query Editor, right-click the **Stock Item** query and select **Reference**.
2. Right-click the **Stock Item** column and select **Remove other columns**.
3. Right-click the **Stock Item** column and select **Remove duplicates**.
4. On the Home ribbon, select **AI Insights** > **Text Analytics**.
5. At the left, select **Extract key phrases**. The configuration is shown in Figure 4-22.
6. Select **OK**.

Once the process finishes running, you should see the results in Figure 4-23, where the first few rows of the table are shown.

The function adds two new columns: a comma-separated list of key phrases in a column called *Extract key phrases*, and individual phrases in a column called *Extract key phrases.Key-Phrase*. Note that the total number of rows has been increased because each key phrase is now in its own row; this is similar to expanding a nested list into new rows in Power Query.

Key phrase extraction is especially useful for comments and whenever similar phrases are repeated in long text values.

FIGURE 4-22 Text Analytics

FIGURE 4-23 Key phrases

Chapter summary

- Conditional formatting in tables, matrixes, and other visuals can help draw your users' attention to insights. In tables and matrixes, you can configure conditional formatting for background color, font color, data bars, and icons in cells. Many other visuals support conditional formatting for data colors.

- Top N analysis can be useful when you want to show only top- or worst-performing items without showing all items. You can perform top N analysis by using a visual-level filter, Q&A, or DAX.

- In addition to column statistics available when performing data profiling in Power Query, you can leverage DAX to create value distribution visuals in Power BI, as well as use basic statistical functions in DAX to explore your data.

- The Quick Insights feature in the Power BI service can be useful if you want to try to find more insights in your data, or when you want to get some inspiration for creating your own visuals in Power BI. If you find a useful visual in the Quick Insights results, you can pin it to a dashboard.

- Reference lines can enhance your charts to make data easier to understand and insights stand out. You can also perform time-series forecasting by using the Analytics pane in Power BI.

- The Play axis in scatter charts can be effectively used to show movements in your data across time.

- In the Power BI service, report viewers can personalize visuals when you enable this feature in a report. Personalizing visuals can include changing the visual type and fields used.

- You can identify outliers—unexpected data points—by using data profiling, Quick Insights, and visuals such as scatter charts, which also allow you to cluster values and group outliers together.

- To enhance your data model, you can group and bin your data by leveraging the Data groups feature in the Power BI Desktop user interface. You can create a group of type List by visually selecting a few data points, or you can create a new data group by manually selecting members for each new group from a list of values. For numerical and date/time columns, you can create bins, which evenly divide values into groups based on ranges. The ranges can be determined by the size of each group or by the number of groups.

- The Key influencers visual can help you understand what makes a certain metric go up or down or belong to a certain category.

- The Decomposition tree allows you to perform root cause analysis or drill down interactively when analyzing a measure.

- With AI Insights, you can apply pretrained machine learning models during the data preparation stage. You can run an Azure Machine Learning model on your data, extract key phrases, score sentiment, detect language, or tag images by using AI insights.

Thought experiment

In this thought experiment, demonstrate your skills and knowledge of the topics covered in this chapter. You can find the answers in the section that follows.

You are a data analyst at Contoso responsible for creating Power BI reports. Management has requested you to analyze data coming from a Power BI dataset built by your colleague. The data model is shown in Figure 4-24.

FIGURE 4-24 Contoso data model

Based on background information and business requirements, answer the following questions:

1. You need to create a bar chart that shows the 10 products that generate the most revenue. Which action should you take? Your solution must involve minimal effort and consider that users may apply date filters.

   A. In the Product table, create a calculated column called *IsTop10* that uses the RANKX function; then use the column in a visual-level filter.

   B. Create a calculated table called Top 10 Products that filters the Sales table.

   C. Set a Top N visual-level filter.

   D. Create a measure that uses the TOPN function.

2. You need to group the Brand values into Brand Group, which is not available in the model. How would you group the Brand values? Your solution must require minimal effort to maintain.

   A. Create a data group of type List.

   B. Create a data group of type Bin.

   C. Create a calculated column in DAX.

   D. Create a custom column in Power Query.

3. You have built a line chart that shows revenue by month. You need to show mean monthly revenue on the same visual. How should you add the value to the visual? Your solution must consider that users may apply product filters and involve minimal effort.

   A. Create a measure that uses the AVERAGEX function.

   B. Add an Average line from the Analytics pane.

   C. Add a Median line from the Analytics pane.

   D. Create a calculated column in the Product table that uses the AVERAGEX function.

Thought experiment answers

1. The answer is **C**. A Top N visual-level filter requires no extra measures and will respond to date filters. Options A and B are both wrong because they won't properly take into account the date filters—both calculated columns and calculated tables will be evaluated before any user filters will be applied. Though it's possible to show top 10 selling products by writing a measure that uses the TOPN function, doing so requires a considerable amount of code—therefore, option D is wrong.

2. The answer is **A**. The data groups functionality provides a user interface that allows you to maintain groups with the least effort. Option B is wrong because the Bin type does not apply to categorical values. Options C and D are both wrong because they require writing formulas, which involves more effort than data groups.

3. The answer is **B**. An Average line will show the mean revenue in the visual, and it will automatically respect all filters. Option A is wrong because it requires writing nontrivial code to mimic the behavior of an Average line from the Analytics pane. Option C is wrong because median is not the same as mean or average. Option D is wrong because the calculated column won't consider any filters that users may apply.

CHAPTER 5

Deploy and maintain deliverables

The Power BI service has many features designed for collaboration and sharing the results of your work with others in a secure way. It also allows you to keep data in your reports up to date efficiently.

In this chapter, we first review the skills necessary to refresh datasets on a periodic basis and how to do so incrementally. We also describe the various ways in which datasets can be secured, which includes segregating access to different parts of the dataset for different groups of people. Since it may be useful to reuse a dataset for different purposes, we also look at how you can raise awareness of a dataset you manage.

In the next part of the chapter, we review how to create and manage workspaces, which are meant for collaboration in the Power BI service. Once you're ready to share the results of your work, you can package the content you created in an app and share it with a wider audience. We conclude the chapter by reviewing data sensitivity labels for workspace content.

Skills covered in this chapter:

- 5.1: Manage datasets
- 5.2: Create and manage workspaces

Skill 5.1: Manage datasets

In the Power BI service, reports and datasets are separate concepts, reports contain visualizations and related information, such as bookmarks, whereas datasets contain only the modeled data. One dataset may potentially have more than one report, whereas one report can be connected to one dataset only.

Keeping data up to date is almost always important, and the Power BI service provides a way to do it at fixed intervals in an efficient manner by refreshing only the latest data, if needed.

You have several options to provide access to a dataset to your users: you can grant full access to the whole dataset, read-only access to the whole dataset, or access to only those rows that you want users to see. Once you are ready to share a dataset with others, you can promote or certify it to facilitate its discovery throughout your organization.

Configure a dataset scheduled refresh

When you build a report, a common requirement is to keep the underlying data up to date. You can refresh a dataset manually in Power BI Desktop or the Power BI service, but this approach isn't viable when you need to refresh data periodically. To address this issue, you can configure a scheduled refresh in the Power BI service.

Accessing on-premises data

If you want to refresh a dataset that uses on-premises data, you need to use a data gateway. A *data gateway* can access on-premises and online data sources when you add data sources to it, which may include the connection details and credentials.

You can download and install a data gateway from the Power BI service by selecting **Settings** > **Download** > **Data Gateway**. You have the option to select from two gateway modes:

- **Standard mode**   Multiple people can use the gateway, and you can use it with other Microsoft services as well, such as Power Automate. This mode is appropriate for corporate environments because you can add each data source once, and then the gateway users will all be able to use it. You can specify generic credentials for data sources.

- **Personal mode**   Only one person can use the gateway, and you can use it only with Power BI. This mode is only useful when you don't plan to share the gateway with others.

> **NEED MORE REVIEW?**   **INSTALLING A GATEWAY**
>
> Full details on how to install, configure, and manage a gateway are out of the scope of this book. If you want to find more information, see "Install an on-premises data gateway" at *https://docs.microsoft.com/en-us/data-integration/gateway/service-gateway-install*.

Once you install a gateway or your Power BI tenant administrator makes you a gateway user, you can use the gateway to refresh datasets that use on-premises data sources. You can select a different gateway for each dataset in the dataset's settings.

To go to the dataset settings, hover over a dataset in the list of workspace items and select **More options** > **Settings**. To see the list of available gateways, as shown in Figure 5-1, select **Gateway connection**.

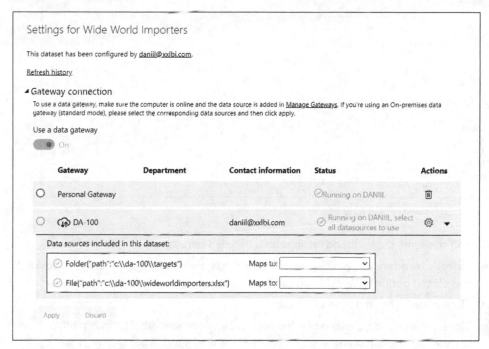

FIGURE 5-1 Gateway connection settings

If you want to use your personal gateway, select it from the list and then select **Apply**. You must also provide the data source credentials in the **Data source credentials** section by selecting **Edit credentials** next to each data source. You need to provide the credentials only once—they will then be securely cached in the Power BI service.

If you select an On-premises data gateway (standard mode), select the data sources from the **Maps to** drop-down lists and then select **Apply**. In most cases, you won't have to provide credentials since you can use the ones that the gateway admin provided.

Configuring scheduled refresh

You configure scheduled refresh for each dataset individually in the dataset settings. For this, expand the **Scheduled refresh** section of dataset settings and switch the **Keep your data up to date** toggle to **On**. You will then be able to configure refresh frequency and other settings, as shown in Figure 5-2.

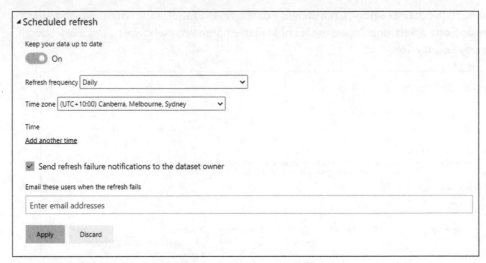

FIGURE 5-2 Scheduled refresh settings

You can configure the following settings for scheduled refresh:

- **Refresh frequency**   Specify how often the dataset will be refreshed: Daily or Weekly. If you set this option to Weekly, you can select the days of the week the refresh will run.

- **Time zone**   The time zone of refreshes.

- **Time**   You can add the time of refreshes in 30-minute intervals. The maximum number of refreshes you can set depends on whether the workspace is backed by a Premium capacity.

- **Send refresh failure notifications to the dataset owner**   This option will send an email to the dataset owner in case of a refresh failure. You can enter email addresses of other users who will receive the notifications, which can be useful when multiple people are responsible for the dataset.

After you adjust settings, select **Apply**. If you select Apply without setting the scheduled refresh time, your dataset will refresh at midnight.

You can see refresh history of a dataset at the top of the dataset settings by selecting **Refresh history**.

Configure row-level security group membership

Configuring row-level security (RLS) is a two-step process. In Skill 2.2: Develop a data model, we reviewed the first step—implementing RLS roles in Power BI Desktop. In this section, we review the steps needed to complete the RLS setup for a dataset; we assign and test roles in the Power BI service.

Assigning roles in the Power BI service

Once you've configured row-level security roles in Power BI Desktop, you need to publish your report to the Power BI service and add members to each role. To do so, go to the dataset security settings by hovering over a dataset in the list of workspace items and selecting **More options** > **Security**. If you don't have any roles defined in the dataset, you'll see the message in Figure 5-3.

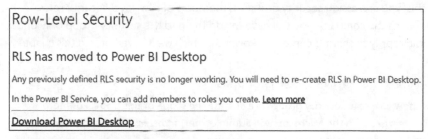

FIGURE 5-3 RLS has moved to Power BI Desktop

If you've created RLS roles defined in the dataset, you'll see a page like the one shown in Figure 5-4.

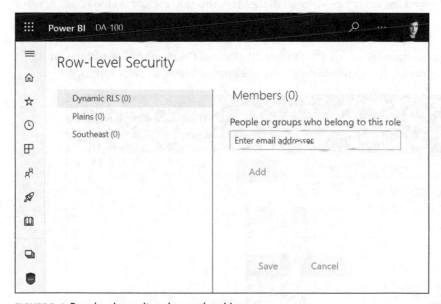

FIGURE 5-4 Row-level security role membership

On the left side of the Row-Level Security page, you can see a list of all roles in the dataset. The numbers in brackets show how many members each role has. On the right, you can view, add, and remove members for a selected role.

To add a member to a role, first select a role on the left, and then enter email addresses or security groups in the **People or groups who belong to this role** field. After you enter new members, select **Add** > **Save**. The changes will be applied immediately.

To remove a member from a role, select the cross next to the member and then select **Save**.

When you use row-level security in Power BI, you can use an email address for each user. Although this solution works, it can be hard to maintain. For example, consider that you have several datasets that use RLS based on the same rules and it's viewed mostly by the same users. If a new user joins your company and you need to give them access to those datasets, you will have to update the row-level security settings for each dataset.

In cases like this, you can assign security groups as members of row-level security roles. When a new user joins the company, you will have to add them to the security group only once. The same principles apply to sharing content in Power BI, which we'll cover later in this chapter.

> **NEED MORE REVIEW?** **CREATING SECURITY GROUPS**
>
> Instructions on how to create security groups are outside the scope of this book. For more details, see "Create a group in the Microsoft 365 admin center" at *https://docs.microsoft.com/ en-us/microsoft-365/admin/create-groups/create-groups*.

Viewing as roles in the Power BI service

As we saw with the *View as* feature in Power BI Desktop, you can test roles in the Power BI service. For this, you need to hover over a role on the Row-Level Security page and select **More options** (the ellipsis) > **Test as role**. You will then see the way a report appears to the members of the role. For example, Figure 5-5 shows what members of the Plains role would see, which you created in Chapter 2, "Model the data." The role applies a filter on Sales Territory.

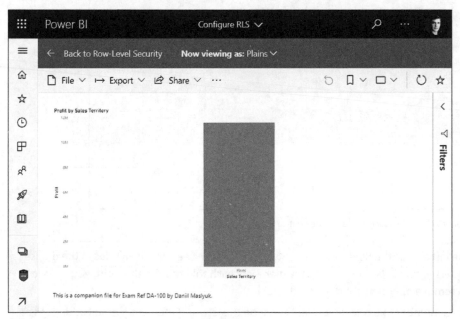

FIGURE 5-5 Testing a role in the Power BI service

If needed, you can test a combination of roles or view as a specific user by selecting **Now viewing as** in the blue bar at the top and selecting the desired parameters. Once you are satisfied with how the roles work, you can select **Back to Row-Level Security**.

Provide access to datasets

The Power BI service enables collaboration between different users. To let other users build reports based on a dataset that you published, you have to share the dataset with them. There are several ways of achieving this, as described next.

Sharing through a workspace

When publishing to the Power BI service, you can publish to your own workspace or a shared workspace. Contributing users of shared workspaces will automatically have access to the dataset you publish.

Sharing through an app

You can also make your dataset available for others when you share an app with them. For this, you'll need to grant the app users the Build permission by selecting the **Allow all users to connect to the app's underlying datasets using the Build permission** check box, as shown in Figure 5-6.

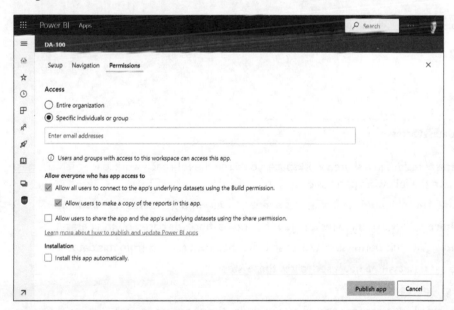

FIGURE 5-6 App permissions

Without the Build permission, users won't be able to connect to your dataset unless they're contributing workspace members or you give access to the individual dataset.

Managing dataset permissions

If you want to share an individual dataset, you can do so by managing dataset permissions. To view the permissions of a dataset, select **Manage permissions** from the dataset menu. You'll then see a list of users who have access to the dataset, as shown in Figure 5-7.

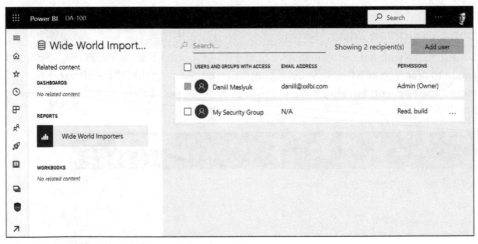

FIGURE 5-7 Dataset access

If the dataset resides in a shared workspace, you'll see the role each workspace member has. Users can have the following permissions:

- **Read** The minimum level of access needed to view reports based on this dataset.
- **Reshare** Allows users to reshare reports and dashboards based on this dataset.
- **Build** With this permission, users can build their own reports from this dataset.

To share a dataset with a new user, follow these steps:

1. Select **Add user**.
2. Enter email addresses or security groups under **Grant access to**.

3. Select the permissions you want to grant. You can allow recipients to either reshare the artifact or build new content from the underlying datasets.

4. Select **Add**.

If you want to change the existing permissions for a user or security group, select **Permission options** (the ellipsis) next to a user or security group and select the desired action, such as add or remove a permission. Note that workspace roles can't be changed here.

> **NOTE WORKSPACE ROLES**
>
> We review workspace roles in Skill 5.2: Create and manage workspaces.

Impact analysis

For datasets you share, it may be useful to know what other reports or dashboards use this dataset. Since Power BI allows you to use the same dataset across different workspaces, the reports and dashboards that use the dataset may reside outside of its home workspace, and the owner of the dataset may not always have access to the workspace. This information is contained in the dataset's impact analysis. To see the impact analysis, in the dataset menu select **View lineage**. You'll see the information shown in Figure 5-8.

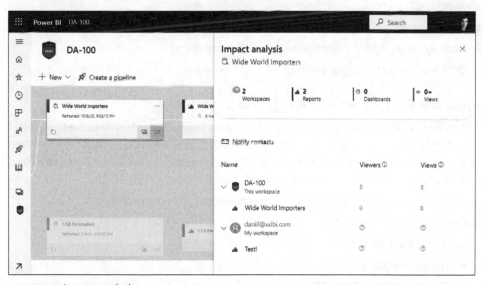

FIGURE 5-8 Impact analysis

Impact analysis shows the list of reports and dashboards across all workspaces related to the dataset. For each item, you can see how many viewers and views it had in the last 30 days, excluding today, and which workspace it's in. Impact analysis is particularly useful when you're making potentially breaking changes to the dataset because you know which items are going to be affected, as well as how popular those items are. You can notify contacts of the affected reports and dashboards by selecting **Notify contacts**.

Configure incremental refresh settings

Power BI allows you to work with datasets well in excess of gigabytes even after Power BI automatically compresses data. However, when you refresh large datasets, you may run into the following issues:

- **Speed**   Dataset refreshes may take a very long time, preventing you from displaying the information in a timely manner.
- **Resource usage**   Transferring and transforming large amounts of data may use up precious RAM, CPU, and network bandwidth.
- **Reliability**   Long-running queries to data sources may time out or fail, resulting in dataset refresh failures.

By using incremental refresh, you can address all these issues at once; you'll only refresh a subset of data, resulting in quicker, more reliable refreshes with lower resource consumption.

Although you can set a different incremental refresh policy for each table in your dataset, to set an incremental refresh policy you'll need to filter a table based on dates. Therefore, usually you'll configure incremental refresh for fact tables that hold time-series data—for example, sales records.

For incremental refresh to work in the Power BI service, you must configure incremental refresh in Power BI Desktop, which involves the following steps:

1. Create the *RangeStart* and *RangeEnd* parameters.
2. Filter by using the *RangeStart* and *RangeEnd* parameters.
3. Define incremental refresh policies.

Creating the RangeStart and RangeEnd parameters

The first step in configuring incremental refresh in Power BI Desktop is to create the *RangeStart* and *RangeEnd* parameters that will be used to filter dates. These parameter names are reserved and case-sensitive—other parameter names won't work properly for incremental refresh. You create the parameters in Power Query Editor in the following way:

1. In Power Query Editor, select **Manage parameters** > **New parameter**.
2. Configure the *RangeStart* parameter as follows:
   - Name: **RangeStart**.
   - Type: **Date/Time**.
   - Current value: **01/01/2020**. Power Query may change the input format of this value later, depending on your system settings.
3. Above the list of parameters, select **New** and create the *RangeEnd* parameter as follows:
   - Name: **RangeEnd**.
   - Type: **Date/Time**.
   - Current value: **31/12/2022**, or **12/31/2022** if your system uses the MDY date format. Figure 5-9 shows the parameters at this stage.

FIGURE 5-9 RangeStart and RangeEnd parameters

4. Select **OK**.

The choice of the current values only matters in Power BI Desktop because parameter values will be automatically overridden in the Power BI service.

Filtering by using the RangeStart and RangeEnd parameters

The *RangeStart* and *RangeEnd* parameters are needed to filter based on dates. For example, let's say you have a table called *Sale* that has a date/time column called *OrderDate*, and you want to incrementally refresh the latest sales records based on *OrderDate*. In this case, you can apply the filters by implementing the following steps:

1. In Power Query Editor, select the **Sale** table from the list of queries.

2. Select the filter button on the **OrderDate** column header and select **Date/time filters** > **Custom filter**.

3. For the first condition, select

   - **is after or equal to** from the first drop-down list
   - **Parameter** from the second drop-down list
   - **RangeStart** from the third drop-down list

4. For the second condition, select

   - **is before** from the first drop-down list
   - **Parameter** from the second drop-down list
   - **RangeEnd** from the third drop-down list

5. Ensure the logic between the conditions is set to **And**. At this stage, the filter conditions should look like those in Figure 5-10.

FIGURE 5-10 Filter conditions

6. Select **OK**.

7. Close Power Query Editor by selecting **Close & apply**.

Although you can also use "is after" and "is before or equal to" as filter conditions, it's important that one of the conditions be a strict inequality and the other one not strict. In other words, if you set one condition to be "is after or equal to" and the other to "is before or equal to," then you'll run into issues, because the edge values will be allocated to different partitions.

> **NOTE FILTERING DATES**
>
> Even though the RangeStart and RangeEnd parameters must be of type Date/Time, the column you filter can be of different type. For example, it's common for data warehouses to store dates as integers, such as 20210523 for May 23, 2021. In this case, you can employ a custom function to convert the parameter values to the required data type, and then you can use the Power Query Advanced Editor to filter the table by using the converted values. The specific implementation steps are outside the scope of this book.

Defining incremental refresh policies

With the *RangeStart* and *RangeEnd* parameters now filtering the table for which you want to apply an incremental refresh—in our example, *Sale*—you can now define an incremental refresh policy in the following way:

1. In the **Fields** pane of Power BI Desktop, right-click the table you want to refresh incrementally.

2. Select **Incremental refresh**.

3. Ensure the correct table is selected in the **Table** drop-down list and switch the **Incremental refresh** toggle to **On**.

4. Select the periods for which you want to store and refresh data. Note that you can set different periods for storing and refreshing data. In our example, you can store the last 10 years of data and refresh the last 15 days of data. Figure 5-11 shows your incremental refresh settings at this stage.

FIGURE 5-11 Incremental refresh

5. Select **Apply all**.

When defining an incremental refresh policy, you can also use the following options:

- **Detect data changes** To make incremental refreshes even more efficient, Power BI can check the maximum value of a date/time column you specify, and data will be refreshed only if the value changes. This column should not be the same column that you filter by using the *RangeStart* and *RangeEnd* parameters.

- **Only refresh complete periods** You can use this setting to exclude incomplete periods from refreshes. In some cases, reporting incomplete periods does not make business sense. For example, if scheduled refresh takes place at 6 a.m. and there's already some data available for the current day, then displaying the current day's figures may be misleading to report users. Excluding incomplete periods may be appropriate in this case.

You can define a different incremental refresh policy for each table in your data model while using the same *RangeStart* and *RangeEnd* parameters.

After you publish your dataset to the Power BI service, the data will be refreshed incrementally. The first refresh may take longer to refresh the whole dataset, but subsequent refreshes will benefit from incremental refresh and will be faster.

Query folding

Incremental refresh is only effective when query folding occurs—that is, when filtering by dates results in the data source returning a reduced set of data. If query folding does not occur, then filtering happens after Power BI retrieves all data, making incremental refresh policies useless. When you define an incremental refresh policy, Power BI Desktop will try to verify whether query folding occurs. If it's unable to confirm query folding, then you'll see the message shown in Figure 5-12.

 Unable to confirm if the M query can be folded. It is not recommended to use incremental refresh with non-foldable queries. Learn more

FIGURE 5-12 Query folding warning

Note that query folding may still occur, though you'll need to confirm it yourself by using query diagnostics. We reviewed query diagnostics in Skill 1.1: Get data from different data sources.

 EXAM TIP

You should know what's required for incremental refresh to work successfully.

Promote or certify Power BI content

When you create Power BI content and share it, you can increase its visibility for other users by endorsing it. For example, other users can search for an endorsed dataset and build reports from it. When many datasets are available in the organization, it's useful to know how reliable each dataset is—some may be created for test purposes only, whereas others may be considered a single source of truth in the company. By default, all datasets look the same when you search for datasets, be it from Power BI Desktop or the Power BI service. In this case, it may be a good idea to endorse datasets—let the reports creators know which datasets are high quality and reliable.

You can endorse datasets, dataflows, reports, and apps. There are two ways to endorse Power BI content:

- **Promote** Promoted content has a badge that signifies that the content is ready to be used by others. Any contributing member of the workspace where the content resides can promote it. Content promotion facilitates the content being reused across the organization.

- **Certify** Content can be certified to show that it is recommended for use, meaning it is highly reliable and curated. Only people selected by the Power BI tenant admins can certify Power BI content.

NOTE **ENDORSING DIFFERENT TYPES OF POWER BI CONTENT**

The process of endorsing all content types is the same. For ilustration purposes, we'll review how to endorse a dataset.

A dataset can be promoted or certified in the **Endorsement** section of the dataset settings in Power BI service, as shown in Figure 5-13.

FIGURE 5-13 Endorsement

Once you select **Promoted** or **Certified**, select **Apply** to save the changes.

If the **Certified** option is inactive, it means you cannot certify datasets yourself. In this case, you should request dataset certification from those who were selected by your Power BI tenant admins to certify datasets. Those who can certify datasets may not always be members of the workspace that contains the dataset. If that's the case, the person who can certify a dataset will need to become a contributing member of the workspace.

You can see the Certified and Promoted badges in Figure 5-14.

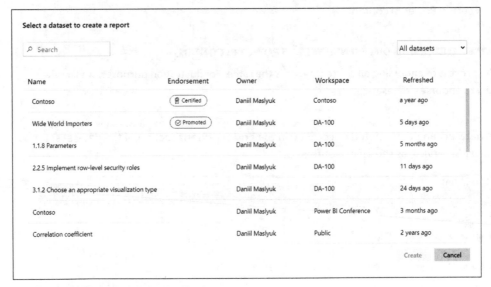

FIGURE 5-14 Promoted and Certified badges

Configure large dataset format

In Power BI Premium, you can enable large dataset format, which can bring the following benefits:

- Datasets can grow beyond 10 GB in size.
- Write operations are faster when using the XMLA endpoint.

You can enable large dataset format for each dataset individually, or you can set it as the default in a Premium workspace.

For a specific dataset:

1. Go to the dataset settings.
2. Expand **Large dataset storage format**.
3. Set the toggle to **On** and select **Apply**, as shown in Figure 5-15.

FIGURE 5-15 Large dataset storage format in dataset settings

To set large dataset storage format as default in a Premium workspace,

1. Go to the workspace settings.
2. Go to the **Premium** section.
3. From the **Default storage format** drop-down list, select **Large dataset storage format**, as shown in Figure 5-16.
4. Select **Save**.

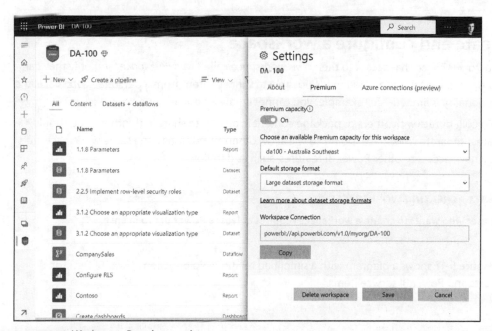

FIGURE 5-16 Workspace Premium settings

Note that with the large dataset storage format, downloading the PBIX file from the Power BI service may not work.

Skill 5.2: Create and manage workspaces

Collaboration in Power BI happens in workspaces, which serve as containers for dashboards, reports, workbooks, datasets, and dataflows. In this section we cover how to create and configure a workspace and illustrate how the Power BI service lifecycle strategy can help you implement phased deployments. We also review the skills necessary to create and manage workspaces, assign roles, publish and update apps and workspace assets, and apply sensitivity labels to workspace items.

> **This skill covers how to:**
> - Create and configure a workspace
> - Recommend a development lifecycle strategy
> - Assign workspace roles
> - Configure and update a workspace app
> - Publish, import, or update assets in a workspace
> - Apply sensitivity labels to workspace content
> - Configure subscriptions

Create and configure a workspace

Each Power BI user has access to their own workspace called *My workspace*, and only they can publish to the workspace. Though it's possible to share content from a personal workspace, the functionality is limited—for example, you cannot create an app in your workspace.

To collaborate with others or package content in an app to share with others, you should create a separate workspace. Doing so will allow others to publish to the same workspace, and you'll have access to other Power BI features, such as dataflows.

> *NOTE* **CREATING WORKSPACES**
> A user who wants to create a workspace requires at least a Power BI Pro license.

Figure 5-17 shows a diagram with a simplified relationship between Power BI Desktop reports and Power BI service items.

FIGURE 5-17 Power BI workspace contents

When you publish a Power BI Desktop to a workspace, you publish the visualizations, which become a report in Power BI service. If there was an associated data model, it would become a Power BI dataset. As discussed in Chapter 3, "Visualize the data," dashboards can have visuals pinned from reports and directly from datasets. We review Power BI apps later in this chapter in detail.

To create a workspace in Power BI service, follow this procedure:

1. From the left-hand menu, select **Workspaces** > **Create a workspace**.

2. Enter the workspace name. The name must be unique in the organization.

3. Select **Save**.

When creating a workspace, you can optionally set a workspace image and enter a workspace description. Furthermore, you can use the following advanced settings:

- **Contact list** You can select who will receive notifications about issues in the workspace. By default, it will be workspace admins, or you can enter specific users and groups.

- **Workspace OneDrive** To have the option to add items to the workspace from a dedicated OneDrive location, you can enter it here. Note that there's no synchronization between the Power BI workspace membership and those who have access to the OneDrive location. You should give access to the workspace to the same Microsoft 365 group that owns the OneDrive location. Managing OneDrive is outside the scope of this book.

- **Dedicated capacity** If your organization uses Power BI Premium and you're a capacity admin, you can allocate this workspace to a dedicated capacity. Administration of Power BI Premium is outside the scope of this book.

- **Develop a template app** You can develop a template app and share it with users outside of your organization. Template apps are outside the scope of this book.

- **Allow contributors to update the app for this workspace** By default, contributors cannot update workspace apps; you can change this by selecting this check box.

Once you've created a workspace, you can change its settings in Power BI service in the following way:

1. From the left-hand menu, select **Workspaces**.
2. Find the workspace of interest, hover over it, and select **More** > **Workspace settings**.
3. Change the settings as desired.
4. Select **Save**.

To delete a workspace, select **Delete workspace** > **Delete** from the workspace settings.

Recommend a development lifecycle strategy

When you develop Power BI reports, typically someone else will test them; once the reports are tested, you make them available for end users. Skipping the testing stage is considered a bad practice, and consumers of the report may raise numerous questions or concerns about the report. The three stages of a development lifecycle are as follows:

1. **Development** Sometimes shortened to *dev*.
2. **Test** Also known as *UAT*, which stands for *user acceptance testing*.
3. **Production** Often shortened to *prod*.

It's not uncommon for each stage to have its own environment with its own data sources. For instance, development data sources may have very little or very old data, whereas test data may be closer to production data. In some cases, developers may not have access to production data due to security concerns.

There are several ways to address the issue of switching between environments, and we'll cover two of them:

- Parameters
- Deployment pipelines

Parameters

When you connect to a data source in Power BI Desktop, you can use a parameter, as you saw in Skill 1.1. You get data from different sources in place of the actual data source address, be it a file, database, or another data source.

For example, you may have a database called Sales on three different servers:

- Development environment—dev.yourcompanyaddress.com
- Test environment—uat.yourcompanyaddress.com
- Production environment—prd.yourcompanyaddress.com

To save the time you'd spend manually editing the server address, you can create a text parameter that holds the three server addresses and use the parameter instead of the server address in your M queries. Once you publish your report to the Power BI service, you can edit the parameters to switch between the environments without republishing the report, which reduces the manual effort. If the database name differs from server to server, you'll need to create a separate parameter for it.

Keep in mind that reports in apps are related to the current version of the dataset even if you don't update the app. Therefore, if you change a parameter of the dataset that feeds a production report to use a development or test data source, then end users will not see the production data. To address this issue, it's a good idea to have separate workspaces for different environments; you can publish the same report to different workspaces and change the parameters right after publishing as needed.

Deployment pipelines

Although using parameters saves time compared to manually editing connection settings in Power BI Desktop, you still need to edit parameters in the Power BI service. To reduce manual effort even further, you can use deployment pipelines, which offer the following benefits:

- **A single view of all stages**   There's a separate workspace for development, test, and production stages. For each stage, you can create or update the corresponding app.
- **Automatic change of data sources and parameters**   You can set up rules that will be followed when deploying from one stage to the next.
- **Selective deployment**   For scenarios where you have multiple reports in the development stage and only some are ready to be tested, you can select those in the deployment pipeline and deploy only them to the next stage. Alternatively, you can deploy all content.
- **Refreshing all datasets at once**   You can refresh all datasets within a single stage with a single click.
- **Content comparison**   You can compare two stages and see the differences between them. Note that you'll be comparing metadata only, not the underlying data.

Using deployment pipelines can be divided into four stages:

1. **Creating a pipeline**   You can create a pipeline from a workspace or from the *Deployment pipelines* menu in the Power BI service.
2. **Assigning a workspace**   You'll need to select one workspace and assign it to a deployment stage (development, test, or production). Workspaces for other stages will be created automatically from the pipeline when you deploy content.
3. **Developing and testing**   Typically, you'll publish to the development workspace, then deploy to testing once the content is ready. Note that you deploy metadata only; you'll need to refresh datasets to populate them with data after deployment.
4. **Sharing with users**   The final step is to deploy from testing to production. Again, you'll have to refresh the datasets after deployment.

You can see an example of a deployment pipeline in Figure 5-18.

FIGURE 5-18 Deployment pipeline

You can share a pipeline with others. Access to a deployment pipeline is managed separately from access to each workspace. We review workspace access next.

Assign workspace roles

You can see the list of users who have access to a workspace by selecting **Access** from the workspace, where you can also add or remove users. To reflect the different needs of users, Power BI offers four workspace roles:

- **Viewers** can
  - View dashboards, reports, and workbooks in the workspace.
  - Read data from dataflows in the workspace.
- **Contributors** can do everything that viewers can do and
  - Add, edit, and delete content in the workspace.
  - Schedule refreshes and use the on-premises gateway within the workspace.
  - Feature dashboards and reports from the workspace.
- **Members** can do everything that contributors can do and
  - Add other users as members, contributors, or viewers to the workspace.
  - Publish and update the workspace app.
  - Share and allow others to reshare items from the workspace.
  - Feature the workspace app.
- **Admins** can do everything that members can do and
  - Update and delete the workspace.
  - Add and remove other users of any role from the workspace.

As mentioned earlier in the chapter, there's a workspace setting that allows contributors to update apps. This setting can be useful when you want a user to be able to update an app but not add other users to the workspace.

Note that giving someone a role in a workspace does not remove the need to give them additional rights, as necessary. For example, you may make a user an admin of a workspace, but unless they have a Power BI Pro license, they won't be able to fully use the role.

IMPORTANT ROW-LEVEL SECURITY

Row-level security applies only to viewers since all other roles have full access to all datasets within a workspace.

EXAM TIP

You should know which role is appropriate for a user based on the business requirements. In most cases, you should follow the principle of least privilege.

Configure and update a workspace app

When you are ready to share your reports and dashboards with users in your organization, you can publish an app. An *app* is a collection of Power BI items, such as a dashboard, reports, and workbooks, packaged together. There can be only one app per app workspace.

When creating or updating an app, you can select which content items appear in the app by toggling the **Include in app** switch to **Yes** or **No**, as shown in Figure 5-19.

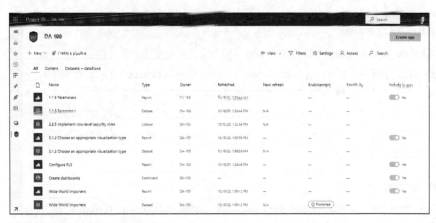

FIGURE 5-19 Include in app switch

Note that datasets and dataflows cannot be included in the app.

To publish an app from a workspace, select **Create app**. If an app already exists, you'll see **Update app** instead. There are three steps in app configuration:

- Setup
- Navigation
- Permissions

Setup

When you select **Create app** or **Update app**, you'll be taken to app setup, as shown in Figure 5-20.

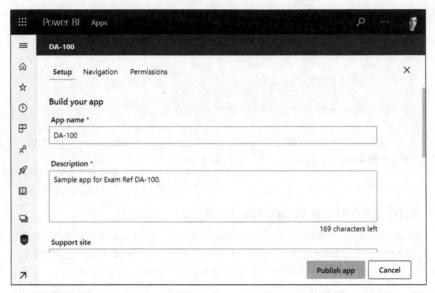

FIGURE 5-20 App setup

To publish an app, specify the app name and description. Additionally, you'll see the following options on the *Setup* screen:

- **Support site** Share where your users can find help related to the app.
- **App logo** By default, the app logo is the same as the workspace image. You can provide a different one here.
- **App theme color** This color will be used for the app menu and navigation.
- **Contact information** You can select the app publisher, workspace contacts, or specific individuals or groups.

Navigation

In the navigation step, you can customize the navigation pane. In addition to selecting the navigation pane width under the **Advanced** options, you can rename, reorder, hide, and group app content items under **Navigation**.

To group app content items, you must create a section first by selecting **New > Section** and giving it a new name. Then you can select an app content item and select a section from the **Section** drop-down list.

Furthermore, you can add links to the navigation pane. For each link, you can select where to open it:

- New tab
- Current tab
- Content area

You can see the *Navigation* screen in Figure 5-21.

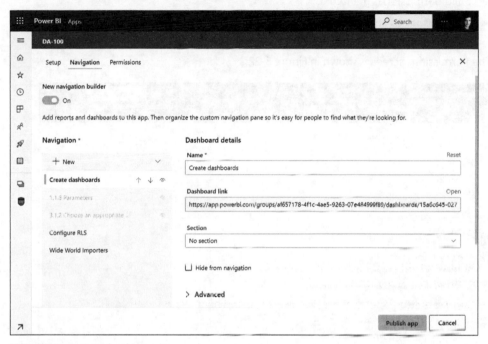

FIGURE 5-21 App navigation

Permissions

On the *Permissions* screen, you can select who has access to the app. You can grant access to the entire organization or specific individuals or groups. If you only grant access to specific individual or groups, you can select **Install this app automatically** so that it automatically appears in the *Apps* section of the Power BI service for each user—otherwise, each user will have to install the app manually from the *Apps* section.

> *NOTE* **ACCESS FOR WORKSPACE USERS**
>
> Users and groups with access to a workspace can access the corresponding app without you explicitly granting them access.

For users with access to the app, you can grant the following rights:

- **Allow all users to connect to the app's underlying datasets using the Build permission** Although the datasets won't show up in the app, this setting allows you to connect to datasets from Power BI or use Analyze in Excel.

- **Allow users to make a copy of the reports in this app** This setting allows users to copy reports to their personal workspaces to customize them. It is available only if the Build permission is granted.

- **Allow users to share the app and the app's underlying datasets using the Share permission** Note that accessing the datasets requires the Build permission.

The Permissions screen is shown in Figure 5-22.

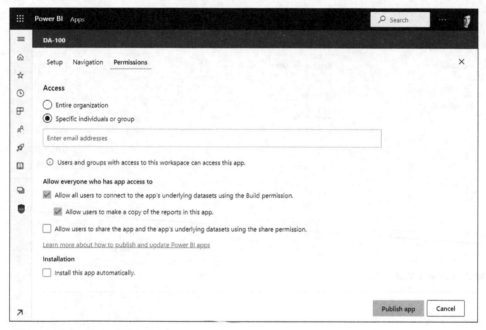

FIGURE 5-22 App permissions

App view

Once you publish an app, the result will look like Figure 5-23.

Note that the interface only has the app navigation; to go back and see the standard Power BI sidebar, you can select **Power BI** in the upper-left corner.

FIGURE 5-23 App view

Update a published app

After you publish your app, you can make changes to it if you are a contributing workspace user. For this, you need to go to the app workspace and make the changes you want; once you have made the changes, go back to the app workspace list of contents and select **Update app**. You can also update the *Setup*, *Navigation*, and *Permissions* settings that you configured when you created the app, and then select **Update app > Update** to propagate the app changes.

Note that on the *Permissions* screen, you will see the app link, as well as dashboard and report links. When you share any of those links, users will see all contents of the app, not just dashboards or reports.

Unpublish an app

If you want to unpublish an app, you can do so from the app workspace by selecting **More options > Unpublish app > Unpublish**. Doing so will not delete the app workspace contents; instead, the app will be removed from the list of apps of each user and become inaccessible.

Publish, import, or update assets in a workspace

You can publish a report to the Power BI service from Power BI Desktop by selecting **Publish** on the **Home** ribbon. To publish a report from Power BI Desktop, you must be signed in. By default, your report will be published to your personal workspace. If you are a contributor in other workspaces, you can select a workspace to publish to.

If the workspace you are publishing to already contains a dataset with the same name, you will be asked if you want to replace it, and you'll see how many workspace items it affects, as shown in Figure 5-24. This feature can be particularly useful when you're updating a dataset that has other reports built from it.

FIGURE 5-24 Dataset impact

An alternative to publishing from Power BI Desktop is to publish from the Power BI service by going to a workspace and selecting **Get data** in the lower-left corner and then selecting **Files**. You'll be given a choice to publish a local file, a file from OneDrive, or a file from Share-Point, as shown in Figure 5-25.

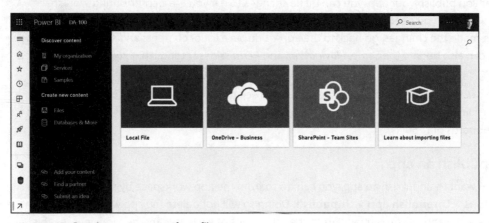

FIGURE 5-25 Creating new content from files

Selecting **Local file** will prompt you to select a file from your computer to publish, whereas **OneDrive** and **SharePoint** options allow you to publish from the cloud. Publishing from One-Drive can be beneficial because you can edit a report locally in Power BI Desktop in a folder that's synced to OneDrive, and it will be published automatically upon saving and closing the file because Power BI can sync published files from OneDrive.

Apply sensitivity labels to workspace content

Within an organization, different data may have different security levels. For example, some data must not leave a specific department, and other data may be shared publicly. To help users understand the sensitivity level of workspace content, you can apply sensitivity labels.

When information protection is enabled in your Power BI tenant, you can set a sensitivity label for a workspace item in the following way:

1. Go to the settings of a workspace item.
2. Select a sensitivity label from the drop-down list under **Sensitivity label**.
3. Select **Apply** or **Save**.

Once you set a sensitivity label, it will be displayed when anyone views the item, as well as in the list of workspace contents, as shown in Figure 5-26.

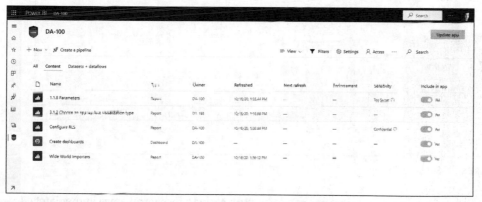

FIGURE 5-26 Sensitivity labels

Note how two reports have sensitivity labels shown in the Sensitivity column. If you hover over a sensitivity label, you'll see its description.

Configure subscriptions

In the Power BI service, you can subscribe yourself and others to individual report pages, dashboards, and paginated reports, which will make Power BI send snapshots of content to your email. When subscribing, you can select the frequency and specific times when you want to receive subscription emails.

Subscribing to content

The process of subscribing to report page or a paginated report is similar to subscribing to a dashboard:

1. Navigate to the content item of interest and select **Subscribe**.

2. In the **Subscribe to emails** menu, select **Add new subscription**.

3. Enter the subscription name, addressees, email subject, frequency, time, start and end times, and other options as needed.

4. Select **Save and close**.

You can create several subscriptions to the same content item. Figure 5-27 shows options available when subscribing to a dashboard as an example.

FIGURE 5-27 Subscription options

When creating a subscription, you can select **Run Now** to receive an email immediately. To disable a subscription without deleting it, switch the toggle next to **Run Now** to **Off**. To delete a subscription, select **Delete** in the upper-right corner of subscription settings. The **Manage all subscriptions** link takes you to a list of all subscriptions you created in the current workspace. Viewing all subscriptions you created is covered in the next section.

NEED MORE REVIEW? **SUBSCRIPTIONS IN POWER BI SERVICE**

For more details on subscriptions, including considerations and limitations, see "Subscribe yourself and others to reports and dashboards in the Power BI service" at *https: //docs.microsoft.com/en-us/power-bi/collaborate-share/service-report-subscribe*.

For details specific to paginated reports, see "Subscribe yourself and others to paginated reports in the Power BI service" at *https://docs.microsoft.com/en-us/power-bi/consumer/ paginated-reports-subscriptions*.

Managing your subscriptions

Only the person who created a subscription can manage it. In addition to viewing workspace-specific subscriptions, you can see all subscriptions you created in the following way:

1. Go to **My workspace**.

2. Select **Settings** in the upper-right corner.

3. Select **Settings** > **Settings** > **Subscriptions**.

Figure 5-28 shows a sample list of subscriptions to manage.

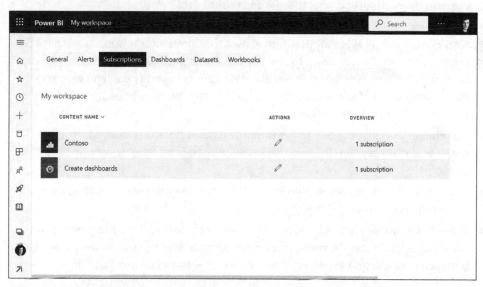

FIGURE 5-28 Subscriptions

While the page says My workspace, it shows subscriptions created across all workspaces. To edit subscriptions, select **Edit** under **Actions**. The Overview column shows how many subscriptions to a content item you have.

Chapter summary

- To ensure that data in your datasets is kept up to date, the Power BI service enables you to configure scheduled refresh. If your dataset is based on on-premises data, you'll need to use an on-premises data gateway. An on-premises data gateway is available in two modes: personal and standard. Personal mode is for use by a single person; on-premises data gateway in standard mode can be used by the whole company.

- To ensure that row-level security (RLS) works on datasets published to the Power BI service, you'll need to add members to RLS roles in the Power BI service. You can also test roles in the Power BI service in a way similar to how you test roles in Power BI Desktop. RLS only works for dataset readers, and it won't work for contributing workspace members.

- Datasets can be shared individually, through an app, or through a workspace. Shared datasets can be used to build reports and dashboards in other workspaces. To track the usage of shared datasets, you can perform a dataset impact analysis.

- When working with large datasets, you can configure incremental refresh to only refresh the latest data while storing the old data. Incremental refresh policies are defined in Power BI Desktop and then applied automatically in the Power BI service. To define an incremental refresh policy for a table, you must use *RangeStart* and *RangeEnd* date/time parameters to filter the table you want to refresh incrementally, and then set the periods for which you want to store and refresh data.

- You can endorse Power BI content by promoting or certifying it to denote that it is high-quality and reliable. Any user with at least the Contributor role in a workspace can promote content that resides in the workspace. Power BI content can be certified only by those who were selected by Power BI tenant admins to certify content, which signifies a higher status of endorsement. Endorsed content has specific badges next to it to differentiate it from other content.

- In Premium workspaces, you can use the large dataset storage format, which allows datasets to grow beyond 10 GB and makes write operations faster when using the XMLA endpoint.

- You can collaborate on developing Power BI content in workspaces. Creating a workspace requires a Power BI Pro license.

- In the Power BI development lifecycle, Microsoft recommends that you have separate workspaces for the development, test, and production stages. You can use parameters to switch data sources between different environments. Deployment pipelines can reduce the manual effort when you are deploying content between stages.

- Four roles are available in Power BI workspaces, listed from least to most privileged: Viewer, Contributor, Member, Admin. Row-level security only works on viewers; other roles can see all data within a workspace and RLS won't apply to them.

- If you want to share content from a workspace with end users, it's best to publish an app. An app includes the workspace content that you select, except for datasets and dataflows. You can customize the navigation of an app further by renaming, reordering, and grouping content items. You can also add links to an app. After you publish an app, you can update or unpublish it.

- You can publish a report from Power BI Desktop. Alternatively, from the Power BI service, you can upload a local file or a file from OneDrive or SharePoint.

- Sensitivity labels allow you to show users the level of confidentiality of each workspace item. To be able to apply sensitivity labels, the information protection settings must be enabled by your Power BI tenant admin.

- You can subscribe yourself and others to report pages, dashboards, and paginated reports. Only the person who created a subscription can manage it.

Thought experiment

In this thought experiment, demonstrate your skills and knowledge of the topics covered in this chapter. You can find the answers in the section that follows.

You are a data analyst at Contoso responsible for creating and distributing Power BI reports. The management requested that you share your reports with a wider audience.

Based on background information and business requirements, answer the following questions:

1. You've created a report that you published to a workspace. A few business users need to have the ability to view the reports. What's the most appropriate way to achieve this? Your solution must consider that the report audience may change in the future and that you've already created other reports in the workspace that will be ready to be shared at a later date.

   A. Share an app with individual users.

   B. Share an app with a security group.

   C. Share report from workspace with individuals.

   D. Give the users the Viewer role in the workspace.

2. You're an admin of a workspace, and you'd like to invite a few users to collaborate with you on reports. They need to be able to update reports and the app but not add others to the workspace. Which role should you give the users?

   A. Admin

   B. Member

   C. Contributor

   D. Viewer

3. You work on a dataset that sources its data from Azure SQL Database. The main fact table contains daily sales data for the last five years. To make the dataset refresh more efficient, you configure incremental refresh for the table by filtering the Sales data column. Upon checking the refresh history in the Power BI service, you notice that the refresh always takes approximately the same amount of time, suggesting that incremental refresh doesn't happen. What could be the reason?

   A. Azure SQL Database doesn't support incremental refresh.

   B. One of the transformation steps breaks query folding before date filtering happens.

   C. The date/time range parameters are called RangeFrom and RangeTo.

   D. The storage mode is set to Import.

4. You create a report based on data from Azure SQL Database. You publish the report to the Power BI service, and you need to ensure that the dataset is updated every day at midnight. Contoso does not use any special network configuration. Which gateway configuration do you need to use? Your solution must minimize the configuration effort.

   A. On-premises data gateway (personal mode).

   B. On-premises data gateway (standard mode).

   C. Two on-premises data gateways: one in personal mode, and one in standard mode.

   D. No gateway is necessary.

Thought experiment answers

1. The answer is **B**. Sharing an app with a security group ensures that users can view only the report you include in the app without exposing other workspace assets. It also minimizes the effort to update the list of viewers because you can update the security group membership, which will be used for the Power BI app access. Sharing an app with individual users, as option A suggests, comes close, but adding or removing viewers will require opening the Power BI website and is not considered best practice. For similar reasons, option C is incorrect; additionally, if you share reports individually as opposed to packaging them in an app, then accessing them will be more difficult for users because they won't be in one place. If you give users the Viewer role in a workspace—option D—they'll see all reports in the workspace. This does not satisfy the business requirements because some reports in the workspace aren't ready to be shared yet.

2. The answer is **C**. Contributors can update reports in a workspace, and they can update the app when allowed in workspace settings; at the same time, contributors cannot add others to a workspace. Options A and B both suggest roles that can add other users to a workspace, which goes against the business requirements. Option D, Viewer, isn't right because viewers cannot update reports or apps in a workspace.

3. The answer is **B**. For incremental refresh to work, query folding must take place. Otherwise, data is filtered after it's loaded, and the refresh time will be the same as without incremental refresh. Option A is incorrect because Azure SQL databases do support incremental refresh. Option C is incorrect because the date/time parameters used for incremental refresh must be called *RangeFrom* and *RangeTo*—other names won't work. Option D is incorrect because incremental refresh is designed for imported data, not other storage modes.

4. The answer is **D**. Since Contoso has no special network configuration in place, the Azure SQL Database can be accessed without a gateway. Options A, B, and C are incorrect because they suggest using an on-premises data gateway.

Index

Plug into learning at

MicrosoftPressStore.com

The Microsoft Press Store by Pearson offers:

- Free U.S. shipping

- Buy an eBook, get three formats – Includes PDF, EPUB, and MOBI to use with your computer, tablet, and mobile devices

- Print & eBook Best Value Packs

- eBook Deal of the Week – Save up to 50% on featured title

- Newsletter – Be the first to hear about new releases, announcements, special offers, and more

- Register your book – Find companion files, errata, and product updates, plus receive a special coupon[*] to save on your next purchase

Discounts are applied to the list price of a product. Some products are not eligible to receive additional discounts, so your discount code may not be applied to all items in your cart. Discount codes cannot be applied to products that are already discounted, such as eBook Deal of the Week, eBooks that are part of a book + eBook pack, and products with special discounts applied as part of a promotional offering. Only one coupon can be used per order.